MODERNISM AND THE MACHINERY OF MADNESS

Modernism and the Machinery of Madness demonstrates the emergence of a technological form of paranoia within modernist culture that transformed much of the period's experimental fiction. Gaedtke argues that the works of writers such as Samuel Beckett, Anna Kavan, Wyndham Lewis, Mina Loy, Evelyn Waugh, and others respond to the collapse of categorical distinctions between human and machine. Modern British and Irish novels represent a convergence between technological models of the mind and new media that were often regarded as "thought-influencing machines". Gaedtke shows that this literary paranoia comes into new focus when read in light of twentieth-century memoirs of mental illness. By thinking across the discourses of experimental fiction, mental illness, psychiatry, cognitive science, and philosophy of mind, this book shows the historical and conceptual sources of this confusion as well as the narrative responses. This book contributes to the fields of modernist studies, disability studies, and medical humanities.

ANDREW GAEDTKE is an assistant professor of English at the University of Illinois, Urbana-Champaign, where he teaches modernist and contemporary literature.

T0364237

MODERNISM AND THE MACHINERY OF MADNESS

Psychosis, Technology, and Narrative Worlds

ANDREW GAEDTKE

University of Illinois, Urbana-Champaign

CAMBRIDGE
UNIVERSITY PRESS

Shaftesbury Road, Cambridge CB2 8EA, United Kingdom

One Liberty Plaza, 20th Floor, New York, NY 10006, USA

477 Williamstown Road, Port Melbourne, VIC 3207, Australia

314–321, 3rd Floor, Plot 3, Splendor Forum, Jasola District Centre, New Delhi – 110025, India

103 Penang Road, #05–06/07, Visioncrest Commercial, Singapore 238467

Cambridge University Press is part of Cambridge University Press & Assessment,
a department of the University of Cambridge.

We share the University's mission to contribute to society through the pursuit of
education, learning and research at the highest international levels of excellence.

www.cambridge.org
Information on this title: www.cambridge.org/9781108406215

DOI: 10.1017/9781108284035

First published 2017
First paperback edition 2022

A catalogue record for this publication is available from the British Library

ISBN   978-1-108-41800-3   Hardback
ISBN   978-1-108-40621-5   Paperback

To Krista, Isobel, and Molly

Contents

Acknowledgments

This book is the product of many generous transmissions of thought and good will, and I am thankful for all of the influences that I have received over the years. I have endless gratitude and admiration for my mentors at Penn whose support and insight made this project possible. Jean-Michel Rabaté has been a model of inexhaustible intellectual curiosity and generosity. His gentle guidance has taught me never to cede on my intellectual desire. Heather Love has been a force for good from the moment that I met her. She has been an inspiring teacher, a brilliant reader, and a humane advisor. Paul Saint-Amour was encouraging before he had reason to be, and his elegant, incisive responses to my work made it more enjoyable for me to write.

I also benefited from a brilliant cohort of friends and fellow graduate students who helped me along the way. Thanks to Ruben Borg, Ian Cornelius, Joe Drury, Paul Franco, Laura Heffernan, Melanie Micir, Ryan Muldoon, Doug Paletta, Joshua Schuster, Rebecca Sheehan, Leif Weatherby, and the entire Mods Group for teaching me so much of what I know about modernism and intellectual community. John Tresch, Mara Mills, and Penn's Science and Lit Group gave me many hours of intense conversation about the history and philosophy of science. Jed Esty and Zack Lesser offered valuable advice and support at crucial, early moments in my career. Benjy Kahan has been the kind of friend that you can't live without. His energy, intelligence, and good humor have kept me going.

In many ways, my fascination with literature and mental illness began at the University of Wisconsin–Madison with the help of Richard Begam, Cyrena Pondrom, and Rebecca Walkowitz, who were generous mentors and tireless advocates whom I cannot thank enough. I would also like to thank Mike Byrd, whose singular combination of humanity and logical rigor taught me to think more clearly. I am grateful to the English Department at Franklin & Marshall College for making my first job so pleasant. Patrick Bernard, Genevieve Abravanel, and Peter Jaros made me feel especially at home. I am also grateful to friends and colleagues who have helped me along the way by offering feedback, exchanging ideas, or organizing venues where I could present and sharpen my work, including Elizabeth Barry, Stephen Burn, Peter Fifield, Joshua Gang, Patricia Gherovici, Ulrika Maude, Steven Meyer, Omri Moses, Michael North, Laura Salisbury, Jason Tougaw, and Tim Wientzen.

At the University of Illinois, Urbana-Champaign, I have gained a community of smart and supportive colleagues who have shaped my thinking and have enabled me to complete this book through their mentorship, advice, and friendship. Thanks to Eleanor Courtemanche, Tim Dean, Sam Frost, Jim Hansen, Melissa Littlefield, Bruce Michelson, Bob Morrissey, Justine Murison, Bob Parker, Curtis Perry, Michael Rothberg, Lindsay Rose Russell, Derrick Spires, and Ted Underwood for making Champaign-Urbana an ideal place for me to live, think, and work. Vicki Mahaffey has been especially supportive, and I am endlessly grateful for her care and mentorship. I would also like to thank the many wonderful undergraduate and graduate students that I have worked with at the University of Illinois who helped me test new ideas in courses, seminars, reading groups, and office hours. A special thanks goes to Rebecah Pulsifer, who has been not only a brilliant student but an invaluable interlocutor.

This book was made possible by fellowships and grants from the Jacob Javits Foundation, the University of Pennsylvania, the Illinois Program for Research in the Humanities, and the Illinois Campus Research Board. Earlier versions of Chapter 2 and Chapter 5 appeared as "From Transmissions of Madness to Machines of Writing: Mina Loy's *Insel* as Clinical Fantasy," in *Journal of Modern Literature* 32.1 (2008): 143–162 and "'Prey to Communications': Samuel Beckett and the Simulation of Psychosis," in *Modernist Cultures* 10.2 (2015): 227–249. Several paragraphs in the Conclusion appeared previously in "Neuromodernism: Diagnosis and Disability in Will Self's *Umbrella*," *Modern Fiction Studies* 61.2 (2015): 271–294. Thanks to the publishers for permission to use this material in the present work.

Thanks to my family – Gary, Jackie, Jason, and Hannah Gaedtke – for all of the years of support, love, and encouragement. It was in my early conversations with Jason that I learned what intellectual enjoyment and friendship through books could be like. I am also grateful for the warmth and hospitality that I have received from the Lampe family, who have always reminded me to take breaks and have fun along the way.

Finally, I am grateful to my amazing daughters, Isobel and Molly, for always reminding me what is most important and for their constant inspiration. My greatest thanks goes to Krista for her inexhaustible laughter, love, and support. Her unique ability to make light of almost any situation and her endless patience have made all the difference. She simply makes everything better. This book is dedicated to Krista, Isobel, and Molly.

Introduction
Three Black Boxes

Modernism was traversed by strange transmissions. In 1919, the Viennese psychoanalyst Victor Tausk published an article entitled, "On the Origins of the 'Influencing Machine' in Schizophrenia," describing a delusion that he found to be common among his patients.[1] These troubled psychotics believed that they were persecuted by a machine operated by a cabal of conspirators. The precise nature of the mechanism exceeded the patients' technological understanding, but they consistently felt that their thoughts had been transmitted to them from the apparatus via electromagnetic rays. For some, these transmissions would produce auditory and visual hallucinations; others would complain that the machine induced unpredictable sexual reactions that they could not control.

In 1933, the year that Tausk's case study appeared in English, an article appeared in *The New Yorker* that describes "an automatic suggestion machine that enables you to direct the vast powers of your unconscious mind during sleep."[2] This "Psycho-Phone" was a modified phonograph designed to play a series of audible messages throughout the night in order to insert messages of self-improvement into the unconscious of its sleeping users.[3] The programs that could be played on the machine promised improvements in the areas of "Prosperity," "Inspiration," "Normal Weight," "Mating," "Normality," "Life Extension," and "Health, Happiness, and Harmony." The "Prosperity" recording included the lines "I desire to prosper. I have complete confidence in the Psycho-Phone. It lulls me to sleep, but my unconscious mind hears and is deeply impressed by these affirmations."[4]

In 1927, the year the Psycho-Phone was trademarked, the British writer, artist, and cultural critic Wyndham Lewis wrote, "People feel themselves being influenced, but their brain and not their crystal set is the sensitive receptive instrument [...] Ideas, or systems of ideas, possess no doubt an organism, as much as a motor-car or wireless set."[5] The observation opens *Time and Western Man*, a monumental attempt to measure the social, psychic, and philosophical transformations that defined the modernist era. The treatise constitutes one volume among several major works of cultural analysis and experimental fiction that Lewis composed in the late 1920s in an ambitious effort to make these transformations available to conscious scrutiny and to renew capacities for self-control and psychological sovereignty against the era's new techniques of unconscious influence. As in the schizophrenic delusions that Tausk describes and that recur in many memoirs of mental illness of the period, Lewis frequently traces those unconscious influences to the effects of new media technology and to emerging, mechanistic accounts of the mind. In a companion volume, *The Art of Being Ruled* (1926), Lewis observes, "The contemporary European or American is a part of a broadcasting set, a necessary part of its machinery [...] at the pressing of a button, all these hallucinated automata with their technician-trained minds and bodies, can be released against each other."[6]

How might we understand such uncanny echoes across the discourses of psychotic delusion, technological media, and literary modernism? All three texts describe remarkably similar versions of a "suggestion apparatus" that exerts an obscure influence on the unconscious of its user or victim, and these examples are hardly unique. Technological thought transmission recurs in many psychotic memoirs across the twentieth century and in many works of experimental fiction. The goal of this book is to open this archive in order to trace the form and logic of a technological paranoia that becomes especially articulate in late-modernist culture. I argue that the fiction of Wyndham Lewis, Mina Loy, Anna Kavan, Evelyn Waugh, Muriel Spark, Flann O'Brien, and Samuel Beckett registered and responded to a convergence of technology and psychology that reconstructed the mind as an informatic machine. Psychoanalytic notions of unconscious "mechanisms" along with early neurological accounts of the mental processes converged toward a view that thought was not fully under conscious control or available to introspection but was governed by automatic systems. The notion these systems could be manipulated by outside influences becomes a prevailing anxiety that recurs in much modernist and psychotic writing.

If it had once been regarded as the seat of human judgment and rational self-control, the mind had been reconstructed as merely another "black box" – an object of technoscientific inquiry that was subject to causal laws not unlike the many information machines that began to appear in the early decades of the twentieth century. Precisely how these machines functioned was often a mystery to their users, and the uncertain status of such "black boxes" made them phantasmatic resources for the work of fiction and delusion. In the novels of Loy, Waugh, Spark, and Beckett, radio often appears as both metaphor and material cause of a new form of passivity to which the human subject had been reduced. In Waugh's *The Ordeal of Gilbert Pinfold* (1957), a novelist suspects that his thoughts are monitored and transmitted to him by strange boxes that may have undisclosed connections to both the BBC and new psychotherapeutic methods. Other writers, such as Samuel Beckett, actively pursued the radio's cultural and phenomenological associations with psychopathology; his BBC radio drama, *Embers* (1959), uses the formal resources and limitations of the medium to reproduce for the audience the hallucinated voices that plague the play's central character. Pamela Thurschwell demonstrates links in the popular imagination between modernism's emerging audio technologies and magical thinking, arguing that, "the possibility of telepathy, legitimated by comparisons to the telegraph and telephone, focused erotic fantasies of minds and bodies merging, as well as utopian hopes for better communication."[7] However, in the logic of utopian fantasies, possibilities of minds technologically merging often manifest as dystopian nightmares.

By the 1930s, several studies of the psychological and sociological effects of radio appeared. Princeton's Radio Research Project produced cultural analyses of the new medium, including essays by Theodor Adorno, who argued that radio had produced "A New Type of Human Being."[8] This new type was the product of a new technological influence that "suffocates the ego and eats away at its innermost constitution through realistic fear."[9] Elsewhere, Adorno writes, "The radio voice, like the human voice or face, is >>present<<. At the same time, it suggests something >>behind<< it. In listening, one lacks a precise and clear consciousness of what this something is."[10] Such suspicions of "something >>behind<<" or beyond the threshold of consciousness bear the structure and valence of paranoia that often recurs in modernist writing about radio. In another prominent study, *The Psychology of Radio* (1935), Hadley Cantril and Gordon W. Allport describe radio as "an agency of incalculable power for controlling the actions of men" and "preeminent as a means of social control and epochal in its influence upon the mental horizons of men."[11] The early media theorist Rudolf Arnheim strikes an equally ominous note in a chapter on "The Psychology of Radio," where he writes, "wireless has absolute mastery and kills all mental initiative,"[12] and "we must speak of the danger of wireless estranging people from life, firstly by making them contented with images instead of the real things in their proper places."[13] Arnheim describes mass acceptance of sensory illusion and an uncanny estrangement from "real things" – language that might describe the forms of auditory hallucination that distinguish extreme mental illness.

Historian Asa Briggs recalls the pitched cultural debates over the pernicious effects of the BBC upon its listeners, particularly a growing concern that "Radio would make people passive."[14] Debra Rae Cohen shows that the BBC's companion serial publication, *The Listener*, managed such anxieties by instructing its audience to listen critically and in groups in order to reduce "the danger of mechanizing thought through broadcasting."[15] Cohen goes on to recount the strange case of Harold Nicolson, a BBC announcer who withdrew from his position because he felt that his voice had taken on a life of its own through the uncanny effects of the medium, claiming that "this broadcasting business creates a strange semblance, an unhealthy *eidolon*, of oneself."[16] The reaction to his statement was so strong that he was forced, "in a letter to the editor after two weeks of such reactions, to attribute his own wireless ailment to individual pathology rather than the contagion of the medium."[17] The strange incident demonstrates the ways in which radio became shrouded in the uncanny valences of psychopathology. If radio's early emergence and adoption prompted such anxious responses, the association of the medium with propaganda during the Second World War only amplified its paranoia-inducing effects.[18]

Cultural responses to new media such as radio constitute only one legible source of the technological delusions that appear in memoirs of mental illness and in modernist fiction. While engineers such as Guglielmo Marconi and A. B. Saliger designed global radio networks and psychological suggestion machines, psychiatrists and neurologists emerged as the new technicians of the mind who claimed to map the dysfunctioning mechanisms of the brain. By the turn of the twentieth century, the foundations of modern neurology had been established: electrical levels were measured in the brains of animals; nerve cells were stained and visualized; several language disorders were correlated with the regions of the brain now known as Broca's Area and Wernicke's Area; the mental disorder associated with syphilis had been linked to the presence of a bacterium in the brain. These developments promised to establish the study of the mind and its disorders on objective, empirical, and materialistic grounds. Lisa Blackman writes, "The orthodoxy within mid-nineteenth- to late twentieth-century psychiatry, was that the psychoses were directly linked to structural dysfunction(s) within the brain, often viewed as progressive, which produced symptoms which could only be addressed through biological processes."[19] However, progress slowed, and early phenomenological psychiatrists, such as Karl Jaspers, dismissed the hope of finding a single neurological cause for complex conditions such as schizophrenia: "[W]e do not know a single physical event in the brain which could be considered the identical counterpart of any morbid psychic event. We only know conditioning factors for the psychic life; we never know *the* cause of the psychic event, only *a* cause."[20] Historian of psychiatry Wayne Shorter writes, "In the 1880s and after, an absolute craze for studying psychiatry with the microscope took possession of the German, Austrian, and Swiss universities. It is generally agreed that this craze led to a dead end, and that the first biological psychiatry died because it detached itself too completely from patients and their world."[21]

This lack of attention to the patient's lived world by an increasingly positivistic and materialist neurology constitutes another source of modernist anxieties of mechanistic depersonalization. The redescription of mental life as the mere epiphenomena of particular neurological systems all but abandoned subjective, first-person perspectives in favor of strictly verifiable, objective, third-person accounts of scientific experimentation. This subordination was especially pronounced in cases of subjects whose self-reports were regarded as manifestly unreliable, such as psychotics. The delusions of such patients often tell the story of the depersonalization that their doctors' positivist epistemology rendered. In modernist delusions of thought broadcasting via some form of radio waves, it is often psychiatrists and neurologists who operate the obscure influencing machines. In Chapter 2, I argue that Mina Loy's novel *Insel* represents a psychotherapeutic relationship as an experience of thought transmission via electromagnetic brain waves.[22] Read in combination with the fiction of their contemporaries, these case studies and memoirs of psychosis reflect the technologization of the mind that had taken hold by the early-twentieth century. The written records of psychotic delusions therefore provide a hermeneutic horizon within which late-modernist fiction may become newly legible.

At the same time, memoirs of mental illness offer more than simply context for understanding works of literature. Psychosis is often marked by failures to maintain fundamental ontological distinctions between self and other, inside and outside, the human and the nonhuman. Memoirs of schizophrenia offer rich accounts of the phenomenology of psychosis as well as attempts to reinstall these fragile ontological distinctions through the ordering work of narration. The graphomania that psychotics often exhibit is spurred by an effort to reestablish these fundamental categories of experience and to reconstruct a livable world – precisely the kind of work that has often been overlooked by reductive forms of psychiatry that, as Shorter puts it, "detached itself too completely from patients and their world."[23] I argue that similar acts of narrative worlding are performed in modernist novels that represent homologous ontological crises. During the composition of *Time and Western Man*, Wyndham Lewis wrote his most formally experimental novel, *The Childermass* (1928), a text that is in many ways the fictional counterpart of his works of cultural analysis.[24] This largely forgotten late-modernist fantasy describes an uncanny afterworld in which undead characters are reduced to behaviorist reactions and mechanical automatisms and show no capacities for volition, agency, or judgment. The epistemic and ontological confusions suffered by these minimalist figures are reproduced for the reader through discursive techniques that render uniquely dysphoric experiences. It is perhaps not surprising that this intractable work has been mostly ignored by scholars, but I argue that the novel comes into focus when read in concert with several memoirs of mental illness and late-modernist fictions that manage similar confusions. Texts such as Daniel Paul Schreber's *Memoirs of My Nervous Illness* (1903) and *An Autobiography of a Schizophrenic Girl* (1951) not only provide invaluable records of a technologically encoded ontological confusion; they also teach us to read novels such as Lewis's *The Childermass*, Loy's *Insel*, and others as attempts to construct narrative solutions to ontological problems.[25]

The notion that storytelling may perform foundational phenomenological work necessary for subjectivity has been proposed by philosophers such as Paul Ricoeur, who argues that narrative renders a "humanization of time,"[26] and Charles Taylor, who writes that self-narrative provides "the inescapable structural requirements for human agency."[27] Cognitive neuroscientist Antonio Damasio argues that an "autobiographical self" is a necessary, although not sufficient, condition for selfhood, and much of his research has been directed toward determining how self-narrating processes fail in extreme pathological conditions.[28] The German philosopher and cognitive scientist Thomas Metzinger has similarly reimagined the ego as nothing more than a useful narrative fiction – a "tunnel" through which phenomena are focalized, organized, and stabilized.[29]

I argue that a repeating chorus can be discerned within a heterogeneous collection of voices that includes novelists, mental patients, psychologists, philosophers, and engineers. Such a search for hidden patterns within these cultural transmissions will inevitably resemble the orderly systems that many psychotic subjects create. This mimetic relation between paranoia and attempts to theorize it has been elegantly articulated by Eve Kosofsky Sedgwick, who writes, "paranoia refuses to be only *either* a way of knowing *or* a thing known, but is characterized by an insistent tropism toward occupying both positions."[30] Perhaps a more productive strategy would be provisionally to acknowledge and affirm this resemblance between cultural analysis and paranoia. That is, we might instead ask, if our cultural analysis begins to resemble certain paranoid sources, might the paranoid sources be read for unacknowledged insights into culture? In this way, the influencing machine delusion may be conceptualized as both symptom and theory: an instance of technologically encoded paranoia that also attempts to explain its own working parts.

Modernism and Madness

Such formal and thematic resemblances between mental illness and modernist literature have drawn the attention of several scholars who have proposed a variety of explanations for these points of contact. Eric Santner finds in Schreber's paranoia the psychological blueprints for the rise of German fascism: as populist movements released repressed social energies, they also produced a crisis of centralized authority by which these forces had been organized, understood, and controlled.[31] In this analysis, both Schreber and German culture more broadly suffered a crisis of "symbolic investiture" – in Lacanian terms, a failure of the paternal function through which social relations had been made coherent and meaningful.[32] The rise of fascism as well as efforts to "cleanse" the nation of supposedly pernicious foreign bodies reflects the paranoiac's need to project outward those intolerable elements that are both internal and threatening. David Trotter similarly identifies the social reorganization of the late-nineteenth and early-twentieth centuries as the cause of a modern paranoia running through the work of several British novelists.[33] For Trotter, the rise of the professional class meant that one's status and place within the social order were no longer simply given but had to be demonstrated through one's work. Social strata were scrambled by this transition from aristocracy to meritocracy in which the potentials for upward and downward mobility made the classification of bodies increasingly difficult. Trotter identifies in the literature and art of the period a will to abstraction and classification that aims to resist this loss of social order.

Santner and Trotter therefore agree that modernist paranoia was motivated by a failure of social hermeneutics – an inability to interpret a person's status. The threat to masculine distinction and respectability posed by universal suffrage and the entrance of women into professional roles contributed to the displacement of a long-standing paternal order and produced a crisis of interpretation. The predominantly male canon to which these critics adhere suggests that paranoia is the burden of modern masculinity and is perhaps the male counterpart to the female hysteria that displaced neurasthenia as the fashionable pathology of the early-twentieth century.[34] However, as I demonstrate in the chapters that follow, many of the most fascinating memoirs and fictions of mental illness were composed by women whose singular accounts of mechanized madness must be incorporated into our histories of both psychiatry and modernist literature.

The rise of modernism was virtually contemporaneous with the emergence of modern psychiatry and its taxonomy of mental illness. Emil Kraepelin first established the nosological category of "dementia praecox" in the late 1890s, and Eugen Bleuler reconceptualized the condition as "schizophrenia" in 1911.[35] While this core psychiatric concept has largely persisted into the present, it was also an unstable and contested category from the very beginning whose scope and rate of incidence expanded and contracted significantly in the last century. Richard Bentall argues that historical rates of mental illness are notoriously unreliable because diagnostic criteria have been inconsistent over time and across national contexts.[36] The very scientific status of "schizophrenia" has been the target of critiques by many psychiatrists, sociologists, and historians of mental illness. Most famously, Michel Foucault argues that for many centuries medical, legal, and psychiatric regimes deployed the notion of madness as an instrument of biopolitics rather than as part of a scientific procedure of treatment or description. He claims that, beginning in the late-eighteenth century, the Age of Reason required the category of "unreason" – a poorly defined stigma that was applied to nearly all nonnormative or undesirable bodies. This would include sexual "deviants," the physically or developmentally disabled, as well as those whom we might now recognize as schizophrenics, all of whom served as scapegoats to be removed and confined so as not to contaminate a rationally ordered social field with their "errors of judgment."[37] While Foucault directs most of his critical attention toward the early-modern era of psychiatry, others have argued that the use of vague and shifting diagnostic categories as blunt instruments of biopolitics continues within contemporary psychiatric systems. Mary Boyle has given reasons to doubt whether "schizophrenia" names a single disorder or natural kind, arguing instead that it has served as a catch-all for a variety of syndromes that may present a broad range of intractable symptoms whose etiologies still have not been clearly established.[38] Similarly, Lisa Blackman writes, "Even when psychiatry operates in its most biophysical mode there is no unified explanation, and many of the causal mechanisms are contested and are far from gaining validity within the discipline"; yet despite this conspicuous lack of empirical explanation, the category of schizophrenia has acquired "the status of 'science-already-made.' "[39] Angela Woods argues that, "psychiatry frames schizophrenia as its sublime object or disciplinary limit point" – it is a condition that has never been properly explained, and it therefore constitutes the perennial problem of the discipline.⁴⁰ The weak coherence of the diagnostic category remains evident in the primary psychiatric guide, *The Diagnostic and Statistical Manual of Mental Disorders* (DSM). Psychoanalyst Darian Leader observes that

> Today, the *DSM IV-R* defines schizophrenia via a selection process: you need to exhibit at least two from a list of five main types of symptoms, including delusions, hallucinations, disorganized speech, disorganized or catatonic behaviour and so-called "negative symptoms", such as lack of affect or volition [...] Critics of *DSM* have pointed out how the diagnostic criteria here are hopelessly vague, as they entail that two people can have schizophrenia without sharing any symptoms.⁴¹

If this lack of consensus or confidence in diagnostic procedures persists today, things were even less certain in the moment of modernism. Boyle and Bentall have suggested that the number of patients diagnosed with schizophrenia in the early-twentieth century was dramatically inflated due to the common misdiagnosis of the condition *encephalitis lethargica* – a neurological disorder that presented symptoms similar to those of schizophrenia, may have been caused by a virus, and swept across Europe from 1915–1927, affecting as many as five million people. Bentall writes: "So varied were the long-term symptoms observed following the epidemic, that *encephalitis lethargica* originally received a variety of other names, including 'epidemic delirium,' 'epidemic disseminated sclerosis,' 'atypical poliomyelitis' and '*epidemic schizophrenia*.'"⁴² While these patients may not have suffered from schizophrenia, the outbreak helped to bring severe mental illness to the forefront of cultural attention and made schizophrenia appear to be a widespread and perhaps even contagious disease.

The historical and cultural picture we have of madness in the early-twentieth century is therefore a cloudy one, made more opaque by shifting diagnostic methods. What is clear is that madness was at the center of late-modernist attention. A 1937 article in *Harper's Magazine* announces "The Age of Schizophrenia" as a new era of "overcrowded asylums and prisons" and links this epochal epidemic to overwhelming technological and scientific developments: "For the mind of man has created a dazzling world of bright light and swift movement and flashing communications in which the man of flesh and blood finds it impossible to make himself at home."⁴³ The cultural fascination and even identification with mental illness was nowhere more evident than in the experimental literature of the modernist era. While writing *Finnegans Wake*, James Joyce consulted Morton Prince's *A Dissociation of a Personality* – a case study of dissociative personality disorder that may have provided a model for the many voices that divide and combine throughout the *Wake*.[44] At the same time, Joyce's daughter, Lucia, exhibited signs of mental illness, was observed briefly by Carl Jung, and was diagnosed as schizophrenic. Virginia Woolf's *Mrs. Dalloway* provides perhaps one of the most memorable fictional renderings of psychotic experience and its inept treatment through the character of Septimus Smith, whose auditory hallucinations were evidently drawn from Woolf's own experiences. Ezra Pound's notorious, paranoid experiments with radio broadcasting are well known. Examples of modernist writers' struggles with mental illness are numerous, and several will be examined in the chapters that follow. Some, such as Anna Kavan, Evelyn Waugh, and Muriel Spark, drew upon their experiences of mental illness to create their most experimental works of fiction. For others, such as Loy and Beckett, encounters with the mentally ill seem to have inspired efforts to narratively reproduce the worlds that psychiatry often dismissed as beyond understanding.

While the works of each of these writers assume unique relations to experiences of auditory hallucination, thought insertion, depersonalization, and paranoid delusion, they share an effort to represent and perhaps manage the similar forms of ontological crisis through the synthetic work of narrative. Therefore, while I would not dispute claims made by Trotter and Santner that radical social transformations produced anxieties over class status and authority, these are not the prevailing concerns of the texts that I discuss. Instead, I argue that the works of Lewis, Loy, Kavan, Waugh, Beckett, and others confront a problem that was perhaps more fundamental than one's location within a shifting social field. What their novels and antinovels share is a radical uncertainty over ontological differences between the human and the machine, the living and the dead, and self and world. These are symptoms not of the low-level status anxiety that Trotter detects in the work of Joseph Conrad, D. H. Lawrence, and T. E. Hulme; rather, such symptoms manifest in subjects who struggle to determine not only what kind of person they are but also what is meant by "person."

Of course, technological dehumanization has been a perennial concern in literature since well before the twentieth century, and modernist and contemporary iterations of the issue have been well observed.[45] However, I argue that in the writings of psychotics we may find a way to reframe this fundamental issue. Read in concert with certain modern and contemporary fictions, these memoirs and case studies prove to be unlikely resources for understanding how the being of the human becomes uncertain and how writing might provide some fugitive order against this ontological confusion. At the same time, I wish to resist temptations to either idealize or normalize those who suffer from extreme mental disabilities. As Angela Woods and Catherine Prendergast argue, schizophrenia has often been appropriated by cultural theory and literature as a form of unmitigated enjoyment or as a strategic model of political resistance, and the effect has often been to subordinate the suffering of actual schizophrenics.[46] Nor should the comparison of their writings to literary texts flatten the singularity of their lived experiences or obscure their histories. While I find in psychotic writing analogues for the ontological problems and narrative techniques that are sometimes engaged by modernist literature, I also wish to underscore the particular histories of suffering as well as the often brutal treatments that distinguish the lived experiences of mental patients from those of their literary contemporaries.

At the same time, I hope to demonstrate the stakes of these patients' writings and the unique discursive methods they produce in order to orient themselves within their vertiginous worlds. These writers develop unconventional modes that stretch the limits of narrative in order to describe and in some instances manage thought disorders that often elude conventional linguistic modes of representation. They are compelled to write their ways through ontological and epistemological uncertainties that also preoccupy much experimental fiction. Further, these memoirs of mental illness are clearly as culture-bound and responsive to historical and psychiatric discourses as any literary text. An examination of these delusional memoirs may disclose the ways that they often adapted their narratives of depersonalization from the often depersonalizing discourses of psychiatry and neurology that purported to explain them.

Mechanizing the Mind

The writings of psychotic patients often demonstrate features more commonly associated with those of philosophers: they exhibit suspicion of basic elements of experience, a propensity for system building, and inventive attempts to resolve problems of being and knowing. Delusions often begin with feelings of "unreality" – an uncanny sense that one's environment and the existence of oneself or of others have become uncertain. The discursive reproduction of this unreality effect and narrative attempts to resolve it are formal features that these memoirs often share with late-modernist experimental fiction. In *An Autobiography of a Schizophrenic Girl*, "Renee" gives an especially lucid description of this experience and of her attempts to explain the feeling of unreality in technological terms: "Around me, the other children, heads bent over their work, were robots or puppets, moved by an invisible mechanism [...] Everything looked artificial, mechanical, electric."[47] In what may be regarded as the founding moment of modern philosophy, another "René" launched his systematic procedure of doubt by tarrying with a similarly nightmarish suspicion. In his "Second Meditation," Descartes considers the possibility that the figures who pass below his window are not humans but are simply clothed automata designed to deceive him.[48] The uncanny indiscernibility between man and machine launches both "Renee" and René on protracted, systematic efforts to determine the being of the human and to construct ways in which this question might be satisfactorily resolved.[49]

Descartes acknowledges that the human body can be explained by analogy to hydraulic machines, but he famously goes to great lengths to establish the sovereignty and integrity of the mind. The action of the body could be explained and even supplanted by machinery, but ontological distinction of thought would remain the privilege of the human. "Renee," however, suspects that even her thoughts are the products of an obscure, electrified System, "a narrow wire passing through the body, or rather through the mind, representing the tension of unreality."[50] This technological framework helps Renee explain her uncanny feelings of unreality, but the terms she uses are not randomly chosen. Her delusion reflects the form of discourse common within a psychiatric regime to which patients like Renee were exposed. Friedrich Kittler, Laura Otis, and others have shown how nineteenth-century physiologists found in telegraph technology useful metaphors for describing the nervous system as an electrified communications network.[51] Such a metaphor would become reality for many patients, such as a woman in the treatment of Carl Jung who believed that the incessant voices in her head were caused by a telephone system running throughout her body.[52] This failure to distinguish literal and metaphorical meaning is a problem that shapes many schizophrenic experiences. The technological metaphors through which doctors explained patients' disorders often supplied the raw materials of the patients' delusional narratives.

This is evident in the famous case of Daniel Paul Schreber, whose *Memoirs of My Nervous Illness* (1905) has garnered as much hermeneutic and theoretical attention as many canonical works of literary modernism. Key elements of Schreber's delusional world reflect the radical materialism that was promoted by his famous psychiatrist, Dr. Paul Emil Flechsig, a leading figure in the late-nineteenth-century German school of "psychophysics." As Friedrich Kittler argues, Flechsig's strictly mechanistic explanation of the brain made the notion of the "soul" an unnecessary hypothesis, and Schreber consequently complains that he is the victim of "soul murder" perpetrated by this doctor.[53] He recalls that his mental breakdown began with the appearance of a strange fantasy in which he imagined experiencing sexual penetration as a woman. Unable to acknowledge these thoughts as his own, he attributed them to some external, malignant influence. "This idea was so foreign to my whole nature that I may say I would have rejected it with indignation if fully awake; from what I have experienced I cannot exclude the possibility that some external influences were at work to implant this idea in me."[54] This suspicion of thought insertion would lead to a more generalized sense of ontological insecurity or contamination in which his psychic boundaries were no longer secure. In Schreber's attempts to explain such obscure external influences and to salvage his ontological integrity, he would devise an elaborate cosmological system that mixes theology, technology, and neurology. It is a cryptomaterialist metaphysical world in which the soul and even God are reducible to nerve tissue. At the center of his delusion is a radiolike system of cosmic proportions in which the sun functions as a transmitter from which God broadcasts his thoughts.[55] In language that draws upon Flechsig's psychophysics, Schreber explains that thought is produced through the excitation of nerves, and he speculates that his unacceptable thoughts were transmitted to him via "nerve communication with rays."[56] Kittler observes, "the patient dissects his own organs and notes their modifications while he is still alive, with a positivism that honors psychophysics."[57] Schreber's account of his experiences assumes not only scientistic explanations but also a pseudoscientific form of writing.

Kittler is right to suggest that Schreber's delusion reflects mechanistic neurological doctrines, according to which mental illnesses are the epiphenomenal effects of dysfunctional nerve tissues.[58] These accounts originated in a German neurological community that was heavily influenced by Hermann von Helmholtz's work on the physics of thermodynamics. In addition to Flechsig, neurologists such as Gustav Theodor Fechner, Ernst Brücke, and Theodor Meynert posited a psychic energy that traveled throughout the nervous system. When that system dysfunctioned, the normal flow of that energy was interrupted, resulting in either an excess or a lack of this electrified force. These hydraulic and electrical metaphors were likely sources for Schreber's technological delusion as well as precursors to Freud's libido theory.[59] Within this mechanistic, explanatory framework, psychological symptoms could be traced to physical causes, effectively making early psychiatrists and neurologists the technologists of the mind. Schreber was certainly not alone in developing a quasitechnological explanation for his experiences. Victor Tausk's paper "On the Origins of the 'Influencing Machine' Delusion in Schizophrenia" generated a great deal of psychiatric interest in schizophrenic patients' tendency to develop machine-centered delusions, and the number of publications describing such cases grew dramatically through the mid-twentieth century.[60]

However, while Freud and his followers made occasional attempts to theorize psychosis, psychoanalysis principally restricted its therapeutic ambitions to the treatment of the milder neuroses, leaving the management of the most severe forms of mental illness to the increasingly biologistic and mechanistic schools of psychiatry. This turn toward biology constituted an attempt to establish the scientific status of the new science of psychiatry on the foundation of objective, empirical evidence. In 1874, the British psychiatrist Henry Maudsley writes, "Insanity is, in fact, a disorder of brain, producing a disorder of mind; or, to define its nature in greater detail, it is a disorder of the supreme nerve centers of the brain."[61] The result was a conception of the patient as a dysfunctioning, depersonalized, biological machine, and modern delusions came to reflect this view. While the first wave of biological psychiatry produced unstable diagnostic categories, no effective treatments, and the hopeless warehousing of the mentally ill, the ambition to explain psychopathology via reference to neuroanatomy only gained momentum over the course of the twentieth century. This incorrigible belief in the absence of evidence that neurological lesions or malformations would be found to correspond with psychological symptoms of schizophrenia was regarded by Karl Jaspers as "brain mythologies."[62] The lack of progress in successfully correlating symptoms with neurophysiology did not deter psychiatrists from a strategic reduction of mind to brain and brain to electrical machine. Ironically, incorrigible beliefs in the absence of evidence would come to be one of the nosological criteria for the diagnosis of psychosis.

By 1921, Eugen Bleuler claims that, "the mutual influence of different psychic functions works like an electric device where functions are switched on and off."[63] If the brain was to be regarded as a system of electrical devices, its dysfunctions suggested electrical forms of intervention and observation. Verena Kuni observes that these were precisely the conclusions drawn by other psychiatric and neurological researchers: "Bleuler's *Elementarpsychologie* ('elementary psychology') provided not only the basis for an 'electro-technically worded psycho-pathology' that his Italian colleague Cerletti would soon use to develop electro-shock therapy. The experiments of Ferdinando Cazzamalli, who tried to prove interference by 'brain waves' and 'radio waves', and to specify different kinds of 'cerebral radio-waves' for patients with diseases of the 'epileptic', 'paranoid', 'hallucinatory' or 'hysterical spectrum', also date from the same period."[64] In 1925, the *New York Times* reported that Cazzamalli, a neurologist at the University of Milan, "treated the human brain as a broadcast station" in order "to see what radio signals sent out by the brain could be picked up by delicate radio receivers."[65] Although Cazzamalli's experiments failed, they may have appeared somewhat less outrageous after Hans Berger successfully measured electrical brain waves with the first electroencephalograph in 1924.[66] Reports of such developments quickly reached a fascinated and sometimes anxious public. Media historian Jeffrey Sconce shows that fantasies and anxieties of neurological manipulation manifested in a wave of 1920s pulp fiction that often imagines a professor whose radio apparatus directly transmits and receives the thoughts of his test subjects.[67] In this context, there are no bright lines between science, fantasy, and delusion; mental patients' suspicions that their thoughts had been technologically observed or inserted via some form of broadcasting device appear to be not without historical foundation.

While psychiatric and neurological discourses manifested in increasingly technological rhetoric, behaviorists such as John B. Watson introduced a psychology that fully eliminated any reference to conscious experience, and announced that its central ambition was the development of techniques for not merely the observation but rather the control of other minds. Watson writes, "The interest of the behaviorist in man's doings is more than the interest of the spectator – he wants to control man's reactions as physical scientists want to control and manipulate other natural phenomena. It is the business of behavioristic psychology to be able to predict and to control human activity."[68] In its efforts to establish a scientific form of psychology based on objective, verifiable evidence, behaviorism replaced any references to consciousness and subjective experience with mechanistic, stimulus–response patterns. It was this psychology without mind that became a target of Wyndham Lewis's sustained and withering critique in the late 1920s, as I will show in Chapter 1.

Edwin Boring, a psychologist who trained as an electrical engineer, articulated behaviorism's guiding, epistemic principle:

> We can always describe what happens in terms of stimulus and response, and that lands us in the realm of mechanism. *We do not need to argue that learning is mechanistic; it is mechanistic by operational definition* [...] You do not understand a psychological phenomenon well until you can generalize the mechanistic properties which are implied by those operations by which the phenomenon is known.[69]

Put differently, behaviorist epistemology only recognizes mechanistic ontology and excludes all other forms of being. The subjective experiences of the subject – or patient – are explicitly foreclosed from this ontological framework and the organism is reduced to a mechanism that could be technologically simulated and manipulated through conditioning. "The advantage of playing this kind of game lies solely in the fact that, if you talk about machines, you are more certain to leave out the subjective, anthropomorphic hocus locus of mentalism [...] Hence the mentalistic concepts need first objective analysis into functions, and then a further test, the test of thinking about them as pertaining to a machine."[70] Confronted with such rhetoric, a psychotic patient could be forgiven for feeling that she had been transformed into a lifeless machine.

Written in 1946, Boring's discussion of the mind as a machine or robot is not merely metaphorical; he claims that this mechanical reduction of the mind "is also a procedure in accord with the spirit of the times. We have heard so much during the late war about electronic brains."[71] If behaviorists regarded actual minds as mechanical black boxes that could be trained, conditioned, and controlled, the emerging science of cybernetics attempted to open those black boxes in order to determine how their automatic, self-correcting operations might function or dysfunction. Some of the earliest "electric brains" to which Boring refers were developed by British psychiatrists Grey Walter and Hal Ashby, whose famous "homeostat" and "tortoise" were regarded as demonstrations that if higher-order mental operations such as "purposive activity" could be modeled in electrical circuits, then the failures or dysfunctions that gave rise to psychopathology could be technologically simulated as well. Historian Rhodri Hayward writes that the cybernetic machine's dysfunctional behavior "could be terminated only if the machine was turned off, rewired or recharged. For their creators, such behaviour had an obvious analogy with the cases they encountered in their medical work."[72] Hayward suggests that the relationship between human mind and electrical device was, for Ashby and Walter, one of "analogy," but it is evident that cybernetic and psychiatric discourses were developing toward one of identity between the two categories. As a biologically oriented psychiatrist, Ashby spent the 1930s studying the structure of the brain before developing his own mechanical devices. Andrew Pickering argues that, "although Ashby's earlier work always aimed to elucidate the functioning of the brain, normal and pathological, he developed, almost despite himself, a very general theory of machines [...] psychiatry was a surface of emergence and return for Ashby's cybernetics, as it was for Walter's," and this is evident in his widely influential 1952 book *Design for a Brain*.[73] In a 1950 report entitled, *Recent Progress in Psychiatry,* Ashby contributed a section on "Cybernetics," in which he asserts, "These methods of treatment [of machines] have analogies with psychiatric methods too obvious to need description."[74]

Pickering describes the cybernetic devices of Ashby and Walter as "ontological theater."[75] Such ontological implications were not lost on others. Norbert Wiener – who published two of the earliest and most widely read accounts of cybernetic theory – declared in 1950 that Ashby's "homeostat" was "one of the great philosophical contributions of the present day."[76] In a famous 1966 interview with *Der Spiegel,* Heidegger was asked what had taken the place of philosophy in addressing his famous question of "being"; his grim response is "cybernetics."[77] Ashby and Walter operated under the assumption, expressed by Boring, that an adequate explanation of a system is accomplished only when its functions have been simulated by mechanical design, and it was this form of "psychology as engineering," already nascent in earlier waves of mind sciences, that eventually gave rise to the cognitive revolution.[78] Regarding the cognitive behavioral therapy that later evolved from this framework, Lisa Blackman writes, "The mind is viewed as a 'system' which processes, stores and codes information or 'input', reified as a repository which has a hardware, metaphors which originate within the 'technological revolution' in computers which accompanied its rise in the psychological sciences."[79]

As computational models of brain functions and dysfunctions were introduced, the paranoid delusions of schizophrenic patients reflected this informatic, explanatory framework. In her memoir, *Operators and Things: The Inner Life of a Schizophrenic* (1958), Barbara O'Brien describes delusional experiences in which she feels herself transformed into a mainframe computer that carries out the commands of unseen operators.

> It was a somewhat startling discovery to me. I had always thought of the unconscious as a whirling pool of repressed emotions, better repressed. Instead, it appeared to be a sort of private Univac, an incredible piece of thinking mechanism, the possession of every conscious mind on earth. The quality of the mechanism differs.[80]

O'Brien describes her experiences of thought insertion in terms of programs running on a UNIVAC, or UNIVersal Automatic Computer, one of the first business computers produced by the Remington Rand typewriter company in the early 1950s. Such a machine was not conceived of as "private" or "personal" but was instead a shared resource that would serve multiple operators logging in from remote locations. The new technology provided an apt framework through which schizophrenic experiences could be explained by both psychiatrists and schizophrenics. Like many of the memoirs and fictions of madness that came before hers, O'Brien's account not only reflects the metaphors and discourses of psychiatry to which she may have been subjected but also includes those mechanistic metaphors among the sources of her anxieties. Ian Hacking writes of the dialectic or feedback loop that often occurs between patient and diagnostician:

> The doctors' vision was different because the patients were different; but the patients were different because the doctors' expectations were different. That is an example of a very general phenomenon: the looping effect of human kinds. People classified in a certain way tend to conform to or grow into the ways that they are described; but they also evolve in their own ways, so that the classifications and descriptions have to be constantly revised.[81]

If simple, linear causality for technological delusions cannot be ascribed to the mechanistic frameworks of twentieth-century psychiatry, neither can those delusions plausibly be detached from those discourses. Many first-person accounts of psychosis describe a flattened affect in which virtually all of the features of mind – beliefs, desires, will, intentions – have been removed or, if they persist, seem no longer to be one's own. In many respects, this is not so different from the account that biological psychiatry, behaviorism, and cybernetics render. As Jean-Pierre Dupuy argues, "The science of mind that cybernetics wished to construct was (to use today's vocabulary) resolutely 'eliminativist.' The mental states invoked by ordinary or 'folk' psychology to account for behavior – beliefs, desires, will, intentions – were to be banned from scientific explanation."[82] In precisely the looping effect between doctors and their patients that Hacking describes, mental patients often came to feel that their minds had been eliminated – replaced by automatic machines – in ways that reflect the technological discourses of the mind sciences. This same flattened affect and absence of folk psychological predicates recurs in much of the modernist fiction that I examine in this book.

Should it appear that psychoanalysis avoided this form of mechanistic modeling of psychopathology, it is worth recalling that Freud's account of the mind's management of drives shares much with nineteenth-century theories of energetics and thermodynamics. Karl Jaspers is equally critical of neurological and psychoanalytic approaches to psychosis for their similar displacements of patient's experiences with what he regards as mythic causal mechanisms, whether somatic or psychological. The English philosopher of mind Gilbert Ryle similarly critiques psychoanalysis's claims to offer scientistic, "para-mechanical" causal explanations that attempt to replicate the methods and prestige of the physical sciences.[83] In the early 1950s, Jacques Lacan was drawn to the new discourses of information theory and cybernetics, devoting several sessions of his seminar to the translation of Freudian concepts into the conceptual framework of cybernetics.[84] Jean-Pierre Dupuy writes that "In so doing he replaced the supposed unconscious death wish with the senseless functioning of a machine, the unconscious henceforth being identified with a cybernetic automaton. The alliance of psychoanalysis and cybernetics was neither anecdotal nor fortuitous: it corresponded to a radicalization of the critique of metaphysical humanism."[85]

Lacan was not alone in pursuing a synthesis between psychoanalysis and cybernetics. Gregory Bateson famously developed a cybernetic model of schizophrenia, and Kenneth Colby, who trained as a psychoanalyst, later became interested in artificial intelligence and designed PARRY – a computer program that simulated the language of paranoiacs so effectively that it convinced several psychiatrists that it was a real patient, and it was purported to be the first artificial system to pass a Turing test.[86] Even Ross Ashby, the British cybernetic psychiatrist, recognized points of fundamental agreement between his cybernetic model of automatic mental operations and the Freudian theory of the unconscious when he wrote in a private notebook, "Others may talk of freewill and the individual's power to direct his life's story. My personal experience has convinced me over and over again that my power of control is great – where it doesn't matter: but at the important times, in the words of Freud, I do not live but 'am lived.' "[87] While it has been rightly associated with interpretive techniques and foregrounding the patient's discourse, psychoanalysis has always had roots in various forms of mechanistic discourse, and at times it clearly enlisted the scientific prestige of thermodynamics and later information theory in order to make its own concepts run.[88] Like much of modernism, psychoanalysis therefore occupied a transitional moment between the monist ontologies of "energy" and "information" – master terms that promised to account for the behavior of human and machine through a single explanatory principle.[89] Many of the texts discussed in the following chapters invoke such monist ontologies.

While Freud, Tausk, and their followers appear to decode psychotic delusions by translating their technological elements into the psychoanalytic vocabulary of unconscious drives and libidinal cathexes, there is equally a sense in which schizophrenic patients often reflect the technological features of the psychological theories through which they are explained. In the closing pages of his essay on Schreber, Freud acknowledges the resemblance between Schreber's delusional theory of "nerve-rays" and his own libido theory, and he anxiously insists that he had developed his own metapsychology prior to reading Schreber's memoirs.[90] In this telling moment, the roles of patient and analyst are inverted: Freud exhibits paranoid anxiety over the originality and integrity of his thoughts, while it is Schreber who theorizes about the operations of the nervous system that underlie his experiences. Methodologically, this book performs a similar reversal of discursive positions: rather than simply applying psychoanalytic theory to literary delusions, I show how the experimental fiction and paranoid memoirs help us to interpret the ontological and phenomenological implications of the period's psychoanalytic, psychiatric, and neurological discourses.

Certain psychiatrists have acknowledged the epistemic limits and ethical consequences of the engineering approach to the mind and its disorders. R. D. Laing observes that his patients "experience themselves as automata, as robots, as bits of machinery, or even as animals. Such persons are rightly regarded as crazy. Yet why do we not regard a theory that seeks to transmute persons into automata or animals as equally crazy?"[91] Karl Jaspers draws a fundamental distinction between "explaining" underlying causal processes and "understanding" a patient's subjective experiences: "Causal thinking impinges on what is alien, non-understandable and on what can be manipulated; understanding of meaning impinges on myself in the other and on what is closest to me in the other."[92] The act of understanding entails the work of empathy that recognizes the human experiences of the patient. At the same time, Jaspers notoriously defined the experiences of the schizophrenic as fundamentally "un-understandable," effectively marking such subjects as beyond the limits of the human. More recently, philosopher of mind Daniel Dennett has reproduced Jaspers's epistemic difference between "explanation" and "understanding" when he distinguishes the "design stance" – an episteme that explains behavior by reference to their underlying functional or material operations – from an "intentional stance" that understands behavior by reference to folk psychological categories such as beliefs, desires, affects, and intentions.[93] Psychologist Richard Bentall argues, "we tend to be thrown on to design stance explanations ('there's something wrong with the brain') when intentional stance explanations fail us (that is, when we say that the behaviour we are observing is 'mad', 'crazy', 'loco' or, in Jaspers' terminology, ununderstandable)."[94] It is behavior that is more difficult to account for via conventional folk psychology – such as the depersonalizing experience of psychosis – that is most often treated as beyond the scope of understanding and is instead "explained" via the function and dysfunction of neurological mechanisms.

This epistemic preference for explanations of mechanical dysfunctions over phenomenological understanding has had significant ontological and ethical consequences, as Bentall asserts: "once we have decided that the patient's experiences are unintelligible, we are given an apparent license to treat the patient as a disordered organism, a malfunctioning body that we do not have to relate to in a human way."[95] Bentall articulates the ways that the history of psychiatry and its often brutal treatments is in many ways a story from which "the human" is excluded. However, Bentall passes over other ethical risks that accompany empathy as well as notoriously fraught categories such as "the human" that demand more thorough reflection. Heather Love writes, "Accounting for the other's interiority always involves a certain violence, whether it is by the hard way of epistemological violence or the soft way of projective identification. It is also perhaps the case that such acts of ethical witness have as their ultimate ground the affective and ethical capacities of the witness, who bathes in the reflected warmth of the other's suffering."[96] Precisely such ethically fraught attempts at empathy and humanization are satirized in Beckett's early novel *Murphy*, in which the title character's desire to know a psychotic patient, Endon, merely reduces the latter to a blank screen upon which Murphy projects his own fantasies. In some instances, the requirements that attend the category of "the human" may be unlivable for certain subjects who conceive of themselves as mechanical systems precisely in order to mediate their relation to others. Once again, it is Beckett who most incisively explores this possibility in *The Unnamable:* "he's getting humanized, he's going to lose if he doesn't watch out, if he doesn't take care, and with what could he take care, with what could he form the faintest conception of the condition they are decoying him into, with their ears, their eyes, their tears and a brainpan where anything may happen."[97] We cannot say in advance what such motifs will mean or how they will be deployed, nor can we say in advance what the category of "the human" may entail for doctor or patient. Instead, Jaspersian "understanding" would require a mode of reading that attends to the particular meanings, pragmatics, and worlds that are developed within each text.

This has not been the standard approach, as is evident in the protocols established by the *Diagnostic and Statistical Manual of Mental Disorders* (DSM).[98] Darian Leader, in his critique of the *DSM*, writes:

> Focusing on external symptoms meant effectively that the individual's own experience was devalued: what mattered was what symptoms they had *rather than how they processed these symptoms, what they made of them, how they bestowed meaning – or not – on their experience* [. . .] The *DSM* classification system that grew out of this consolidated the emphasis on surface and visibility.[99]

The priority of externally observable and supposedly easily legible "surface symptoms" over patients' lived experiences, acts of meaning making, and particular cultural contexts has had consequences not only for the ways that psychiatrists have framed mental illness but also for the patients' self-understanding. After enumerating the brutal treatments to which psychotic patients have been involuntarily subjected – including insulin injections, electroconvulsive shock therapy, solitary confinement, and prefrontal lobotomy with ice picks – Bentall argues that "without regarding psychosis as *ununderstandable* (to use Jaspers' terminology), it would not have been possible to deny psychiatric patients a voice, which might otherwise have been raised in protest against these horrors."[100] The novels and memoirs of mental illness discussed in the following chapters attempt to give voice to such limit experiences of mechanical reduction and depersonalization. Like memoirs of mental illness, avant-garde forms of late-modernist fiction often exhibit idiosyncratic narrative methods and occupy positions at the limit of what has been regarded as "understandable." If experimental literature expands those limits in order to represent experiences and conditions in ways that more conventional forms cannot, such works may help us to understand the voices of those who have been systematically regarded as no longer worth listening to.

Narrative Worlding

One alternative would be an approach that resists both the temptation to disregard the discourse of the mentally ill as epiphenomenal nonsense (as biological psychiatry has often done) and the temptation to rewrite or translate the patient's narrative into a preferred theoretical idiom (a tendency that is arguably evident in the certain forms of psychoanalysis, including Tausk's analysis of the "Influencing Machine Delusion," in which the patient's discourse is often converted into the libido theory). Scholarly attention to patients' narratives in general and to the discourse of the mentally ill in particular has been renewed by the fields of disability studies and medical humanities, and one of the goals of this book is to contribute to these lines of research. Lisa Blackman writes, "If we were to follow these moves then one implication would be that we would no longer be interested in mapping underlying internal psychological or neurological mechanisms, and would instead concentrate on the different ways in which the voice-hearing experience is mediated through culturally available narratives."[101] In this vein, the writings of the mentally ill might be read as records of the devastating experiences of unworlding as well as provisional, reparative acts of narrative worlding.

If a tacit system of relationships, purposes, and categories normally constitute our conventional sense of "being-in-the-world," the experience of schizophrenia may be understood as a loss of such a tacit order, and the language of "unworlding" recurs in many first-person accounts of mental illness. Of course, experiences of radical unworlding are not limited to the mentally ill. In an account of such experiences, including that of receiving information at a distance via radio, Martin Heidegger writes:

> The terrifying is unsettling; it places everything outside its own nature. What is it that unsettles and thus terrifies? It shows itself and hides itself in the *way* in which everything presences, namely, in the fact that despite all conquests of distances the nearness of things remain absent.[102]

The "nearness of things" that is lost is a sense of familiarity and kinship with the contents of one's environment – a sense in which one is at home with things. For Heidegger, the terror that arises from the loss of this feeling of dwelling is an effect of the increasingly technological mode of discourse that extends to the description and treatment of the mentally ill as dysfunctioning machines. Perhaps the most lucid discussion of a schizophrenic experience of unworlding can be found in *An Autobiography of a Schizophrenic Girl*, in which "Renee" recalls,

> An awful terror bound me; I wanted to scream [...] Everything looked artificial, mechanical, electric [...] But behind this wall of indifference, suddenly a wave of anxiety would creep over me, the anxiety of unreality. My perception of the world seemed to sharpen the sense of the strangeness of things. In the silence and immensity, each object was cut off by a knife, detached in the emptiness, in the boundlessness, spaced off from other things. Without any relationship with the environment, just by being itself, it began to come to life.[103]

Renee describes a terrifying experience of "unreality," in which objects and persons can no longer be distinguished or integrated within a sensible, familiar environment. Her account shares much with Heidegger's description of the ontological terror that he attributes to a modern, technological framework. After describing her feelings of unreality and unworlding, Renee develops an elaborate, technological, delusional narrative through which her experiences are explained, and a coherent if dystopian world is reconstructed. She writes, "some time after, I discovered that the Persecutor was none other than the electric machine, that is, it was the 'System' that was punishing me. I thought of it as some vast world-like entity encompassing all men."[104] More than simply meaningless symptoms, delusions might be understood as pragmatic responses to this terrifying experience. Such narratives may both register the texture of this unworlding and reconstitute some provisional or ad hoc world from the available cultural fragments.

The claim that we may learn much from the altered forms of narrative world construction evident in such cases of mental illness is a recurring, if minoritarian, view within the history of the mind sciences. Some have begun to advance a "narrative turn" in their fields – a line of research to which literary studies has much to contribute. Jerome Bruner has critiqued the displacement of what he called the study of "human meaning making" by more mechanistic models of "information processing" that dominated early cognitive science, and Bruner has advocated for a narrative turn in cognitive psychology. Several recent studies have attempted to identify the neural correlates of narrative formation, including one that begins from the premise that "our everyday engagements in tasks, conversations and narratives only become meaningful to the extent that we can integrate and profile local information in relation to larger coherent situation models and story plots."[105] The notion that delusional narrative may be understood as not only a symptom of schizophrenia but also as a reparative procedure has recurred in numerous psychiatric and phenomenological approaches to mental illness. Dan Zahavi suggests that "Elaborate storytelling might serve a compensatory function; it might be an attempt to make up for the lack of a fragile self-identity."[106] Shaun Gallagher observes that "Not all schizophrenic narratives go wrong. For example, someone suffering from schizophrenic symptoms of thought insertion or delusions of control may correctly complain or describe these feelings in a coherent narrative."[107]

Writing within the phenomenological tradition of Husserl, Heidegger, and Merleau-Ponty, Paul Ricoeur asserts the role of narrative in the formation and maintenance of subjectivity. He presents this position as a direct response to the reduction of the human to an impersonal array of informatic processes in which the "self" is regarded as a vestigial and specious remainder of folk psychology. In a response to a version of that reductionist position articulated by philosopher Derek Parfit, Ricoeur asserts that "It is because mental states and bodily facts have at the outset been reduced to impersonal events that the self appears to be a supplementary fact. The self, I will claim, simply does not belong to the category of events and facts."[108] Instead, Ricoeur argues, the self and its world are effects of narrative, and it is through narrative that biological life becomes human life in which the temporal succession of discordant events is reconfigured into an experience of concordant, diachronic unity. Anthony Giddens recasts this as a historical condition of late modernity when he argues, "A person's identity is not to be found in behaviour, nor [...] in the reactions of others, but in the capacity to keep a particular narrative going."[109] This entails a disciplinary and normative understanding of what counts as "narrative" and "identity," and many late-modernist novels and memoirs diverge from conventional modes of self-report and storytelling. Altered forms of narrative entail altered forms of subjectivity, and this is evident in the range of formal and phenomenological structures rendered in the texts that will come under examination. Some texts, such as Beckett's *The Unnamable*, eschew linear development and consistency of identity and instead manifest disruptive events and unresolved episodes that resist both integration within a single plot and attribution to a single character. Other texts render a more rigid, global configuration of experience through paranoid delusions that reduce all phenomena to the same univocal or, in Ricoeur's term, "concordant" meaning. In many memoirs and self-reports, paranoid psychotics' heterogeneous experiences are assigned univocal significance within a persecutory and/or megalomaniacal plot that locates the self at its center. Such delusional narratives often perform the work of worlding that restores some sense of concordant order within which the subject can locate herself.

Freud advances a similar view that delusions are "attempts at restitution or recovery" when he writes, "a fair number of analyses have taught us that the delusion is found applied like a patch over the place where originally a rent had appeared in the ego's relation to the external world."[110] This act of worlding through delusional narrative is often explicitly thematized as in Schreber's famous memoir, which includes an elaborate outline of his "Order of the World."[111] If Freud was among the first to describe delusional narratives as reparative acts, he was hardly the last. The Russian neurologist Alexandre Luria describes *The Man with a Shattered World*, the writings of a patient who suffered severe brain trauma, as a "neurological novel," and in a foreword to the text, Oliver Sacks observes "the way in which, through constructing his own narrative he managed to recapture, and reappropriate, the sense of a life-world."[112] Psychologist Larry Davidson has proposed narrative analysis as a resource for understanding the phenomenology of schizophrenia.[113] James Phillips discusses one case within a taxonomy of schizophrenic forms of discourse: "a man with rather flamboyant delusional experiences, represents a style of self-narrative in which the challenges of developing a self-narrative are resolved through the creation of a delusional narrative."[114] In similar vein, Paul and John Lysaker and others have developed clinical approaches that demonstrate the role of narrative cognition in schizophrenia and the ways that the dialogical development of narratives may have positive therapeutic outcomes.[115]

Such examples extend to many modernist writers whose works were often implicated in their own struggles with mental illness. An understanding of paranoid delusions as "attempts at restitution or recovery" should prompt a rethinking of Eve Kosofsky Sedgwick's influential opposition of "reparative" to "paranoid" modes of thought: for some, paranoia can be a form of psychic and even ontological repair, even if it trades negative feelings of persecution for a provisional sense of being-in-the-world.[116] The precarious status of these delusional formations demands forms of listening and reading that differ from the modes of suspicion and critique that have long dominated literary studies. It is perhaps uninstructive and dismissive to rehearse the observation that schizophrenics' conceptions of self and world are the effects of delusion and error; more interesting would be an approach that asks what pragmatic work those "errors" perform for the subjects in question, from where the fragments of their worlds may have been derived, and how those fragments are refashioned in attempts to resolve fundamental problems – questions that could be applied equally to texts conventionally categorized as "literary" or "pathological."

In advocating for similar approaches to narratives of illness, Ann Jurecic argues, "The academy has long rewarded readings that dismantle literature's illusions but, with regard to literary and amateur illness memoirs, it is also evident that critics need other options, interpretive approaches that enable them to assemble meaning in the face of life's fragility."[117] For a model of alternative hermeneutic practices, Jurecic points to Bruno Latour's essay, "Why Has Critique Run Out of Steam," where he argues, "The critic is not the one who alternates haphazardly between antifetishism and positivism [...] but the one for whom, if something is constructed, then it means it is fragile and thus in great need of care and caution."[118] Indeed, care, caution, and recognition of pragmatic effects – rather than critique – may be especially valuable modes of engagement with the fragile worlds and selves that are constructed through narrative delusion. Darian Leader observes that "It is left to each psychotic subject to invent their own solution to these problems, and the styles of response can allow us to differentiate and define the different forms that psychosis can take."[119] I would suggest that the different forms that these narrative solutions may take are shaped not only by the specific disorders but also by the historical discourses that are available to the subject. "Hence there is a search for an alternative, something like a code or a formula or even *a gadget* that would bring order and meaning to the world."[120] The recurrence of certain technologies at the center of modern psychotic delusions suggests that such devices provide resources through which uncanny and unspeakable experiences can be explained.

At the same time, as will become evident in subsequent discussions of both literary texts and memoirs of mental illness, acts of worlding and self-repair through narrative do not always succeed, or such "success" may appear only partial and provisional. Nor can we say in advance what narrative forms such "success" might take. When these fragile worlds fail in a collapse of meaning, order, and self-identity, an unmediated heterogeneity of experience often returns – an experience akin to "the terrifying" to which Heidegger often refers. Ricoeur observes that something resembling this catastrophic loss of narrative orientation manifests with marked frequency in modern fiction, such as Robert Musil's *The Man without Qualities*: "That the crisis of character is correlative to the crisis in the identity of plot, is amply demonstrated by Musil's novel. One could say generally that as the novel approaches this annulling of the person in terms of sameness-identity, the novel also loses its properly narrative qualities."[121] Similar patterns of plotlessness, or "hyponarrativity," and identity-loss are recurrent formal features of the experimental fiction of Wyndham Lewis, Samuel Beckett, and others whose works empty the novel of its narrative structure while all but evacuating character.

Yet, even when character and emplotment collapse, these fundamental narrative features continue to haunt these texts through their often metafictionally marked absence. In many late-modernist novels, figures often flicker in and out at the edge of personhood. Ricoeur suggests that the status of this pre- or postnarrative "non-subject" cannot quite be dismissed, and his recommendation might extend beyond works of fiction to memoirs of those who have sometimes been denied the status of personhood.

> A non-subject is not nothing, with respect to the category of the subject. Indeed, we would not be interested in this drama of dissolution and would not be thrown into perplexity by it, if the non-subject were not still a figure of the subject, even in a negative mode. Suppose someone asks the question: Who am I? Nothing, or almost nothing is the reply. But it is still a reply to the question *who*, simply reduced to the starkness of the question itself.[122]

It is in this dimension of narratological concerns that the technologically deterministic approach to modern psychosis and modernist writing advanced by Friedrich Kittler falls short. His recognition of the role that materialist psychophysics and communications technology played in Schreber's delusion remains an invaluable starting point; however, Kittler's insistence that writing in the "1900 Discourse Network" is reducible to automatic "transposition of media" in which signal is not distinguished from noise and the brain is simply another informatic device that risks the reduction of such writing to the meaningless and the "un-understandable."[123] It fails to acknowledge the extent to which the resources of narrative, fiction, fantasy, and delusion may be improvised and modified to reconstitute a range of possible phenomenological worlds.[124] Schreber's memoir, like *An Autobiography of a Schizophrenic Girl* and many other memoirs of mental illness, is a record not only of the experience of unworlding but also of the conspicuous work of reconstituting a world through narrative. These formal consistencies and their cultural sources can be located within the history of early psychiatry and its dismissal of narrative forms of understanding.

Psychiatrist and medical ethicist John Sadler has criticized the *DSM*'s diagnostic regime for its "the marginalizing of the narrative, 'storied' dimension of human existence."[125] Sadler argues that this "hyponarrativity" of some forms of psychiatry is often reflected in the discourse of patients. Sadler describes a "Ms. Y" who "could not couch her life in terms of a narrative [...] She could not place herself into a narrative line in which she was an actor among an interplay of other actors with their own motivations, beliefs, concerns, and histories."[126] The suggestion that the self-descriptions of patients like Ms. Y exhibit an internalization of hyponarrative diagnostic methods implies that Hacking's looping effect may manifest not only in the contents of a patient's discourse but also in its formal structure. "Ms. Y's compulsion to evaluate herself and others makes her both the embodiment of the DSM ontology and a hyponarrativity. Her self-talk appears to be tailored for DSM diagnostic criteria."[127] Those criteria often include a functional analysis of the patient that reduces the subject to a loose system of normative cognitive and emotional operations modeled upon information-processing systems. Giovanni Stanghellini explains how, when internalized and turned upon oneself, such a functional analysis might result in the form of self-reification that recurs in schizophrenic delusions:

> My gaze turns into an event that happens in my own mental space, becoming "objectified" by the fact that I'm looking at it. My gaze is now an object that I can analyse, and it starts to detach itself from me. What is disturbing about this experience is that the immediacy of my seeing gets lost along the way, that it starts to seem somewhat foreign, and no longer familiar.[128]

Excessive reflection upon normally tacit processes often results in an interruption of the feeling of immediacy and self-identity, as Stanghellini argues:

> The next stops on this road are the *concretization* of one's own experience of depersonalization ("It's not me who's looking; its a machine that's looking in my stead") and the phenomenon of passivity – one's psychic life is under an alien control ("Someone is manipulating my gaze, and that's why things seem so strange").[129]

Stanghellini conceptualizes such an experience of depersonalization as the reduction of one's own thoughts to objective processes with no narrative center or temporal trajectory. Such a reduction, suggest Sadler and others, is consistent with the functionalist, mechanistic approaches to mental illness that dominated twentieth-century psychiatry. Like Stanghellini, Louis Sass argues that psychosis is not the result of diminished "reality testing" but exhibits a heightened awareness of psychological processes that are normally carried out without reflection:

> Yet it seems these reifications or concretizations may actually indicate not a lack but an exaggeration of reflective distance and self-consciousness: psychological processes and ideas the normal person would experience only tacitly or abstractly (such as kinesthetic sensations in the jaw, or the meaning of "meaning") are focused on and thereby transformed into phenomena having some of the qualities of actual physical objects existing separate from the self.[130]

In this way, the writings of schizophrenics and the parapathological narratives of modernist fiction describe the phenomenal worlds that emerge when a foundational lack of information is disclosed. Steven Connor takes this position when he argues, "Schreber's madness is not the madness of a rampant and irruptive unconscious, but rather that of a psychototalitarian hyperconsciousness, convinced that he is entirely responsible for himself, capable of coinciding with or precisely doubling himself, letting himself be known in its entirety."[131] Schizophrenic patients experience explicitly and concretely those psychological processes that are normally tacit; the hyperreflexive techniques of modernist fiction often render similar effects. Patricia Waugh has observed this unreality effect in psychological fiction that attempts to represent mental processes that are not normally regarded as objects of reflection:

> The problem of how to *represent* an experiencing mind is the problem of preserving a sense of the tacit flow of feeling and consciousness that anchors

the individual in an environment, while accepting that in order to build such a picture in a verbal medium, what is normally tacit must of necessity be explicitly constructed and selected and therefore carries the potential to disturb the "flow" by intruding the act of representation and an ontological awareness of the condition of fictionality, the status of "as if."[132]

What Waugh calls the "ontological awareness of the condition of fictionality" shares much with the feeling of unreality that defines schizophrenia as well as the sense that one's thoughts have been composed by some foreign agent, mechanism, or authority. Waugh cites Muriel Spark's novel *The Comforters* (1957), in which the central character often feels that her thoughts have been inserted by some unseen agent. Eventually, she becomes convinced that she is a character in a novel – a realization that precipitates an ontological crisis and a feeling of artificiality: "Her sense of being written into the novel was painful."[133] Evelyn Waugh, who also explores the ontological convergences of fiction and delusion in *The Ordeal of Gilbert Pinfold*, argued in his review of *The Comforters* that "The area of her mind which is composing the novel becomes separated from the area which is participating in it, so that, hallucinated, she believes that she is observant of, and observed by, and in some degree under the control of, an unknown second person."[134] Like schizophrenics, characters in many late-modernist novels have trouble maintaining a single world or become split across worlds.

Precisely these formal qualities of unworlding, hyperreflexivity, and depersonalization are signature features of much late-modernist fiction. While there is a limit to the usefulness of increasingly fine-grained periodizing distinctions, the "late modernism" that is assembled here could be said to differ from both the first wave of modernist experimentation and from what Fredric Jameson has identified as the "emptied" or "flattened" aesthetics of postmodernism that often ironizes the modernist urge toward formal order and stylistic mastery.[135] Late modernism can be seen as a moment that is burdened by its reflections on the successes, failures, and mounting exhaustion of modernism's first two decades of experimentation. It is marked by a heightened reflexivity and a spirit of stock taking without forfeiting a sense of aesthetic and formal urgency. As Tyrus Miller argues in his classic articulation of late-modernist aesthetics, "The choices for artists working in the wake of modernism had real stakes, and these stakes have not been sufficiently recognized in the rush to postmodernism."[136] By the late 1920s, modernist culture had become a thing that could be retrospectively remembered, reconstructed, and evaluated. This dialectical orientation toward earlier moments in modernism is evident in Wyndham Lewis's works of cultural analysis such as *Time and Western Man* and *The Art of Being Ruled* and in his memoirs of modernism such as *Blasting and Bombardiering* and *Rude Assignment*.[137] These works share with memoirs of mental illness the urgent project of reassembling a world in the aftermath of a traumatic event. While this may resemble the vocation of post–World War I fiction, for many late-modernist works, the disruptive event that would require the work of reconstruction is the legacy of aesthetic experimentation and provocation inaugurated by modernism itself. As Paul Saint-Amour has suggested, late-modernist works exhibit a sense that the disruptive event – whether military, aesthetic, or psychological – has not fully ended so that any achieved formal order carries a distinctly provisional and precarious status.[138] This anxious, unpredictable rhythm of worlding and unworlding is the condition under which both late-modernist fiction and memoirs of mental illness labor. The increasing rate of such upheavals under the conditions of both retrospective and anticipatory knowledge marks a dialectical difference between many late-modernist works and their precursors. For second-generation Irish modernists such as Flann O'Brien and Samuel Beckett, the burden of writing after Joyce meant that new ways of "making it new" were required. In the works of Lewis, Beckett, Loy, Spark, and others, this often manifests as a weakening of narrative's capacity to achieve sustainable coherence along with the persistent requirement for such impossible acts of worlding.

As in the discourse of many schizophrenic patients, a heightened sense of reflexivity often yields an interruption of world-building and world-sustaining narrative operations. The worlds of the late-modernist fiction are often marked by precarity and destitution that are only exacerbated by second-order reflections upon their fragile constructions. Many of the works that I examine therefore not only reflect the conditions of psychic collapse at the level of thematic content but also through their fragile and hyperreflexive narrative forms. Beckett's work often exhibits the crises of plot and character that Ricoeur associates with the "dark nights of personal identity," and these experiences are frequently located within the context of mental illness and psychiatric institutions. In Muriel Spark's work, feelings of "unreality" are explicitly marked as effects of both fiction and delusion. Flann O'Brien's metafictional novels reflect upon the resemblances between delusion and fiction and move anarchically among multiple ontological registers or worlds.

If narrative may provisionally resolve certain ontological problems, it may also introduce others in its proliferation of worlds. Related questions have been raised by narratologists such as Lubomír Doležel, Marie-Laure

Ryan, and Ruth Ronen, who have adapted concepts from modal logic and possible worlds theory in order to address questions regarding the strange ontology of fictional narratives.[139] Ryan writes, "The theory has two concepts to propose to textual semiotics: the metaphor of 'world' to describe the semantic domain projected by the text; and the concept of modality to describe and classify the various ways of existing of the objects, states, and events that make up the semantic domain."[140] Such concerns are also central to any understanding of delusion as well as of hyperreflexive narratives that render worlds while scrutinizing the ontological status of the objects and events internal to those worlds. Ryan writes: "Fiction is characterized by the open gesture of recentering, through which an Alternative Possible World is placed at the center of the conceptual universe. This APW [alternative possible world] becomes the world of reference."[141] I argue that delusion performs a similar "recentering" within an alternative possible world, but this center often does not always hold. Instead, there is often a vacillation among several alternative possible worlds or frames of reference, and such vacillation makes manifest an "as if" status of "possibility" but not "actuality." This is evident in what Renee often calls "unreality" and in Schreber's discussion of "fleetingly-improvised men" that seem to lack full existence.[142] Delusional accounts are often accompanied by the patient's commentary and modal reflections, as when Renee recalls, "at that time, according to my concept of the world, things didn't exist in and of themselves, but each one created a world after his own fashion."[143]

Eric Hayot argues, "Literary critics have usually, however, focused on the artwork's world-content, not world-form, trusting the general concept of aesthetic or generic form to address the work's relation to worldedness. This pattern of thought means that the world-forming quality of the work, though often sensed or felt, has rarely been directly looked at."[144] The writings discussed in the following chapters do not allow their readers to pass over the tacit act of narrative worlding – indeed, the difficulty of that act is often explicitly thematized as the central problem that their writings both perform and undo. These are texts that construct conspicuously broken worlds, and, in Heideggerian fashion, that which is broken is what rises up for conscious, thematic reflection.[145] Many psychiatrists accepted Jaspers's claim that the nature of psychotic experience is fundamentally "un-understandable" – too broken to constitute a knowable world. The hermeneutic acts of understanding that would allow one to inhabit a schizophrenic patient's experience and therefore to recognize its worldedness have often proven prohibitively difficult. Jean-Luc Nancy writes, "a world is only a world for those who inhabit it."[146] Perhaps an aesthetic mode predicated on experimentation and difficulty such as modernism may provide discursive and hermeneutic portals into such worlds. The following chapters attempt to reconstruct such hermeneutic portals. By locating a recurrent form of technological madness at the center of late-modernist literature, this book presents fiction's critical and creative responses to the mechanistic constructions of the mind and of mental illness; it demonstrates the uses to which narrative is put in both fiction and delusion for the construction of phenomenological order and personhood; and it establishes an alternative account of the modernist psychological novel as a form defined not by epistemic deficits but by hyperreflexivity and its consequences.

In Chapter 1, I show how Wyndham Lewis's work often performs this paranoid synthesis with a level of anxiety that sometimes rivals Schreber's apocalyptic prose. In *The Art of Being Ruled* (1926) and *Time and Western Man* (1927), Lewis launches vicious attacks on trends in modern culture that conspire to reduce the human to a passive automaton. Chief among these perceived conspirators are Freud with his doctrine of the "mechanical subconscious," the behaviorists, and the BBC, which he suspects of a wireless "hypnotism" of the British population.[147] In *The Childermass* (1928) and *Snooty Baronet* (1932), Lewis satirizes the mechanized bodies that F. T. Marinetti had fetishized in the early years of modernism. I read this text in light of *An Autobiography of a Schizophrenic Girl*, Martin Heidegger's critique of the technological world picture, and Theodor Adorno's dystopian analysis of wireless in order to locate Lewis's fiction within a broad discursive range of technological paranoia.

In Chapter 2, I offer one of the first readings of Mina Loy's posthumously published novel *Insel* (written in the late 1930s). I read this strange work as a surrealist revision of the Freudian case study that recasts the transferential relationship between doctor and patient as a form of thought transmission that closely follows the rubric of the "Influencing Machine" delusion. In *Insel*, these uncanny experiences are transformed into writing that reflects the narrative form of the case study. However, Loy's text concludes with a melancholic meditation on the loss that occurs in this transformation from Insel's transmissions to the writing machines that the characters have become. The "Influencing Machine" delusion is nowhere more evident in late-modernist fiction than in Evelyn Waugh's semiautobiographical novel *The Ordeal of Gilbert Pinfold*, in which a writer feels that his thoughts have been broadcast to him by an obscure psychotechnological "Box." His delusion expands to include the BBC and psychiatrists who observe his thoughts and transmit voices to him at a distance. While the novel exhibits the features of a distinctly modern form of psychosis, it also reflects upon the reparative function that delusional, narrative world building might perform for both character and mental patient.

In Chapter 3, I examine the work of Anna Kavan and Muriel Spark – writers whose hallucinatory narratives pose questions about the ontological status of both fictional and delusional worlds. Both authors suffered periods of acute mental illness that became avowed sources for their experimental fiction. Kavan, a writer who has been all but forgotten by scholars of literary modernism, spent time as both a patient and as a nurse in several psychiatric hospitals, and her short stories collections *Asylum Piece* (1940) and *I Am Lazarus* (1945) reflect those experiences as well as the influence of earlier modernist writing, especially the paranoid narratives of Franz Kafka. I explore a similar formal convergence of fiction and memoir in Muriel Spark's *The Comforters* (1957), which reflects the author's experiences of drug-induced psychosis and delusions of technological thought insertion. The works of Kavan and Waugh make overt comparisons between the composition of fiction and the construction of delusion, and this chapter explores the reparative work of worlding that these discursive modes may perform.

Chapter 4 demonstrates the ways in which Flann O'Brien satirizes the immense authority that scientific and technological discourses often acquire over a population that increasingly takes the claims of those discourses on faith alone. In *The Dalkey Archive* (1964) and *The Third Policeman* (1967), the half-understood concepts of twentieth-century physics, psychology, and technology become the material of an absurd scientistic faith that generates strange worlds that often resemble delusion. Confronted with a deficit of expertise in these increasingly specialized areas of knowledge, one character complains, "Anything can be said in this place and it will have to be believed."[148] I therefore show how O'Brien's work explores the persistent roles of both belief and narrative in cultures that claim strict scientific empiricism.

In Chapter 5, I argue that much of Beckett's work may be understood as literary simulations of madness that were inspired by his early encounters with the Surrealists, his extensive research in psychology, as well as his own encounters with mental illness. Psychosis is foregrounded as a mirage of psychic withdrawal from the torsions of neurotic desire in *Murphy* (1938). In his subsequent works, the links between the dissolutions of narrative form and character identity become apparent as *The Unnamable* devolves into a reverberating chamber of hallucinated voices. Having pushed the novel to its formal limits, Beckett turned to other media such as radio in order to simulate for his audience the experience of auditory hallucination that his earlier novels only described. The radio drama *Embers* (1959) uses the phenomenological resources of the technological medium to recreate a schizophrenic environment.

In the book's Conclusion, I survey the legacy of the late modernism that this book assembles in an emergent wave of contemporary fiction that revisits the historical moment and the formal techniques of literary modernism in order to manage renewed concerns over the cultural influences of the brain sciences. I demonstrate how the rise of the neuronovel responds to the growing prestige of this new discourse of the brain by reactivating many of the narrative methods and conceptual problematics of late-modernist fiction. I show that the narratives of madness that I have assembled help to clarify the techniques, anxieties, and sources of several neuronovels. Conversely, I suggest that it is impossible for us to conceptualize modernism's engagement with the early mind sciences without considering the ways that those earlier texts are now mediated by the demands, conflicts, and fictions of our present moment.

Over the course of the following chapters, I argue that technopsychic delusions recur in the work of these late-modernist writers because they occupy a historical moment in which emergent mind sciences and information technology had fundamentally altered one's relation to one's own thoughts.[149] These writers do not resign themselves to the passive reception of phantasmatic influences but exert a critical pressure upon the historical changes that they register. Wyndham Lewis articulates the ambitions that motivated his work in this regard:

> Such an invention as wireless, for example, which, in the first years of its appearance, runs wild, left to its own devices, as it were, will certainly in the end be subjected to critical discipline, for the good of all of us. It is the philosophical intelligence, broadly, that reviews the claims of such a phenomenon of mechanical creation for survival and fixes the terms.[150]

The writings that I analyze in the chapters that follow – works of fiction, philosophy, psychology, engineering, or memoir – engage in such applications of intelligence to obscure influences that threaten to erode any ontological difference between mind and machine. I read them as participants in a discursive contest to "fix the terms" by which the nature of these black boxes would be understood.

CHAPTER I

Fables of Regression
Wyndham Lewis and Machine Psychology

Perhaps no modernist writer responded to the displacements of conscious thought in modernist culture with more insight and vitriol than Wyndham Lewis. In the sprawling analyses of *The Art of Being Ruled* (1926) and *Time and Western Man* (1927), Lewis critically evaluates the effects of numerous cultural and intellectual developments, ranging from new forms of psychology such as behaviorism and psychoanalysis; to the rise of mass media such as radio; to transforming conceptions of gender, sexuality, and disability; to the experimental techniques of his fellow modernists such as Gertrude Stein, James Joyce, and Charlie Chaplin. The fragmentary, dialectical, and sometimes contradictory logics of these ambitious treatises make any general summary of their positions incomplete; however, if those cultural transformations shared some common, disturbing feature for Lewis, it was their attenuation of a particular notion of rational consciousness and the subjection of the mind to forces that operate above and below the scale of the individual intellect. In his memoir *Rude Assignment* (1950), Lewis reflects on his earlier, satirical treatment of D. H. Lawrence's promotion of embodied, unconscious, irrational impulses: "*Paleface* attacked the visceral philosophy – 'the consciousness in the abdomen', which (as I wrote) removes 'the vital centre into the viscera; taking the controls out of the grasp of the 'hated intellect.'"[1] Lewis sometimes appears to be modernism's quintessential antihumanist whose fiction does not represent characters so much as unthinking automata. While there is much evidence to support this view, I suggest that it must be understood as part of his satirical campaign *against* what he perceived to be anti- or posthumanist cultural developments, and his resistance often manifests in a distinctly paranoid structure of thought.

Nowhere is this more evident than in Wyndham Lewis's underread novel, *The Childermass* (1928) – his most formally experimental work that hypostasizes an uncanny world shaped by many of the cultural developments that he critically assesses in *Time and Western Man* and *The Art of Being Ruled*. The novel formally and thematically intervenes in late-modernist debates over new models of the mind and personhood that Lewis had already identified in modern psychology, philosophy, and experimental literature. Bodies are fragmented into modular, mechanical systems that function and dysfunction with little centralized, executive control; characters are swept up into swarms of bodies that are governed by unthinking reflexes and mass psychology. The result is a mass of figures whose actions are reduced to puppetry by invisible forces and whose minimal cognitive functions are both epiphenomenal and ineffectual. Thought is all but eliminated in favor of the stimulus-response loops of behaviorist psychology that preoccupied Lewis for several years. *The Childermass* can therefore be read as a satirical *reductio ad absurdum* of the doctrines of behaviorism, psychoanalysis, and Bertrand Russell's monist philosophy of mind – rendering a world in which action and agency are virtually impossible and new forms of cognitive disability and psychopathology are universalized.

The novel is set in a modernist purgatory in which the dead of the Great War assemble and await entrance into the "Magnetic City" of heaven. Judgment is made not on the basis of any moral assessment but through an obscure ontological determination that the primary characters do not fully understand. The scene of judgment is administered by the Bailiff, a bureaucratic functionary who articulates many of the cultural and intellectual discourses that Lewis attacks in his cultural criticism, including a form of anticartesian materialism. In one of his many speeches, the Bailiff mocks "the old deep-seated dualism which attached disgrace to physical nature [...] there is no mind but the body; and there is no singularity but in that."[2]

Doubt is cast on the Bailiff's authority by a bold interlocutor who assumes the name of the Greek rhetorician, Hyperides. In his view, this modern, mechanistic monism must be subjected to rational scrutiny, and the novel stages a Socratic dialogue in order to evaluate competing metaphysical positions. Hyperides claims that the Bailiff's agenda is "to overthrow our human principle of life, not in open battle but by sentimental or cultural infection so that at last indeed there will be nothing but these sponges of your making left."[3] Elsewhere, Hyperides argues, "What is your object, from the standpoint of your Paradise over there, in reducing all these creatures to the dead level of some kind of mad robot of sex?"[4] Hyperides clearly recapitulates many of the claims made in *Time and Western Man* and the *Art of Being Ruled* when he suggests that the Freudian doctrine is merely a ruse for the displacement of the rational intellect.

In response, the Bailiff acknowledges that the figures before him are fractured and incomplete. They are, in his view, "split-men" who must combine in order to constitute the quantum of "substance" necessary for entrance. He advises, "we are practically nothing – we can only *half* make you believe, only *half* if that, as we can only produce you as split-men or slices, not persons [...] we too are only half-makers of split objects – realize our impotence."[5] If the figures that populate this afterworld are unthinking automata and partial objects that lack the unity of full personhood, it appears to be belief in a form of materialist monism that makes it so.

The effects of the Bailiff's rhetoric can be observed in the delirious and nightmarish experiences of two central characters that manifest the symptoms of such a schizoid "split man."[6] Pullman (or "Pulley") and Sattersthwaite ("Satters") are old schoolmates and veterans of the Great War who happen to reunite and explore the unstable, hallucinatory afterworld that is conditioned by the discourses that the Bailiff propagates and that Lewis satirizes. Pulley is introduced as a figure "who multiplies precise movements, an organism which in place of speech has evolved a peripatetic system of response to a dead environment. It has wandered beside this Styx, a lost automaton rather than a lost soul."[7] If Pulley's physical actions are reduced to mechanical automatisms, so are his higher-order capacities for language and cognition. When he first encounters his friend, Satters, his speech is compared to the electrified staccato of the telegraph: "his tongue, suddenly galvanic, raps out its response" [...] "The nondescript brevity of clattering morse hammers out on his palate message and counter-message, in harsh english."[8] What might be understood as the internal lives of these figures are no less automatic and mechanical than their external behavior: "Their minds continue to work in silent rhythm, according to the system of habit set in motion by their meeting."[9] Elsewhere, Pullman's behavior is presented as the output of an algorithm: " '[I]t's best to keep moving' Pulley's formula mechanically asserts."[10]

The characters' capacities for perception are decentralized and distributed into the physiological mechanisms that appear to function independently and are insufficient for complex intellectual work.

> The effort to understand is thrown upon the large blue circular eyes entirely: but the blue disk is a simple register; it has been filled with a family of pain-photisms, a hundred odd, it is a nest of vipers absolutely – oh, they are unreal! What are these objects that have got in? signal the muscles of the helpless eye: it distends in alarm; it is nothing but a shocked astonished apparatus, asking itself if it has begun to work improperly.[11]

In a satire of experimental psychology, perception is construed as a mere physiological, mechanical process that lacks phenomenological understanding. The sense organs are inadequate prosthetic devices that are inadvertently disconnected, shut off, or forgotten like articles of clothing while clothing is regarded as essential to one's identity. Pulley explains:

> "Once I left this stick at my kip when I went out. I might as well have left my head! I soon went back for it I promise you! That's the way it is. We are organic with the things around us. This piece of cloth" – he takes up a pinch of his coat sleeve – "is as much me as this flesh. It's a superstition to think the me ends here. [...] Yes, it's easy to leave [your coat] off. But you leave yourself too."[12]

Pullman's discourse articulates many of the claims made by recent post-cognitive philosophers of mind such as Andy Clark, David Chalmers, and Edwin Hutchins for ecologically extended and distributed forms of cognition – topologies of mind that are not restricted to human consciousness or to a single organism.[13] In *The Childermass*, similar forms of distributed cognition result in the reduction of character to a loose system of organic and inorganic prosthetic devices with little ontological distinction, centralized control, or identity.

Lewis's critical assessment of these conditions often functions by linking them to forms of cognitive disability and to shattering conditions of psychopathology. Satters witnesses figures appearing and disappearing and experiences a general sense of unreality, leading him to wonder in frantic discourse that is ambiguously both internal and externalized: "Am I mad I wonder if I am, why do I see things that are not there? It must mean something or is it nothing it's silly to notice as you say? [...] I'm just a fool of course. I've no grey matter they left it out, all the same I know there's something wrong."[14]

In ways that may be linked to the Bailiff's anticartesian, materialist doctrine, Satters lacks the necessary matter for sustained, rational inquiry. Pulley, a former teacher, demonstrates greater capacity for thought, but his reasoning often invokes the modern discourses that Lewis acerbically attacks. At times, Pulley performs the role of a psychoanalyst, diagnosing Satters with a "fear complex" or "hysteria," though the infantilized Satters is unable to concentrate long enough to follow Pulley's diagnoses. These vague categories often stand in for all forms of mental illness, but the symptoms that Satters and others experience – depersonalization, hallucination, paranoia, and unreality – conform more closely to the more extreme conditions of psychosis.[15]

The symptoms suffered by Lewis's modern "split-man" also manifest clearly in memoirs and case studies of schizophrenia – a nosological
category that literally indicates a "split-mind." In *An Autobiography of a
Schizophrenic Girl,* Renee recounts the feeling that she and her classmates
have been reduced to the kinds of unthinking automata that Pulley and
Satters encounter.

> Around me, the other children, heads bent over their work, were robots
> or puppets, moved by an invisible mechanism. On the platform, the
> teacher, too, talking, gesticulating, rising to write on the blackboard, was
> a grotesque jack-in-the-box [...] An awful terror bound me; I wanted to
> scream.[16]

Like the "split-men" in *The Childermass,* the schizophrenic girl encounters
only bodies deprived of minds. In order to make sense of her impressions, Renee generates a complex narrative delusion that draws upon the
explanatory discourses available to her. This vacillation between radical,
schizophrenic dissolution and paranoid narrative recurs often in first-
person accounts of psychosis, and a similar double-movement between
dissolution and paranoid reconstruction structures the textual world of
The Childermass. Renee's delusion functions as a kind of prosthetic world –
a rigidly organized, persecutory, and fragile totality within which phenomena may be assigned meaning. This worlding process becomes especially
legible as Renee's memoir of mental illness develops its curiously technological explanatory system:

> Some time after, I discovered that the Persecutor was none other than
> the electric machine, that is, it was the "System" that was punishing me.
> I thought of it as some vast world-like entity encompassing all men. At
> the top were those who gave orders, who imposed punishment, who pro-
> nounced others guilty. But they were themselves guilty [...] Everyone was
> part of the System. But only some were aware of being part.[17]

Renee fashions a world structured by an obscure, persecuting force of
judgment and order that operates materially through a dimly understood
electrico-magnetic mechanism – features that resemble the world of *The
Childermass* in both form and content. In attempting to account for his
hallucinatory and depersonalizing experiences, Pulley speculates that those
who await entrance to the Magnetic City are somehow remotely controlled
by a similar technological system that obscurely materializes an act of judgment. "The magnetism out here again requires stamina of a particular sort;
at bottom it's electricity all the way through, magnetic and electric, this is
all nothing but that."[18]

What are we to make of this uncanny resemblance between this schizo-phrenic's world and that of the "split-men" in *The Childermass*? Psychotic delusions are as culture-bound as any literary novel, and both can be seen as responses to constructions of the human that reduce its ontological dis-tinction from other mechanical systems. These ontological confusions of the human and the nonhuman, the living and the dead, and interiority and exteriority are common symptoms of psychosis, but for Lewis they are the logical consequences of the modern discourses of the mind that he satirizes.

In *The Art of Being Ruled*, Lewis makes explicit what is only implicit in *The Childermass*, suggesting analogies between mental illness, deper-sonalization, and the anticartesian materialism of modern psychologies that reconstruct the thinking human as an unthinking material object. He diagnoses "the anxiety of a disillusioned person to escape from himself and merge his personality in things; verging often on the worship of things – of the non-human, feelingless, and thoughtless – of such experiences and tendencies is the delusion composed."[19] In using pathological language, Lewis assumes the role and discourse of a cultural psychiatrist: he regards the writings of his fellow modernists as performances of mental illness and cognitive disability that are always at risk of devolving into actual illness and disability. Regarding Gertrude Stein's use of unconventional syntax and repetition in her experimental writing, he argues:

> What she is exploiting in her method is the processes of the demented. For anyone less strong-minded than Miss Stein this might prove a dangerous occupation [...] The exploitation of madness, of ticks, blephorospasms, and eccentricities of the mechanism of the brain, is a thing of a similar order in language to the exploitation of the physical aspect of imbecility in contem-porary painting.[20]

Lewis regards affectations of childishness and mental illness as evidence of psychological or cultural regression. As Reeve-Tucker and Waddell argue, "*Time and Western Man* suggests that he discerned within this quest a destructive pathology: 'How *the demented* also joins hands with the child, and the tricks, often very amusing, of the asylum patient, are exploited at the same time as the happy inaccuracies of the infant'."[21]

Lewis regards these literary simulations of mental disorders as the result of discourses such as behaviorism and psychoanalysis that, in his view, attenuate or fully eliminate the roles of consciousness and the rational intellect. "The *Lunatic*, or the *Demented*, and the *Child* are linked together by psycho-analysis, the link being its dogma of the Unconscious."[22] If disability and psychological regression are universalized in *The Childermass,* it is because the novel satirizes a perceived universalization and perhaps fetishization of these conditions that had emerged in modernist culture. "A sort of clinical religion is being built up to accommodate us, the priesthood of which is recruited principally from the ranks of the alienists. In every case it is our weakness, our smallness, our ignorance, or our dementia that is catered for."[23] *The Childermass* represents a world that not only accommodates but rather cultivates dementia and disability, and this regression is linked to what he calls the "cult of the child." Lewis's treatment of modernist culture is at once satirical and diagnostic, condemning what he regards as pathological obsessions with psychopathology.

Lewis's conspiratorial account of this "cult of the child" identifies Stein, James Joyce, and Charlie Chaplin as participants in a univocally pathological modernism. He produces a sweeping, diagnostic vision of cultural decline that owes much to the discourse of degeneration that had been popularized for more than a generation. Ironically, in constructing such a broad and embattled vision of a pathological modernist culture, Lewis's thought exhibits uncanny affinities with paranoid thought. Eve Sedgwick famously identifies paranoid thought as a form of "strong theory" due to "the size and topology of the domain that it organizes."[24] Sedgwick owes this distinction between strong and weak theory to the cognitive psychologist Silvan Tomkins, who writes, "To the extent to which the theory can account only for 'near' phenomena, it is a weak theory, little better than a description of the phenomena which it purports to explain. As it orders more and more remote phenomena to a single formulation, its power grows [...]"[25] The scalar expansion of such paranoid, strong theory is evident in *Time and Western Man, The Art of Being Ruled,* and *The Childermass* – volumes that were written after the failure of Lewis's short-lived journal *The Enemy* and that synthesize and attack a rather diverse range of modern cultural and intellectual developments. Like Renee, whose memoir of psychosis constructs a systematic, persecutory world within which she can locate herself, Lewis exhibits his own paranoid, world-building impulses when he acknowledges that modernist culture has become a vast conspiratorial system: "Everything assumes an increasingly associational form. A vast system of interlocking syndics – pleasure syndics, work syndics, sex and age syndics, vice and race syndics, health syndics, and valetudinarian syndics – is imposed."[26]

Such paranoid patterns have been noted by other critics.[27] David Trotter traces these tendencies to Lewis's anxiety over his uncertain status as a "professional" writer and to his outsider status with respect to other groups that Lewis perceived as opposed to his work – especially the Bloomsbury circle.[28] Much has been written about Lewis's tortured and rather confused politics, but it may be more productive to read his work of the late 1920s as a form of ontological activism, waging a rhetorical and satirical battle against psychological and cultural discourses that reduce or eliminate older conceptions of the mind – and with it, the human – from its "disintegrating metaphysic."[29]

Radio and the Cult of the Child

Although he is not primarily known as an early media theorist, Lewis's analyses of the psychic and phenomenological effects of radio and other forms of mass communication comprise some of the most potent sequences of *Time and Western Man* and *The Art of Being Ruled* – analyses that arguably anticipated the better known media theory of Marshall McLuhan, whose early work was devoted to Lewis. Hal Foster notes that, "McLuhan was influenced by Wyndham Lewis: he sought Lewis out in St. Louis in the early 1940s, published an essay on his work in 1944, and founded a journal in homage to *Blast* called *Counterblast*."[30] Many of the provocative analyses of mass media technology that McLuhan would go on to perform in works like *Understanding Media* have much in common with Lewis's late-1920s writing.[31] In *The Art of Being Ruled,* Lewis warns that, "The contemporary European or American is a part of a broadcasting set, a necessary part of its machinery."[32] His claim reverses the logic of prosthesis, so that the radio is described not as an extension of its listener; instead, the listener becomes a mere component in a new informatic assemblage.[33] The techno-psychic system that Lewis describes also anticipates a discussion of radio by Theodor Adorno during his work in the late 1930s for the Princeton Radio Research Project:

> Radio technicians hold that the structures of the microphone and of the ear are similar. The diaphram of the microphone corresponds to the diaphragm of the human ear. To this diaphragm the voice coil is connected which conveys the electric >>intelligence<< further on its way. To the diaphragm of the ear the series of small bones is connected which convey the auditory stimulus through the nervous system.[34]

What begins with an apparently simple comparison of the anatomical structure of sensory organs to the components of broadcasting apparatus ultimately erodes any clear distinction between machine and organism. Human consciousness and critical awareness are displaced until even intelligence becomes "electric" and is unconsciously transmitted across copper, air, and nerve. Adorno continues: "However, the subtler those objective characteristics and the deeper they are engraved in the phenomenon facing the listener, the better is their chance of reaching him at the very layers of his own unconscious life which correspond to the unconscious elements of the object, without being >>censored<< by his critical Ego."[35] Like Lewis, Adorno appears profoundly concerned that the structure of subjectivity may be transformed by modernism's new media, and this transformation entails the erosion of the ego and rational, critical faculties.

Given Lewis's notorious interest in fascism in the late 1920s and early 1930s, any resemblance in his cultural analyses to the critiques of the Frankfurt School should seem surprising. However, as Andrzej Gasiorek argues, "the parallels between Lewis and Adorno, for example, are strong. They both saw popular culture in unremittingly negative terms, partly because they considered it to be unquestionably aesthetically inferior to the achievements of high culture, and partly because they saw its social function as solely ideological, the means by which false consciousness was organized and then kept in place."[36] Adorno and Lewis are in agreement nowhere more than in their analyses of radio as a potential mechanism of unconscious manipulation and as a symptom of a mass cultural desire for infantilization – the subject of both *The Childermass* and much of Adorno's writing on radio.

In this way, Lewis rivals Adorno in his pessimism over the possibility of any sustainable intellectual resistance to the effects of mass media that infiltrates even the work of modern writers and intellectuals such as himself: "they only had *one* personality between them to 'express' – some 'expressing' it with a little more virtuosity, some a little less. It would be a *group personality* that they were 'expressing' – a pattern imposed on them by means of education and the hypnotism of cinema, wireless, and press."[37] Even singularly expressive writers are distinct only for their virtuosic expression of increasingly univocal cultural formations. As in Adorno's discussion of the unconscious effects of radio, Lewis's mention of "hypnotism" suggests that the rapid adoption of this new medium has outstripped the audience's capacity to consciously mediate its unconscious effect.

In his frequent discussions of wireless, or the "crystal set," Lewis often locates the technology's popularity as a manifestation of the modern "cult of the child." In his view, the infantilizing effects of radio demonstrate the desire of the population to cede control to the authoritarian forces that remain unidentified. The radio is therefore the appropriate toy of this generation of infantilized adults. "So you are recommended to remain 'children' – to remain 'kids,' and not outgrow your own 'kids,' but share their nursery with them and quarrel with them over wireless sets owned in common."[38] In almost identical terms, Adorno wages a scathing critique of the infantilizing tendencies of broadcast technology almost ten years later: "In my special section of the project, music, an idea has impressed itself upon me which I should prefer to call, at first, the idea of >>infantile<< listening. Compared to developed music-listening, listening to radio music shows definite infantile features."[39] In Adorno's view, it is not simply an uncritical mode of reception and vulnerability to unconscious influences but also the fetishization of the apparatus itself that constitutes these "infantile features" of the "Radio Generation" in precisely the form that Lewis had identified thirteen years earlier in *The Art of Being Ruled*: "for a theory of radio such as we contemplate will have to analyze all forms of fetishes which are reaffirmed or created by the new tool."[40] Developing his account of this infantile fetishism, Adorno argues:

> Throughout the entire sphere of radio a certain type of person is to be found. I call this type of person the >>*Basteler*<< – a German word which is not quite expressed in the expression >>radio amateur<<. The *Basteler* is that type of individual – mostly to be found among youngsters – who is more interested in the radio apparatus and its function than he is in the form and content of the broadcasts. I should like to draw the attention of our colleagues to this type, as I regard it as one of the main manifestations of the >>infantile<< attitude of radio listeners, especially since it is fostered by the mechanism of radio.[41]

The device itself, Adorno warns, has acquired an auratic charge for its users, while the droning radio voice does its work in the background and below the threshold of conscious or critical mediation.

Lewis would of course agree. Adorno's diagnosis of "infantile listening" would fit well within Lewis's theory of the "cult of the child," which he finds evident in everything from Gertrude Stein's stammering prose and Charlie Chaplin's diminutive tramp to the increasingly fetishistic orientation toward the radio apparatus; this strong cultural theory assumes a distinctly paranoid tone when it posits an evil genius, obscured from view yet orchestrating the behavior of the masses through unconscious influences made possible by devices like the radio. Lewis writes that the figure of the child becomes a "mechanical, subconscious obsession that in the fashions takes such ridiculous forms that it is impossible not to suppose that there is a mind at the back of them capable of appreciating a joke, perhaps too well (though the 'wisdom' of this comedian can be doubted)."[42] Here, the "subconscious" appears in Lewis's critique as the seat of this "mechanical obsession" and the hand-hold for those who might manipulate the masses like so many puppets.

While Lewis attacks Freud as a theoretical source (and symptom) of the cult of the child, he goes further to suggest that oedipal desire has been achieved to disastrous, pathological consequences. That is, in the fantasy of returning to the womb, Lewis identifies a possible structure for the ontological crisis of the human that preoccupied him for so many years. Lewis recognized a similar fantasy allegorized in the Futurist myth of rebirth by machine, in which the eroticized automobile carries and delivers the Futurist artist who then merges seamlessly with his technological source. In this instance, the technologization of the human is a fantasy of regression toward a primal union. Lewis finds this fantasy most clearly articulated in Freudian theory in which the subject emerges through the process of "castration" – when, in the mythic schema of the family triangle, the attachment to the mother and full satisfaction are interrupted by the interdiction of the father. Lewis identifies the rise of the modern "cult of the child" with a historical reconfiguration of this family drama, which results in a form of regression and disindividuation. "So *there is no longer any family*, in one sense: there is now only a collection of children, differing in age but in nothing else. The last vestige of the *patria potestas* [paternal power] has been extirpated."[43] Lewis's point is not simply a reactionary rejection of feminism (despite apparent misogynist tendencies, he sometimes promotes the dissolution of reified gender roles). Instead, Lewis's anxiety is directed toward what arrives with the loss of the paternal interdiction, which, Freud suggests, establishes subjectivity by prohibiting the child's desire to return to the mother and by protecting the child from the mother's potentially overwhelming desire.[44] The failure of this interdiction is precisely what precipitates psychosis in certain psychoanalytic accounts – including Lacan's – and Freud similarly associates psychosis with developmental regression.[45] In his treatment of the cult of the child as a psychopathological form of regression, Lewis also appears to operate within the terms of psychoanalytic theory even as he critiques it.

In a similar vein, Adorno's analysis of radio's psychic effects relies upon Freudian models of subjectivity in order to suggest that the device may induce a cultural form of psychopathology. Members of the "Radio Generation" are no longer Oedipalized or properly individuated but are fully reduced to some disindividuated mass by the hypnotic voice of the wireless announcer: "The individual seems to be on the way to a situation in which it can only survive by relinquishing its individuality, blurring the boundary between itself and its surroundings, and sacrificing most of its independence and autonomy. In large sectors of society there is no longer an 'ego' in the traditional sense."[46] Like Lewis, Adorno suggests that radio has induced a process of psychic regression to a state prior to individuation that is akin to psychoanalytic models of psychosis. With the collapse of any mediating third term, subject and object become indistinct.

Lewis does suggest that with the dissolution of the paternal function, a compensatory, derivative figure of authority has emerged in the form of the purveyor of mass culture. However, this avuncular figure has perversely inverted the logic of the paternal law: in place of the interdiction against forbidden desire that separates subject from object, this perverse, substitute figure encourages the masses to pursue infantile desires, a condition that Lewis – like Adorno – recognizes in the cultural obsession with the radio. Adorno identifies this figure with the voice of the radio itself: "Radio has its own voice inasmuch as it functions as a filter for every sound. Due to the comprehensiveness of its operation as a filter, it gains a certain autonomy in the ears of the listener: *even the adult experiences the radio voice rudimentarily, like the child who personifies radio as an aunt or uncle of his.*"[47]

A similar, avuncular voice appears in *The Childermass*, where subjects and objects collapse into one another. In place of a divine figure of absolute authority, the Bailiff holds court as a perverse voice whose rhetoric appears to hypnotize the masses of childlike figures. Pulley and Satters learn that the criterion for passage into the Magnetic City of Heaven is that they must constitute an adequate quantity of matter. "Substance, then, it is our aim to secure."[48] The Bailiff recommends that, given the condition of the many "split-men" who seek entrance, "combining" may be the best way to meet this condition. The Bailiff announces, "Individuality then is identity without the idea of substance. And substance we insist on here, nothing else can hold any real interest for us, that is a cardinal fact about which you should all be perfectly clear."[49] Consequently, the figures lose their identity and merge into masses of raw material that collectively constitute the quantity of substance sufficient for passage into the Magnetic City to which they are unconsciously drawn.

Pullman and Satters experience a profound terror in reaction to their imminent depersonalization that results from the form of materialist monism that the Bailiff advocates. In *Men Without Art* (1934), Lewis attacks all forms of ontological monism.

> There are, on the market today, patterns of belief extending from the extreme position, on the one hand, that there is in fact no traceable psyche, but only *one stuff*, out of which our mind is composed, properly neither "mind'"nor "matter"; to the extreme position of the other, which as a matter of fact is much the same as the former, only with a more strongly marked flavoring.

The basic single stuff is more soulful at that end than it is at the other, the deterministic end, that is all.[50]

With his call for "substance," the Bailiff articulates such a reduction of mind and body to "one stuff" – an ontological monism that erodes fundamental distinctions such as mind and matter and, in *The Childermass,* self and other.[51] The merging of the masses and subsequent passage into the Magnetic City may be read as Lewis's satirical reconstruction of the Futurist, technological rebirth and as an ontological degradation. The Bailiff describes the process in explicitly scatological terms, "they reach the anus symbolized by the circular gate over there more cloacal even than at the moment of their engulfing on their earthly deathbeds."[52] The masses combine finally to lose their personhood and to become shit: an undifferentiated substance passing through the anus of a perversely modern afterworld. The Bailiff clarifies the ontological consequences of this transformation: "Heaven is not, I need hardly say, a drainage system into which you drop but a system of orthodox post-humous – if you will excuse the pun, *post-human* life."[53] The moment constitutes one of the first articulations of the "post-human," which, for Lewis, is the logical consequence of the ontological monism that structures modern thought.[54]

Lewis's evaluation of these patterns of modernist culture signal a turn toward a late-modern moment from which earlier avant-garde enthusiasms could be critically evaluated. The Bailiff's speeches may have been lifted from the Futurist rhetoric of F. T. Marinetti, who famously fetishized the mechanization of the body and mind and the elimination of individual identity in favor of a modernized mass movement predicated on violence, force, and speed. "We systematically destroy the literary *I* in order to scatter it into the universal vibration and reach the point of expressing the infinitely small and the vibration of molecules [...] Thus the poetry of cosmic forces supplants the poetry of the human."[55] In a later manifesto, Bruno Corradini and Emilio Settimelli offer a Futurist account of the mind that reflects the reduction of all mental activity to the monist ontology of energetics that dominated nineteenth-century physics and neurology:

OBSERVATION NO. 1. Every human activity is a projection of nervous energy. This energy, which is one of physical constitution and of action, undergoes various transformations and assumes various aspects according to the material chosen to manifest it. A human being assumes greater or lesser importance according to the quantity of energy at his disposal, and according to his power and ability to modify his surroundings.

OBSERVATION NO. 2. There is no essential difference between a human brain and a machine. It is mechanically more complicated, that is all.[56]

The post-human, mechanical reduction of subjectivity to a form of physicalism had already been promoted by avant-garde provocateurs against whom Lewis spent much of the late 1920s engaged in a lengthy rebuttal.

Lewis's response to Futurism's posthumanism is most clearly articulated in *The Childermass* by Hyperides, who challenges the Bailiff's monist reduction of the human to mechanistic and mindless disorder:

> Is not your Space-Time for all practical purposes only the formula recently popularized to accommodate the empirical sensational chaos? Did not the human genius redeem us for a moment from that, building a world of human-divinity above that flux? Are not your kind betraying us again in the name of exact research to the savage and mechanical nature we had overcome; at the bidding, perhaps, of your maniacal and jealous God?[57]

Hyperides gives voice to the ontological anxiety that recurs throughout Lewis's work in the 1920s that the distinction of the human had been eroded. In a structure that recalls Daniel Paul Schreber's delusion, Hyperides posits a "maniacal and jealous God" who stands behind the Bailiff's doctrine of degraded, disindividuated being. Whereas Descartes posited God as the guarantor of the subject–object relation (a triangulation that is homologous to the foundational separation of subject and object in psychoanalytic theory), Hyperides suspects a jealous and threatened divinity has instead collapsed this distinction, rendering the subject indistinct from object. Elsewhere, Lewis observes this transformation or dislocation of the symbolic, prohibitive father in the infantilizing dynamics of mass culture where subject and object are not only brought into closer proximity but appear to merge. "The trinity of God, Subject, and Object is at an end. The collapse of this trinity is the history also of the evolution of the subject into the object or of the child back into the womb from which it came."[58] In *The Childermass*, the result of this failure of triangulation is represented as a collapse of human subjectivity which resembles the hallucinatory, depersonalized condition of psychosis.

Jacques Lacan developed a strikingly similar account of the collapse of subjectivity in one of his last seminars entitled, "... *ou pire*," which punningly equivocates between "... either a father/ ... or worse."[59] The implication is that either one's subjectivity is mediated (and stabilized) through a law that separates subject from object and coordinates their relation, or, worse, one is submerged in the chaotic condition of psychosis in which all ontological distinctions are lost or some delusional form of symbolic organization is improvised through a paranoid system. Bruce Fink writes, "Lacan does not assert that the father should be propped up in our society. Rather, he issues a warning: to reject the father's role, to undermine the father's current symbolic function, will lead to no good; its consequences are likely to be worse than those of the father function itself, increasing the incidence of psychosis."[60] In *The Childermass*, Lewis stages these consequences and pessimistically diagnoses what he regards as the prevailing ontology of his historical moment as pathological. If the regression of the "split-men" in *The Childermass* may be understood as the schizoid disintegration of identity, Lewis explores the paranoid, megalomaniacal alternatives in his later novel *Snooty Baronet*, where it is not psychoanalysis but rather behaviorism that becomes the target of Lewis's satirical critique.

The Psychology of the Machine: Behaviorism

In a key sequence of *Time and Western Man*, Lewis outlines an intellectual and cultural genealogy beginning in the late-eighteenth century in which the conscious subject fades from philosophical and psychological discourses. A chapter entitled "The Subject Conceived as King of the Psychological World" surveys this displacement of consciousness by increasingly mechanistic or physiological accounts of human behavior, and behaviorism recurs in Lewis's argument as the logical culmination of this trajectory.

The ambition of John B. Watson, the founder of behaviorism, was to establish a properly "scientific" psychology that would be firmly grounded in strictly empirical, verifiable, and objective methods of observation. The behaviorist approach was offered as a corrective to the excessively subjective and interpretive techniques of introspective psychology. For Watson, the organism was to be treated as a black box that could be studied only through the correlation of external stimuli and visible, behavioral responses – data that could be objectively observed and verified in accordance with proper scientific methods. Any reference to first-person experience, psychological interiority, or consciousness was to be strictly avoided.[61] In his 1913 paper, "Psychology as the Behaviorist Views It," often regarded as the behaviorist manifesto, Watson argues, "The time seems to have come when psychology must discard all reference to consciousness; when it need no longer delude itself into thinking that it is making mental states the object of observation."[62] Any claims to access the conscious states of other subjects are compared to delusions, and Watson proposes that in the future, psychologists should "never use the terms consciousness, mental states, minds, content, introspectively verifiable, imagery, and the like."[63] What begins as an epistemic principle evolves into a more radical ontological claim when he writes:

> Since, according to my view, thought processes are really motor habits in the larynx, improvements, short cuts, changes, etc., in [sic] these habits are brought about in the same way that such changes are produced in other motor habits. This view carries with it the implication that there are no reflective processes (centrally initiated processes) ...[64]

It is not only that one cannot observe the internal, mental states of others; Watson suggests that consciously directed mental states do not exist but are rooted in the subconscious motor mechanisms of the body. The result is not only an attack on introspectionist psychologies but the assertion of a physicalist monism that eliminates mental predicates entirely.

This is precisely what draws Wyndham Lewis's attack in several works of fiction and cultural analysis. As Paul Scott Stanfield writes, "behaviorism was messily cathected to everything else Lewis feared and loathed," because "Lewis most dislikes [...] what he considers the regicidal exclusion from consideration of the reasoning, reflecting, creating mind. In his view, the behaviorists completed a demolition of mind-as-entity that had already been proceeding on several fronts."[65] The refusal of behavioral psychology to posit any psychological interiority, restricting itself to objectively observable behavior, may be one source of the automata that populate the world of *The Childermass*. As Satters observes, "One would say one was hollow!"[66] David Trotter argues that "we need also to acknowledge a certain equivalence between the doctrines of behaviorism and Lewis's aversive technique, which often treats human beings as though they were animals, or machines."[67] While it is true that the representation of the human as a mechanical system is essential to Lewis's aesthetic, I would suggest that this mechanical aesthetic cannot be detached from his rigorous and relentless ethic of satire – a satirical aesthetic whose purpose only comes into focus when its objects of critique are made clear.

Lewis observes that behaviorism treats complex thought as little more than the delayed response to multiple stimuli. This delay introduces complexity and indeterminacy that make the "objective" correlation of external behavior to stimuli problematic. In his characteristically acerbic mode, Lewis regards behaviorism's reductive approach to the mind as especially well suited to the modern capitalist mechanization of human labor:

> [T]he "mind" is action: the human being a machine into which you drop a penny in the form of a stimulus – and sooner or later the figure works. And

the *sooner* the *better*! Let there be a clear understanding about that at once. Quickness is his motto – *time is money*: the Tester's master is a money-man. When the figure works slowly, you call it "thought." When it works quickly, you call it "reflex." But they are the same thing. There is no "mind": men are "reaction masses." The whole bag-of-tricks is contained in physiology.[68]

Lewis's figure of the "Tester" refers to the methods of psychometric testing that came to be associated with Watson's strictly empirical, positivist psychology and that was proposed during the First World War as a method for scientifically managing the growing military's new recruits. Lewis's language underscores the industrial, military, and commercial applications to which behaviorist methods would be put.

Watson's avowed agenda did not stop with the goal of establishing his discipline's scientific credibility through strict, empirical methods but extended to rhetoric of "mental engineering" that would afford "the prediction and control of human activity."[69] Progress toward these goals was accelerated during the First World War, which Watson regarded as a large-scale laboratory for testing new scientific methods for the management of large populations. Harvard psychologist R. M. Yerkes, who worked with Watson in developing behaviorist applications for military training and troop management, hoped to adapt these techniques to civilian life, and in his report to the National Research Council, he writes, "Great will be our good fortune if the lesson in *human engineering* which the War has taught us is carried over, directly and effectively, into our civil institutions and activities."[70] Lewis cites and responds to the Yerkes report at several points in *Time and Western Man*, offering it as evidence of behaviorism's ambitions to perfect methods of social and psychological control:

> Whether, then, the War once done, and its feats of "human engineering" – its mechanizing of millions of mankind – it is advisable that its spirit and methods should be perpetuated, is a subject on which many different opinions must be held. The 'captains of industry' (and no doubt also the general staff) are of one mind: the military organization of the vast masses of people militarized during the War must be carried over into "civil life." We are naturally not of that opinion.[71]

While Lewis's rhetoric may reflect the totalizing and persecutory features of paranoid thought, he finds extensive evidence for his anxieties in behaviorism's often hyperbolic rhetoric. Yerkes writes, "two years ago mental engineering was the dream of a few visionaries. Today, it is a branch of technology which although created by the war, is evidently to be perpetuated and fostered by education and industry."[72]

Lewis was hardly alone in his critical reactions to behaviorism's elimination of mind from the purview of psychology, its reduction of the human to a mechanistic automaton of stimulus/response circuits, and its technocratic aspirations to "mental engineering." In response to Watson's foundational paper, "Psychology as the Behaviorist Views It," prominent members of the American and British psychological communities articulated concerns that aligned closely with Lewis's objections. Kerry Buckley notes that E. B. Titchener's "fundamental criticism of behaviorism was that its practical goal of the 'control of behavior' gave it 'the stamp of technology.' In Titchener's opinion, 'to exchange a science for a technology' was 'out of the question.' But this was precisely what Watson was asking."[73] This distinction between science and technology would become a central point for the satirical critique of behaviorism that Lewis would develop in his novel *Snooty Baronet.* Watson's efforts to ground psychology in strict empiricism and to abandon much of the field's inherited conceptual vocabulary also gained the interest of Bertrand Russell, who was developing his own monist philosophy of mind. However, Russell articulated concerns over the technocratic agenda of behaviorism in a letter to Watson. Buckley writes, "This notion of control in behaviorism disturbed Bertrand Russell. Although he supported Watson in his efforts to demystify the thinking process, Russell saw potential for abuse by a technocratic elite. Exploitation of behavioristic techniques of control, he warned, could result in a society wherein an official class of 'thinkers' dominated a passive class of 'feelers.' "[74]

It was Watson's expressed goals of psychological manipulation and social control that also disturbed Lewis, who writes, "It is only a step from observing a man engaged in a very clear-cut 'stimulus-response' (rigidly-habitual, readily-observed) type of action, and to persuade him to continue doing that harmless simple thing till the machine stops. For 'the control of organized society' is always at the bottom of his mind."[75] The paranoid register of Lewis's assessment shares much with the reaction of many mental patients who, having been exposed to the instrumentalization of modern psychiatry, often describe feeling that they have been somehow reduced to a bare mechanism that could be manipulated in ways that subvert conscious awareness or intervention. The pathological valences of these suspicions are not lost on Lewis, but he reframes this manifestation of paranoia as a cultural rather than a singularly psychological symptom: "Most reasonably sane societies wish if anything to have their habits broken up, not stereotyped [...] The feeling of almost insane uniformity produced by this must be highly displeasing to anyone except a habit-adept."[76] If

the elimination of personhood and feelings of mechanization are common experiences of mental illness, the historical evacuation of the subject
within a mechanistic psychology that refuses to recognize consciousness is,
Lewis suggests, symptomatic of a cultural form of madness.

Paul Edwards also observes Lewis's generalization of mental illness in
his postwar writings, though in Edwards's view such rhetoric is a consequence of wartime shell shock and widespread cultural trauma rather
than a response to reductive psychological discourses: "Such psychological
effects have, Lewis intimates, moved into, and affected, society as a whole.
The shock of war manifests itself in society not only as an infantilism and
refusal of the traditional masculine gender-role, but also in all those cultural phenomena that encourage a return to pre-Oedipal bliss, before self
and other have separated."[77] While I agree that Lewis excoriates the fantasy
of regression to pre-Oedipal states, and wartime trauma clearly brought
forms of psychopathology and involuntary behavior to cultural attention,
it is also clear that, for Lewis, the emergent discourses of psychoanalysis
and behaviorism only deepen the sense of crisis.

Lewis generalizes delusion as a cultural-historical symptom when he
reverses conventional distinctions between the "normal" and the "mad."

> What is most generally meant, no doubt, when the average man employs
> the word "mad," is something that could most accurately be applied to him-
> self: for if to be the victim of a constant indestructible delusion is to be
> insane, then certainly we all are fairly insane: and further than that, those
> most "normal" are the most mad. The greater part of men and women live
> plunged in the depths of the great naif hallucination that causes them to
> struggle passionately for what, regarded dispassionately, would be strictly
> nothing, and that passion is surely insanity, if anything is.[78]

Adopting the position of behaviorism for a moment, Lewis suggests that
the belief that one exists as a distinct, experiencing, and self-determining
agent who is not subject to mechanistic laws of causation or manipulation may be regarded as delusional. The fearful suspicion that one may
not be a subject is a recurring feature of many psychotic delusions, and
it is precisely this grim possibility that Lewis often stages in his fiction.
In *The Childermass*, Pullman and Satters encounter numerous, robotic
"peons" who seem to lack any cognitive or verbal ability and who often
appear only as a single aggregate "group-mechanism" that is involuntarily
pulled toward the Magnetic City.[79] While Satters suspects that these figures reflect his own mindless state, Pullman insists that he retains all of
the capacities and ontological distinctions of personhood. When the two
encounter the apparent shape of a deceased friend, their debate over his

existence leads to growing uncertainty over the status of their own sanity and subjectivity:

> "Well, did I just imagine Marcus – you know what I mean, or don't you? – I'm afraid!" ...
> "Did *you* create Marcus, do you mean?"
> "Why not? In your dreams you create all sorts of people. Why not in the other thing?"
> "Why not in the what?"
> "Why, in the other dream."
> Pullman looks up. Satters gazes into a sallow vacant mask, on which lines of sour malice are disappearing, till it is blank and elementary, in fact the face of a clay doll.
> "Why, you are a peon!"[80]

The hallucinatory status of others redounds upon the novel's central characters, who are forced to acknowledge that their confidence in their own ontological status may be only a delusion. Pullman attempts to maintain belief in his own subjectivity against all evidence that he has been reduced to involuntary automatisms: "Pullman is the iron girder supporting these delicate unstable effects, refusing collapse. *He* is there! That is sufficient. He puts his foot down. *Not*. Not that."[81] His subjectivity is grounded in a delusional refusal of identification with the mechanized peons, but Satters ultimately admits, "I believe we only think we're so different."[82] The moment serves as a grim parody of Hegelian recognition: as in many of Lewis's fictional worlds, one does not gain subjectivity through the recognition of the other; instead, awareness of the other as object reflects one's own condition as a mere thing similarly deprived of subjectivity. Rather than achieving individuation and separation, Satters and Pullman at times appear to merge into one another – a "group mechanism" not unlike the novel's titular masses of childish bodies. Fredric Jameson usefully adopts the Beckettian concept of the "pseudocouple" to describe the loss of distinction between Pullman and Satters.[83] Together, they paradoxically seem to number both more and less than one. While the hallucinatory instability of their experiences casts doubt upon their sanity, Lewis applies the language of delusion to the incorrigible belief in the persistence of one's own subjectivity.

Hugh Kenner saw a contradiction between Lewis's view that behaviorism, "in reducing the person to a set of predictable gestures, was insulting to the human race," while he went on to produce "a body of fiction on the premise that people were nothing else."[84] Some, such as Erik Bachman, have argued that Lewis demonstrated sympathies with behaviorism and that his own formal techniques demonstrate an alliance with behaviorist methods: "Considered simply as a methodology, behaviourism seems the ideal shell for Lewis' brand of literary modernism."[85] Others suggest that Lewis viewed humanity as fundamentally divided between the masses who were accurately described by behaviorism and those few who demonstrated greater complexity of thought. This is the claim that Stanfield makes when he argues, "That Lewis attacked behaviorism in his polemical works while presenting characters in his fiction as automata is thus not really a contradiction, for he believed that almost all people were exactly as behaviorism described them. Behaviorism, however, allowed for no exceptions, and for Lewis it was precisely on the exceptions that all depended."[86] Evidence that Lewis maintained such "exceptions" is present in *The Art of Being Ruled*, where he exhibits the influence of Nietzsche's theory of the *Ubermench* and articulates a protofascist political vision that he would later regret. The distinction that Lewis draws is not only a moral one but also an ontological one.

> Goethe had a jargon of his own for referring to these two species whose existence he perfectly recognized. He divided people into *Puppets* and *Natures*. He said the majority of people were machines, playing a part. When he wished to express admiration for a man, he would say about him, "He is a *nature*." This division into *natural* men and *mechanical* men (which Goethe's idiom amounts to) answers to the solution advocated in this essay. And today there is an absurd war between the "puppets" and the "natures," the machines and the men. And owing to the development of machinery, the pressure on the "natures" increases. We are *all* slipping back into machinery, because we *all* have tried to be free.[87]

The passage considers exceptions to increasingly reductive and mechanistic accounts of the human that Lewis critiques while suggesting that the historical possibility of such exceptions has waned. The fiction that he would compose after *The Art of Being Ruled* includes scenes, like the exchange between Pullman and Satters, that suggest that those who believe themselves to be exceptions to behaviorist forms of descriptions and manipulations are the most deluded. Therefore, Kenner's sense of a contradiction in Lewis's work and Stanfield's resolution of that apparent contradiction do not tell the full story of Lewis's evolving and increasingly pessimistic attitudes toward the historical transformation of human subjectivity. The target of his satirical attention dialectically shifts from those who fully conform to behaviorism's reductive account to those who believe themselves to be exceptions to that account – especially, and ironically, behaviorists themselves.

This satirical critique is especially evident in *Snooty Baronet,* the novel that most explicitly takes up the consequences and the contradictions of behaviorism. Its central character, Michael Kell-Imrie, has achieved a modicum of fame for two books that were written under the influence of John B. Watson's behaviorist methods. In applying this doctrine to both his work and private life, Kell-Imrie regards his friends and lovers as little more than a collection of puppets to be manipulated through behaviorist techniques of observation and control. Like Pullman and Satters, he regards others as fundamentally lacking personhood or even reality. In a description of Humphrey, his friend and literary agent, Kell-Imrie observes, "His imagination was quite nerveless, it had no power to *grasp* whatever it might numbly handle. – Humph was, as I have said, not real."[88] However, as Stanfield suggests, the novel's narrative technique ironizes the psychological poverty of Kell-Imrie's behaviorism as well as his failure to embrace the full consequences of its reductionism:

> The novel's first-person narration also repeatedly wanders from the plot in a way that insistently foregrounds Kell-Imrie's conscious mind, its judgments, its volitions, its intentions, whatever of it there may be that is irreducible to observable behavior. Kell-Imrie's foregrounding of his own interiority is surprising, since as a behaviorist, interiority is precisely what he ought to consider ruled out of discussion. That "mind" is reducible to "behavior" is both what Kell-Imrie holds as an article of faith and what, in his own particular case, he takes drastic measures to disprove.[89]

Evidence of Kell-Imrie's inconsistency is hard to miss when he declares, "The inner meaning of 'Behavior,' as a notion, got in motion within my consciousness."[90] That "Behavior" might have an "inner meaning" is precisely what behaviorism denies, along with the very notion of consciousness.

However, what is at stake is not simply a contradiction between Kell-Imrie's behaviorism and the impressionistic form of his self-narration; instead, the novel demonstrates the intellectual inconsistency of behaviorism's claims to the status of both science and technology. While Watson boldly announced his brand of psychology as a strictly objective, empirical description of external behavior that posited no mental states such as intentions, desires, or purposes, these same mental states are reserved for the behaviorist who carries out the technocratic agenda of "mental engineering." Lewis's novel stages the critique that Bertrand Russell had leveled against Watson that his psychological technology would entail two classes: the thinking behaviorists and their unthinking subjects. This is evident in Kell-Imrie's megalomaniacal self-narration, in which he distinguishes himself as the sole "plotter" against all of Mankind:

> What I suppose I was doing was to hatch a plot against Mankind, a plot that had only one plotter: for I rapidly discovered that I was alone, with my hard vision, and there was no one alive I could trust. But I kept my own counsel. I never opened my mouth.[91]

If Kell-Imrie has a unique status in the "hard vision" of his behaviorist gaze, it is in part because he directs that reductive gaze at all but himself. "Snooty," as he is known by others, arrogates to himself the status of an ontological exception, which renders a solipsistic and megalomaniacal storyworld in which he alone is granted full subjectivity. This is a common narrative pattern of many delusions that often exhibit the paranoid structure of thought that is evident in Kell-Imrie's pronounced distrust of others.

While he maintains an instrumentalizing attitude, he also demonstrates a growing suspicion that he may be the object of others' machinations, and his narrative discourse alternates between paranoid and conspiratorial modes. Such paranoia introduces the possibility that his "hard vision," which refuses to recognize mental operations in others, has overlooked something that may lie beyond the immediate appearances of their outward behavior. He comes to suspect that his lover and his literary agent, both of whom he intended to abandon, somehow have been plotting against him. If he underestimated their possibility for such conspiratorial forethought, it follows that he may have also overestimated his own ontological difference from them. "As to me, in the charge of these machines, they should – up to the last moment – have their way with me. [...] They desired me to be their automaton! *I would in the end become their Frankenstein!*"[92] In a paranoid, zero-sum logic, Kell-Imrie's nightmarish suspicion of other minds precipitates his own sense of instrumentalized vulnerability to the potential manipulations of others.

This suspicion leads to a feeling of unreality in which he detects an uncanny transformation of his environment, the obscure meaning of which centers on him. "Nothing could ever persuade me that what next took place was not a deliberate trap set by destiny. The natural and familiar scene had been tampered with, and who would deny that everything pointed to its being on my account?"[93] Snooty comes upon a shop window display that contains an elaborate mechanical puppet. The automaton bows, removes its hat, and appears to meet the gaze of Kell-Imrie. As he observes the automaton, the windowpane reflects his image back to him, rendering a superimposition of the two forms. In this moment of reflection, he is prompted to apply the techniques of behaviorism to himself and is forced to recognize his similarity with the automaton. Kell-Imrie becomes aware of the uncanny facial expression that he assumes when lost in thought, along with the strange reaction that his own inscrutability must induce in others around him. "That in its turn affects people's behavior to me, as you can guess. They look at my frowning and puzzled stare and they act accordingly. That is only natural. And I act back – that's only good sense too. That's 'Behavior.'"[94] Kell-Imrie observes a causal circuit of involuntary automatisms that enfolds Snooty's inscrutable look – the outward expression of internal thought – along with the inscrutable responses of others. While stimuli and responses are observed, no meaning is exchanged. Behaviorism begins with the failure of any theory of other minds.

In this dense moment of mirroring and identification, Kell-Imrie reflects upon his own failure to know not only the contents but also the very existence of other minds. This epistemic limitation is elicited by the automaton's successful mimicry of human behavior.

> I watched him with a painful amazement, attempting to penetrate what he meant, by being what he was ... The fellow was playacting – and what I resented in this comedy was the fact that I knew (or thought I knew) that he was not *real*. There was something abstruse and unfathomable in this automaton.[95]

Kell-Imrie's need to "penetrate what he meant" violates the protocols of behaviorism by positing some meaning beyond or beneath the surface of ostensible action. The source of anxiety is both epistemic and ontological: Kell-Imrie doubts whether he can determine with certainty, on the basis of strictly behaviorist methods alone, whether the automaton is "real," and, in the logic of his identification with the automaton, he suspects that the automaton's apparent unreality only reflects his own. This ontological anxiety is exacerbated when a pedestrian gestures toward Snooty's prosthetic leg and suggests that he resembles the window manikin. His feeling of unreality appears to metastasize.

> Was not perhaps this fellow who had come up beside me a puppet too? I could not swear that he was not! I turned my eyes away from him, back to the smiling phantom in the window, with intense uneasiness. For I thought to myself as I caught sight of him in the glass, smiling away in response to our mechanical friend, *certainly he is a puppet too!* Of course he was, but dogging that was the brother-thought, *but equally so am I! –* And so I was (a very thoughtful and important puppet ...).[96]

No longer confident that he is distinguished or "alone" in his "hard vision," Kell-Imrie suspects that his own behavior is as absent of subjectivity as that of the automaton whose unchanging grin becomes, like that of Lewis Carroll's fading Cheshire cat, an expression without a subject which expresses nothing. The reduction of such gestures to mere "behavior" without meaning is, for Lewis, the effect of behaviorism.

If such depersonalization is the logical consequence of modernist discourses of the mind, it is also an experience that is commonly described by psychotics who were often exposed to such frameworks. R. D. Laing observes this looping effect between the experiences of the schizophrenics and the ontological framework of twentieth-century psychiatry and psychology:

> Seen as an organism, man cannot be anything else but a complex of things, of *its*, and the processes that ultimately comprise an organism are *it*-processes. There is a common illusion that one somehow increases one's understanding of a person if one can translate a personal understanding of him into the impersonal terms of a sequence or system of *it*-processes.[97]

It is this reduction of the human to objective, impersonal "*it*-processes" that Lewis finds in Watson's behaviorism, and his fiction represents the first-person experience of such reduction in ways that resonate with experiences of mental patients, described by Laing as "the dread, that is, of the possibility of turning, or being turned, from a live person into a dead thing, into a stone, into a robot, an automaton, without personal autonomy of action, an *it* without subjectivity."[98] In *An Autobiography of a Schizophrenic Girl*, Renee lucidly describes the dread of this vision as she observes a school friend:

> So I accompany her a little way, waiting, hoping that a miracle will restore reality, life, sensibility. I look at her, study her, praying to feel the life in her through the enveloping unreality. But she seems more a statue than ever, a manikin moved by a mechanism, talking like an automaton. It is horrible, inhuman, grotesque.[99]

Elsewhere, Renee's references to an "invisible mechanism" that seems to animate the lifeless puppets that surround her indicate her exclusion from systems of meanings and protocols that govern normative social behavior as well as from any access to the mental states of others that might be motivating their behavior. In *Snooty Baronet*, Kell-Imrie describes a similar feeling of unreality as he observes the window manikin's simulation of polite greetings and gestures of welcome – simulations that seem as unreal and without meaning as his own performances of expected "behavior."

To me *nothing* seemed natural. Often I have smiled upon occasions of that sort. Every day I was smiling hard at such common or garden things. Everything that passed as natural with him, looked exceedingly odd to me. The most customary things in the world struck me continually as particularly ludicrous. *How* ludicrous – or how normal on the other hand – would depend upon how I was feeling at the moment.[100]

Like Renee's memoir, the passage describes an experience of unworlding: when behavior is reduced to "it-processes," experiences of everyday life – "the most customary things" – seem suddenly uncanny, artificial, and indecipherable. This loss of the meanings and purposes of everyday objects and actions is at the core of many accounts of schizophrenic "unworlding." As phenomenological psychiatrists such as R. D. Laing and more recently Louis Sass have argued, the everyday integration of things into a world organized by the needs and projects of the human subject is often a way of being-in-the-world that becomes abruptly foreign to many patients. As a result, the difference between objects and people becomes obscure and uncanny. An object normally experienced as a tool with a particular relation to "normal" activity within a subject-oriented world may be encountered as indecipherable, uncanny presence. Conversely, persons may be seen as lacking the characteristics that might conventionally distinguish humanity (intelligence, emotion, independence), appearing instead as so many automata, dancing in unison to a rhythm that the psychotic is unable to hear. All phenomena are in this sense collapsed into a single, uncanny ontological status. Renee describes her terrifying experience of this uncanny unreality.

> This existence accounted for my greatest fear. In the unreal scene, in the murky quiet of my perception, suddenly 'the thing' sprang up. The stone jar, decorated with blue flowers, was there facing me, defying me with its presence, with its existence. To conquer my fear I looked away. My eyes met a chair, then a table; they were alive too, asserting their presence. I attempted to escape their hold by calling out their names. I said, "chair, jug, table, it is a chair." *But the word echoed hollowly, deprived of all meaning; it had left the object, was divorced from it, so much so that on one hand it was a living, mocking thing, on the other, a name, robbed of sense, an envelope emptied of content.* Nor was I able to bring the two together, but stood rooted there before them, filled with fear and impotence.[101]

In this experience, what is felt to be threatening is the very *being* of these objects that are no longer tacitly organized into familiar places in an everyday ecology. What is lacking is their "sense" – their meaningful place in relation to the subject's world of purpose and value – all of which are features of experience that are categorically excluded from behaviorist accounts. Renee, the author of this memoir, recalls the difficulty she had performing the routine tasks of sewing and cleaning: "Varied as these subjects were, they presented similar problems, so that more and more, despite my efforts, *I lost the feeling of practical things.*"[102] What replaces a practically organized world is the sense that things simply move *automatically* according to a logic that is inscrutable and unavailable to the psychotic observer.

Like Renee, Kell-Imrie is unable to grasp any distinction between the automaton and the human. "There was something *absolute* in this distinction, recognized by everybody there excepting myself. I alone did not see it. What essentially was the difference however?"[103] Kell-Imrie appears to acknowledge a pathological dimension to his experience – it "would depend upon how I was feeling at the moment." However, these feelings of unease are not merely the results of his psychological state but appear to be the effects of his behaviorist doctrine, which resolutely forecloses any reference to mental states. As in *The Childermass*, what follows is a struggle to establish one's own reality within an impoverished ontology. "And must I confess it? I was very slightly alarmed. I saw that I had to *compete* with these other creatures bursting up all over the imaginary landscape, and struggling against me to be *real* – like a passionate battle for necessary air, in a confined place."[104] The hallucinatory figures that somehow lack reality within an "imaginary landscape" recall the world of *The Childermass* as well as the "fleetingly-improvised men" that plagued the psychotic Daniel Paul Schreber.[105] Such a paranoid contest for precarious existence is also described by Laing, who recounts the delusional strategies of one schizophrenic patient:

> He turned the other person into a thing in his own eyes, thus magically nullifying any danger to himself by secretly disarming the enemy. By destroying, in his own eyes, the other person as a person, he robbed the other of his power to crush him. By depleting him of his personal aliveness, that is, by seeing him as a piece of machinery, rather than as a human being, he undercut the risk to himself of this aliveness either swamping him, imploding into his own emptiness, or turning him into a mere appendage.[106]

Laing's account summarizes well the anxious struggle that dominates novels like *Snooty Baronet* and *The Childermass* – texts that stage the distinctly ontological terrors that arise from behaviorism's "hard vision." In his fiction and in his works of cultural analysis, Lewis suggests that such experiences are not restricted to the delusions of the mentally ill but are the logical consequences of increasingly influential psychological discourses that explicitly announce their ambitions to reduce the human to engineered automata. While *Snooty Baronet* explores the internal contradictions of a behaviorist rhetoric that aspires to both detached, objective description and instrumentalizing control, it also makes vivid the feelings of unreality and paranoia that such visions produce without remedy.

The text may introduce an ambiguity as to whether Kell-Imrie's singular insight is reducible to his vacuous behaviorist ontology of the human or to his own precarious psychological state. That the novel merges these two visions suggests a technological delusion at the core of behaviorism. Lewis's satirical treatment of this discourse suggests that extricating oneself from this mechanizing understanding of being is not possible through mere disavowal. If Lewis fails to locate a satisfactory position for himself, even through the series of schizoid and paranoid narratives that comprise his late-modernist literary corpus, he deftly succeeds in articulating the structures and sources of a distinctly modern form of madness.

CHAPTER 2

Modernist Influencing Machines
From Mina Loy to Evelyn Waugh

In 1937, Mina Loy was sent by her son-in-law Julien Levy to consider the work of Richard Oelze for his New York art gallery. Oelze was a reclusive German surrealist painter who cultivated a mysterious persona, even by the standards of an aging avant-garde Paris. The stories of drug use and suspected madness that surrounded this marginal figure piqued Loy's curiosity, and when she finally met him she was struck by the impression that the emaciated figure seemed to barely hold together, physically and psychologically. Despite or perhaps because of the warnings she had received from mutual acquaintances about his erratic behavior, Loy soon took Oelze in. The ambiguously maternal, romantic, and perhaps psychotherapeutic relationship that ensued would become the material for Loy's posthumously published novel *Insel*.

Although finally rescued from the archives by Elizabeth Arnold and published by Black Sparrow Press in 1991, this strange novel has suffered the same disregard within contemporary modernist studies that it faced when Loy failed to find a sympathetic publisher.[1] Perhaps it is not entirely surprising that a late-1930s literary world exhausted by avant-garde provocation was not receptive of a "novel" that showed minimal narrative development or structure, incorporated a cast of only two primary characters, and indulged in hallucinatory interactions that defied the neorealist tendencies that were beginning to dominate. Still, I would insist that the rediscovery of this text remains a crucial event for our understanding of literary modernism's engagements with madness and technological anxieties that recurred in the years of late modernism.

Whether it is possible or even useful to diagnose the historical Oelze as schizophrenic, it rapidly becomes clear that Loy's title character Insel is the monadic island of insanity that his name suggests. The novel is launched by the strange fact that Insel is accessible only for the Loy-like narrator, Mrs. Jones. It is only Jones, a somewhat unstable writer and artist in her own right, who is able to achieve a bizarre, technologically encoded communication with Insel that makes him knowable. To the extent that an arc of development can be plotted through the novel, it is the progress of this strange transferential relationship between an otherwise unreachable subject and the narrator – a development that appears to end in a fundamental shift in the symptoms that had defined Insel.

All of this would suggest that over the course of the novel a kind of "lay analysis" has taken place. While *Insel* refuses generic features that might be expected even of a late-modernist novel, it does exhibit many characteristics of psychoanalytic case studies: the text is largely constituted by a catalogue of bizarre symptoms and a transferential dynamic that ends in some change in a character's behavior and enjoyment. In this sense, the structure and aim of the case study are carefully embedded in the construction of *Insel*. However, while clinical writing may have been a possible resource for Loy's literary production, the novel also exerts an active, transformative pressure on the form of the case study. What is most remarkable about this strange text is not simply its initial resemblance to the Freudian corpus – the ways that it might neatly fit into that canon of quasinovelistic case writing – but rather the ways in which it knowingly differs and departs from that modernist genre. In this sense, the novel invokes the case study as genre in order to measure its own critical limitations. One critical departure from psychoanalytic frameworks is the curiously technological or somatic form of transference achieved between Jones and Insel, which bypasses the linguistic exchange crucial to the scene of analysis. Such uncanny features of the novel resist the strong temptation to reconstruct *Insel* as merely a kind of lay psychoanalytic case study.

Therefore, the task of this chapter will be twofold. First, in order to understand these strangely technological features of Jones's "treatment" of Insel, we will have to look beyond the Freudian doxa to a longer history of psychotherapies and theories of mind that may have been sources for the strange transmissions. Secondly, I will argue that these technological elements lead toward a critique of the Freudian clinic as a machine of text production. Among other questions, the novel asks, What is the relation between psychological treatment and the writing that it makes possible? If the case study is generically distinct for the way that it is underwritten by the work of analysis, what might be its cost to the patient? Before considering the novel's answer, we must first examine the oblique means by which it is able to pose these ethical questions.

The novel unfolds through a catalogue of observations and symptoms that arise over the course of Mrs. Jones's experiences with the strange figure. Initial descriptions begin where Lewis seems to have left off in *Snooty*

Baronet, locating Insel somewhere between human and machine but a machine that seems to be in an entropic state of decay and dissolution. "A wound up automaton running down, Insel ceased among the clatter of our amusement."[2] Later, Jones remarks, "as I watched, I had the sensation of a 'breaking point,' an expectance [sic] of a spring flying loose to whirr insanely."[3] While this precarious, lifeless condition has an alienating effect on others, Jones experiences a magnetic pull toward Insel – a strange attraction that is encoded in the discourses of modern mechanization and new media. Insel's social isolation is further compounded by a peculiar linguistic ineptitude: not only does he not speak French or English, but he seems at times congenitally deficient of a capacity for speech. At one moment, he explains to Jones, "As a child I would remain absolutely silent for six months at a time."[4]

Despite this symptomatic failure of language, Jones becomes capable of a mysterious, direct access to Insel's psychic interiority. This ambiguous communication is accomplished through the bizarre *Strahlen* or "rays" that Insel seems to transmit from his body – rays that only she is capable of detecting, receiving, and perhaps reciprocating. "Some infrared or invisible rays he gave off, were immediately transferred on one's neural current to some dark room in the brain for instantaneous development in all its brilliancy. So one saw him as a gray man and an electrified organism at one and the same time."[5] Upon reception of these rays, Jones gains access to Insel's hallucinatory world, an experience that she describes as "the telepathic, televisionary machinery of our reciprocity."[6]

If these mysterious rays seem to function as channels of communication, they also appear to operate as material instantiations of the dynamic libidinal flows and cathexes that pass between Insel and Jones. When Insel's rays are transmitted or invested in Jones, she is overwhelmed in a sublime and terrifying experience of *jouissance*: "I was overcome by a rush of nervous sublimity carried by the air. 'If this is madness,' I said to myself, breathing his atmosphere exquisite almost to sanctification, 'madness is something very beautiful'."[7] The result of this cathexis on Mrs. Jones is that Insel's own fragile ego is decathected and becomes unstable. In the libidinal geography of the novel, the word "Insel" paradoxically comes to name a densely empty space.

> The flat seemed emptier for his being there, until I found that further off it was filled to a weird expansion with emanations drifting away from Insel asleep [...] In the room at the end of the corridor their force of vitalized nothingness was pushing back the walls [...] Why should Insel, less ponderable than other men, impart perceptible properties in the air?

> Was he leaking out of himself, residuum of that ominous honey he stored
> behind his eyes into which it was his constant, his distraught concern to
> withdraw?[8]

For Jones, Insel's singular quality is his unstable ontological status. Her
account suggests that he is forever in danger of disseminating and dissolving into nothingness. A dialectic emerges over the course of the relationship
in which his *Strahlen* move between investment in her and a narcissistic
reinvestment in his own precarious ego – all of which Jones and Insel can
somehow visually observe in the form of auratic, electromagnetic rays.

> Insel, intently keeping watch, had moved his stool some distance away as
> if to find his range for an inverted "Aim of Withdrawal." Spinning himself
> into a shimmering cocoon of his magnetic rays, introvert, incomparably
> aloof, "They're mine," he exulted as clearly as if he were crying aloud.
>   Too simple to fully imagine the effect of these rays, he had, it would
> seem, only an instinctive *mesmeric* use for them. He might even feel them
> as a sort of bodily loss compensated perhaps by rare encounters with one
> able to tune in.[9]

Feeling threatened by the rare psychic investment in Jones, Insel with-
draws into a monadic carapace of his own libidinal construction. Insel
jealously guards his *Strahlen* as if they were constitutive of his precarious
being. Jones, implicitly positioned as his analyst, seems to understand
the status and nature of these *Strahlen* more than Insel himself, who
only unconsciously distributes and redistributes this hallucinated energy.
Jones recognizes that the "transmission" of these rays compromises Insel,
but that this corporeal or psychic loss is somehow repaid by the connection he is finally able to achieve with the rare interlocutor able to
"tune in."

In the language of the novel, then, Jones is at once analyst and radio
receiver to Insel's uncanny transmissions. Elsewhere, her role is described
in cinematic terms as she offers something like the mute, blank surface
onto which Insel is able to project his fantasy. However, Freud famously
regarded psychotic patients as generally unreachable through the transferential relationship on which psychoanalytic technique is grounded.
In a 1928 letter, he writes, "I did not like those patients [...] They made
me angry and I find myself irritated to experience them so distant from
myself and from all that is human. This is an astonishing intolerance which
brands me a poor psychiatrist."[10] If the goal of transference is to activate
the neurotic's repressed unconscious drives toward a more livable libidinal
experience, Freud suggests that such an operation is not only impossible
but perhaps even undesirable in the case of the psychotic.[11]

If the transferential relationship is implied at times in *Insel*, at the same time, the strangeness of the novel refuses such a simple identification. Indeed, there is something resolutely illegible about the oddly material connections that occur in the novel – an inscrutability that may be overcome through a more complete sense of the therapeutic practices that may have informed the text. Freud was not the first to develop a transferential rapport as a means to therapeutic progress. While Loy appears to have read Freud's work and was even read by him (he once declared her work "analytical"),[12] *Insel* suggests knowledge of a longer history of therapies that preceded and competed with psychoanalysis. The description of Insel's rays as "mesmeric" sends us back to earlier, materialist treatments of mental and nervous illnesses.

Historians of psychoanalysis and psychiatry have long demonstrated the important role mesmerism and hypnotism played in early dynamic psychology.[13] It was in part the bizarre, altered states that these techniques induced in their patients that made theories of the unconscious a necessity. What may be especially illuminating about these earlier movements in relation to Loy's novel are their distinctly materialist and often technological understandings of psychological behavior and its treatment. Mesmer and his followers famously hypothesized the existence of a "neuric fluid," a vaguely material component of the body that resembled electromagnetic energy and that was said to emanate from various orifices.[14] Many symptoms that could not otherwise be treated by conventional medical techniques were attributed to an imbalance of this "neuric fluid." Mesmer's solution was the application of large magnets to affected parts of the body. This often resulted in remarkable recoveries, and Mesmer's practice grew into a large, cultlike following. Many guides to proper mesmeric procedures were published in the nineteenth century, some recommending ideal physical orientations between doctor and patient for the proper, corrective flow or transfer of the "neuric fluid" between the two. It was often recommended that the mesmerist sit facing the patient with her knees between his, their eyes locked into a deep stare as he passes his hands over her face and torso in order to effect the corrective transfer of neuric fluid from his body to hers. Insel's neurological transmissions may come into focus when interpreted in light of these techniques.

Once properly magnetized, patients would enter into an altered state in which they often claimed to see the "neuric fluid" emitted from the bodies of those around them in the form of rays of light. The mesmerists also found that subjects in this condition were especially susceptible to suggestion, something that was at once useful for therapeutic purposes and extremely controversial. Patients often seemed to fall under a peculiar spell cast by their mesmerists, and those suspicious of the practice recommended that husbands be present when their wives were magnetized.

The medical community, such as it was in late-eighteenth-century Paris, largely regarded Mesmer and his followers as charlatans, and the technique was soon discredited by an investigative committee headed by Benjamin Franklin. Still, treatment by magnetism continued late into the nineteenth century, when it became evident that the source of its success was the force of authoritative suggestion rather than any material influence. In spite of this explanatory shift, fascination with these altered states only continued into the late-nineteenth and twentieth centuries. Publications on hypnotism and efforts to theorize these altered states of consciousness, or the unconscious, followed at a rapid pace. While the materialist explanation of the mesmeric or hypnotic state lost favor, its vestigial traces can be found in psychological writings around the turn of the twentieth century. Conversely, as John Durham Peters points out, early developers of radio technology pursued the possibility of mental transmissions:

> In the 1880s and 1890s, every major physicist involved in the development of radio flirted with the notion of wireless "thought-transference." In Britain, Lord Rayleigh, the leading acoustician of the late 19th century, J.J. Thomson, the discoverer of the electron, William Crookes, the inventor of the cathode ray tube, and Oliver Lodge, the inventor of the radio coherer, all took an active interest in what was called "psychical research."[15]

While mesmerism's influence on popular and clinical culture constitutes a possible source for the *Strahlen* that pass between Insel and Jones, the narrator invokes modern communications technologies to describe and explain her nonverbal rapport with her "patient." She is able to "tune in" to rays transmitted by him to "some dark room in the brain for instantaneous development in all its brilliancy."[16] The effect of this reception is a kind of auditory and visual hallucination that Jones compares to more common experiences of media technology that had been adopted by the 1930s. Loy was not alone in recognizing the similarities between the altered states of madness (often explained through materialist discourses) and the flood of new, quasihallucinatory experiences that these media technologies could produce, often at a distance.

As Friedrich Kittler and Pamela Thurschwell have argued, experimental and paranormal psychology sometimes merged in the popular imagination with half-understood theories about these new communications technologies.[17] For the less spiritually oriented, radio offered a materialist, technological explanation for the strange communications that were taking place during this "neo-mesmeric renaissance."[18] If the possibility of communication with the dead inspired fascination, the notion that the machinery of one's mind was vulnerable to the manipulation of others became a source of growing anxiety. The intimate powers of knowledge and influence that mesmerists and hypnotists might wield over their subjects became evident when Hyppolite Bernheim's hypnotism became a popular stage show for the general public in the late-nineteenth century.[19]

The convergence of these two forms of influence – clinical and technological – became explicit in the delusions of many paranoid psychotics in ways that closely resemble the surreal world of *Insel*. Victor Tausk describes the recurrent delusion that one's thoughts had been transmitted

> by means of waves or rays or mysterious forces, which the patient's knowledge of physics is inadequate to explain. In such cases, the machine is often called a "suggestion apparatus." Its construction cannot be explained, but its function consists in the transmission or "draining off" of thoughts and feelings by one or several persecutors.[20]

In the patients' accounts of their delusions, the "suggestion apparatus" or "influencing machine" was often operated by their doctors. The delusions seem to synthesize the anxieties of influence that had been provoked by "suggestion therapies" and the increasingly technological descriptions of the brain that had become increasingly common within neurological discourse. Further, the delusional accounts draw upon the emergent media technologies that made new experiences akin to visual and auditory "hallucination" a mass-cultural experience: Victor Tausk reports that several patients describe visual hallucinations that manifest as two-dimensional, cinematic projections on a wall.[21] At times, Jones and Insel are characterized less as doctor and patient than as reciprocal transmitters and receivers: "Behind this fragile front lies a delicate radio-raceiver [sic] of cosmic urges which canalised, intricated, misconstrued by his brain, compose the rhythm of his individuality."[22] Elsewhere, Jones observes that, "Taking on another aspect, emitting electric waves, he broadcast his thoughts which were returned to him conditioned by their effectiveness; ideas, operative as hands, shaping events."[23] John Durham Peters argues, "each age gets the form of madness it deserves and that every form of madness is a parody of the reigning form of reason. Pathology reveals normality. In the same way, each format or technology of communication implies its own disorders."[24]

What is perhaps most troubling to these patients, and a central anxiety that repeats in *Insel*, is the sense that one's thoughts are no longer one's own.

Tausk observes that the suspicion that one's perceptions, emotions, and cognitive processes had been directly manipulated often results in the subject's loss of sovereignty and self-identity:

> This symptom is the complaint that "everyone" knows the patient's thoughts, that his thoughts are not enclosed in his own head, but are spread throughout the world and occur simultaneously in the heads of all persons. The patient seems no longer to realize that he is a separate psychic entity, an ego with individual boundaries.[25]

The remarkable homology between the experience of the psychotic – marked by a sense of thought manipulation and ego loss – and experiences of emergent technology in the early-twentieth century suggests that Tausk's patients might offer insight into not only the conditions of their private psychic formations. The threats to psychic integrity and sovereignty – whether in the form of suggestion therapy or new media technologies – converge and multiply. Each apparent threat becomes overcoded and synthesized with the other not only in the language of psychotic delusions but also in late-modernist works such as *Insel*.

Even for those who had not been subjected to the institutional regime of psychiatry, the very notion of an unconscious – a psychological component that governs one's behavior in ways that a doctor might understand and mediate more easily than the patient herself – introduced a challenge to one's personal sovereignty and self-control at the core of one's being. In this way, the delusions of the "influencing machine" only made explicit what was implied by newly articulated dimensions of mental life such as "automatisms," the "subliminal," and the "unconscious." In Tausk's view, the influencing machine did not simply encode the relationship between doctor and patient; it also reflected the alienation felt by the patient when confronted with the automatic operation of her own libidinal drives – an operation independent and even defiant of any conscious control or intervention.

> The evolution, by distortion of the human apparatus into a machine, is a projection that corresponds to the development of the pathological process that converts the ego into a diffuse sexual being – or, expressed in the language of the genital period, into a genital, a machine independent of the aims of the ego and subordinated to a foreign will. It is no longer subordinated to the will of the ego, but dominates it.[26]

For Tausk, the machine represents an external projection of the unconscious and its uncanny drives over which the subject has little control – a theory similar to the one Freud offered of Daniel Paul Schreber's description of divine influence via "nerve-rays." The same features inhere in both the influencing machine and the psychoanalytic theory of the unconscious: they name an uncanny force exerted on the subject that is felt to be alien, anterior, and challenging to consciousness.

The many uncanny elements of Mrs. Jones's strange rapport with Insel may now seem rather timely in light of this context of materialist treatments and descriptions of the mind and their integration in the popular imagination with the modern media ecology. The novel is evidence of a syncretism of clinical and technological discourses – a syncretism that had already been performed by many paranoid psychotics. The resemblances between the paranoid memoirs and Loy's novel may therefore be read in two directions. The delusions provide a hermeneutic horizon for the surreal phenomena that manifest in *Insel*, while Loy's novel retroactively transforms those delusional narratives into valuable resources for understanding certain cultural anxieties of the moment.

The novel also anticipates ethical questions about the micropolitics of therapeutic relations – many of which are more commonly associated with the antipsychiatry movement of the 1960s and 1970s than with the era of modernism. Some of these concerns are already manifest in the delusions that Tausk presents, but in his efforts to make those delusions conform to the libido theory – "the machines always stand for the dreamer's own genitalia" – he often overwrites or ignores the patients' attempts to communicate.[27] Elsewhere, Tausk observes, "The machine serves to persecute the patient and is operated by enemies. To the best of my knowledge, the latter are exclusively of the male sex. They are predominantly physicians by whom the patient has been treated."[28] His interpretation of the influencing machine as a figure for the patient's unconscious moves quickly past the expressed anxiety over the power dynamics of the gendered therapeutic relationship. Indeed, the gender coding of this asymmetrical relationship is neither neutral nor innocent. A familiar narrative of the birth of psychoanalysis has it delivered by a genius male doctor from the suffering and stuttering bodies of so many female hysterics. The delusions of those suffering the persecutions of the "influencing machine" in fact testify in quite legible ways to the felt violence that might emerge from such an asymmetrical relationship. Writing at a clinical remove, Tausk does not fully acknowledge the way that he may be cast by the delusions in the potential role of a persecuting clinician.

However, *Insel* makes clear the potential threat posed by the doctor for the patient. If the novel locates itself within a history of psychotherapies by telling the story of a particular therapeutic relation, it also exerts a critical force on that history by ethically assessing the risks of certain therapeutic relations to their subjects. This critique manifests through the novel's unorthodox rearrangement of the therapeutic roles of doctor and patient. The novel integrates the complaint of the psychotic during the anxious scenes of "treatment" and accordingly restructures that relationship in radical ways. This reorganization involves a shared psychological risk and burden for both "patient" and "doctor" such that these roles begin to lose their distinction. Finally, this restructured relationship demands an alternative understanding of authorship of the document that will record the progress of that relationship. Jones's singular rapport with Insel – her capacity to "tune in" to his hallucinated *Strahlen* and observe his dynamic investment and dissolution – is itself an impossible fantasy of every analyst. She claims to have achieved precisely that which endlessly frustrated the father of psychoanalysis, and at one point she declares that she has "superseded Freud."[29] What further distinguishes Jones's approach is her failure, or perhaps refusal, to definitively establish and maintain the asymmetrical relationship between analyst and analysand. Set in the first person, the novel offers only Jones's vision of these hallucinations – hallucinations that Insel seems not to apprehend fully. It follows that Insel may become Jones's object of fantasy or, further, an element of her own delusion: "By then, all that remained of Insel was a vague impression of *trompe l'oeil.*"[30] Elsewhere she seems to acknowledge that she may have assumed the role of patient: "Had I recalled the earlier iridescent Insel, it could only have been as a figment of *my* insanity."[31] The two characters' positions appear to reverse unexpectedly, relocating Insel in the role of doctor: "I had become for him a strange specimen, to whose slightest gesture he pinned an attention like that of a vindictive psychiatrist."[32] Jones's exposure to Insel's *Strahlen* seems to have adverse effects on her own mental stability. She begins to suspect that her thoughts have been compromised – that her words are not her own but are transmitted to her via Insel's rays: "But I was beginning, myself, to feel unnatural. I distinctly detected my voice in ventriloquial emulation echo the wistful, surf-like swooning singing of his – '*Sterben – Man mu-u-uss – Man mu-u-uss*'" [die – one must].[33] This trajectory reaches its apex when she describes an experience of depersonalization that follows an extended encounter with him:

> The painless buoyancy lasted well into the night when, as I sat calmly at work in my hotel bedroom, I unexpectedly disintegrated. My body, which had hitherto made upon itself the impression of a compact mass, springing a multiplicity of rifts, changed to a fractional covering I can only compare to the spines of a porcupine; or rather vibrant streamers on which my

> density in plastic undulation was being carried away – perhaps into infinity.
> A greater dynamism than my own rushed in to fill the interstices. Looking
> down at myself I could *see* my sensation. The life-force blasting me apart
> instead of holding me together. It set up a harrowing excitement in my
> brain. An atomic despair – so awful – my confines broke down. I lost con-
> tour. Once more I found myself in the "impossible situation" in which one
> cannot remain – from which there is no issue. I cognized this situation as
> Insel's. A maddening with desire for a thing I did not know – a thing that,
> while being the agent of his – my – dematerialization alone could bring
> him together again. A desire of which one was "dead" and yet still alive …[34]

By an effort of empathy, Jones assumes Insel's precarious form of being.
Jones visually observes her own ego loss as a material and corporeal disintegration. An imaginary identification with Insel has occurred such that
his pain has become her own. The price of this mimetic dissolution is that
Jones's relation to the world becomes unstable.

> I had found myself without any instrument with which to contact the uni-
> verse […] But now I was at the mercy of an imperfect instrument. The
> antennae of the contact with the world in some way crippled for their func-
> tion seemed – like the umbilical cord in abnormal birth – to be wound
> round my brain in a fearful constriction, implacable as iron barriers.[35]

Jones's only channel of communication with the outside world is her
reception of the hallucinatory transmission from Insel, embodied in her
own "imperfect antennae." As in the discourse of schizoid regression that
haunts Wyndham Lewis, Jones's convergence with Insel into madness is
figured as an umbilical cord wrapped around her brain. If her care for Insel
seemed strangely maternal, this image might suggest that she is now being
reborn through him, nurtured and at the same time crushed by his "life
force."

Later, Jones suggests that her moment of crisis and literal self-sacrifice
becomes the condition of possibility for Insel's reconstitution: "my dema-
terialization alone could bring him together again."[36] Having experienced
radical subjective destitution and the uncanny mode of existence that she
had identified in Insel, Jones begins to work back toward some more conventional form of what she calls "sociability," hoping to bring Insel with
her. If this relationship can be described as a therapeutic practice, it is one
in which both share the risk and suffering that are normally reserved for
the patient alone.

Jones's reception of Insel's thought broadcasting and her apparent
entrance into his delusion recall a moment within the history of psychoanalysis in which a similar dynamic was proposed. As Pamela Thurschwell

shows, the Hungarian psychoanalyst Sandor Ferenczi differed with Freud on the possibility of treating psychotic patients and claimed to enter into obscure, telepathic relations with them that literalized and materialized the figurative exchange of thought and emotion that Freud's theory of transference was meant to establish through the mediation of language. Thurschwell writes that Ferenczi's "theories relentlessly broke down the barriers between bodies and minds; for him thought transference was a bridge between the material and psychic. By suggesting that identification and empathy were made possible by a permeable psyche, he formulated a psychotic scene for psychoanalysis."[37] Ferenczi was regarded as deranged by Ernest Jones and became increasingly marginalized by the psychoanalytic community. Thurschwell argues that, "what Jones saw as Ferenczi's psychosis – for instance, his belief 'that he was being successfully psychoanalyzed by messages transmitted telepathically across the Atlantic from an ex-patient of his' – was connected to this same desire to break down mental and physical barriers."[38] The attempt to go "beyond Freud" that is represented in Loy's surreal novel therefore has parallels in the history of psychoanalysis.

The fantasy of such direct, material, psychic effects has other analogues beyond Ferenczi's delusional claims. On several occasions, Insel lapses into a near-mesmeric state in which he becomes preoccupied with a singular experience of time. At one point, Jones spontaneously decides to view a lengthy film with a group of friends. Upon exiting the Parisian cinema, she remembers that she had planned to meet with Insel hours earlier. When she finally arrives, he seems completely unaware that he had been waiting for hours. Through the second half of the novel, this altered relation to the passage of time becomes a central symptom of Insel's condition. As Mrs. Jones enters deeper into Insel's world, she also experiences the lapse of temporal orientation that distinguished Insel.

> I could not make out whether the cause was a shift in the relative tempos of a cosmic and micro-cosmic "pulsation," whether *my* instant – the instant of a reductive perceiver – passed through some preponderant magnifier and enlarged, or whether a concept (become gnarled in one's brain through restriction to the brain's capacity) unwinding at leisure, was drawing my perception – infinitely soothed – along with it. For again this novel aspect of time seemed, like light, to arrive in rays focusing on the brain at a minimum akin to images on retinas; and the further one projected one's being to meet it, the *broader* one found it to be. Anyway, it was useless trying to analyze it. This alone was certain. It was absolutely engrossing to the mind, although nothing brief enough for us to cognize *happened* in this longer time.[39]

In her altered state, Jones is able to visualize an oceanic flow of time – an experience, it seems, that is available only to those with instruments of reception sensitive enough for its detection. If the madness that Jones has assumed on behalf of Insel entails a crisis of being, it also affords peculiar epistemological faculties. It appears that Jones has indeed moved beyond Freud. In breaking with more familiar forms of "treatment" of mental illness, the novel puts pressure on the condition's very status as "illness." Other theorists of the mind offered likely sources for Loy's critique and understood madness as not simply a state of deficiency or defect but as perhaps something else entirely. The passage preceding offers clues to several sources that assisted Loy in her move "beyond Freud" in understanding this borderline-psychotic way of being in the world. The emphasis on an expanded sense of "duration" must be read as a reference to Henri Bergson, whose work was a great source of inspiration to Loy. His theories of mind, along with those of Bergson's occasional colleague Frederic Myers, constitute additional threads in the long history of psychology woven into the fabric of *Insel*.

While symptoms of mental illness became taxonomized as pathological conditions by the psychiatric community, Frederic Myers found in these cases evidence of psychological abilities yet to come. Myers was the leader of the British Society for Psychical Research, an organization that, while somewhat marginal for the breadth of its investigations, was nevertheless well respected by the international psychological community around the turn of the twentieth century.[40] Experiences generally associated with mental illness were, for Myers, evidence of new mental faculties that were the most recent products of human evolution. In his quasi-Darwinian account, humanity had only begun to fully investigate these new epistemological faculties that were to be encouraged and fostered through proper scientific means rather than stigmatized. Myers's work offers a likely source for the notion, expressed at times by Jones, that Insel's symptoms might not simply be pathological breakdowns but signal emergent qualities of a form of human yet to come:

> The surrealist man is very long, stretching like a live wire from 1938 as far into the future & through equally numerous stages of evolution as he reaches into the past. His beginning is a speck of transparency, impinged upon by the sun. His ultimate presence would have been virtually invisible to a twentieth-century eye.[41]

In this and similar passages, the "surrealist man" is described as a highly evolved, electrified organism whose mode of being extends deep into the future in ways that are only made recognizable by Jones herself. In a related fragment, she describes her relation to him as one of reverse engineering: "Now I was engaged with a kind of surrealist man. Constructing, demolishing him kaleidoscopically, hoping to demonstrate how he 'worked.' "[42] In another archival fragment related to the manuscript for *Insel*, this figure is described as a kind of cyborg that has fully incorporated the functions of early-twentieth-century media technologies into itself so that devices such as radio and television are no longer needed – their operations are now carried out by the brain itself.

> His way is strewn with stone implements, embedded bones & machinery he discarded as superannuated models of functions he slowly develops within himself. Transport telepathy, radio, & television together with surprising future facilities are effected by "centres" in his cerebellum controlling the various potentials of the life-ray. The religious symbols of the precocious visionary in his early days, translated, become the "scientific" commonplace of his further condition.[43]

In the novel's present moment, Insel's mind appears miraculous for its telepathic transmissions, but the narrator implies that this religious understanding only marks the limits of current scientific understanding that will ultimately grasp the operations of his highly evolved brain. The novel implies that its titular character embodies a possible future form of the human, suggesting a potential revaluation of the "illness" as instead something like an evolved gift or talent. However, such a gift is an ambivalent and ambiguous combination of singular capacities and painful burdens. As the novel refuses to resolve this ambiguity, it clearly departs from the tradition of clinical writing that is comparatively univocal in its diagnosis and pathologization. In this ambiguity, we find the novel resisting its generic proximity to the form of the case study. If *Insel* does not offer a final and decisive evaluation of its title character's condition, it does demand that "madness" be written and read in many voices. While the narrative reconfigures and collapses the roles of doctor and patient and invokes the genre of the clinical case study only to abandon it, it also provokes a reconceptualization of its authorship and production.

If Insel exhibits anxiety about the influence that Jones might acquire over him, this anxiety is only compounded when Jones proposes to write his story. The offer raises concerns over who is authorized to tell his story and what mode of discourse would be most appropriate. The uneasy relationship between Jones and Insel is therefore repeated in a contest between the generic forms of the novel and the case study. *Insel* therefore asks what may be the cost of such a document to the troubled subjects that it treats if the conditions of its production are not experienced as beneficial but instead as persecutory.[44]

In the context of these questions, the novel's technological poetics gain added significance: the Jones–Insel rapport becomes a machine of writing, the product of which may not be the patient's relief but rather a work freighted with cultural and professional capital. While these two goals have not always been mutually exclusive in the history of psychiatry and psychoanalysis, neither have they been fully coterminous. To verify this distinction, we need to only consider the number of case studies that have become famous, thereby earning their authors cultural capital, without indicating any therapeutic improvement in their patients. This potential difference between the patient's relief and the writer's professional success as operative goals becomes an ethical concern in Loy's novel and a concern that may extend to the clinical history that shadows the novel.

Yet, these two agendas – the therapeutic and the literary – often seem consonant in their overdetermination of Jones's behavior. She prompts Insel to read from autobiographical notes he has kept, and her request provides material for her narrative while also advancing her attempt to restore him to "sociability." The return from the nonverbal communion via his "*Strahlen*" to more conventional linguistic exchange precipitates a shift in Insel's condition that resembles the procedures of "the talking cure." Assuming a clinical voice, she observes, "This communication of an actual transcription of a mental process had reinforced his sociability. His contacts ordinarily depending almost entirely on his *Strahlen*, for the moment our companionship was complete."[45] Incrementally, Jones brings Insel back into the fold of the symbolic from the brink of psychotic depersonalization through the project of writing his story.

Friedrich Kittler argues that writing within the modern media ecology dislocates the role of author as sole creator and is best described as the "transposition of media" in which the mind becomes simply another technological medium in a network that includes radio, cinema, and print.[46] It is tempting to interpret the text as not simply Jones's creation but instead as a transposition of media by which the Insel's thought transmissions become textualized through his assemblage with Mrs. Jones. This would suggest that the roles of patient and analyst have been displaced in favor of a complex writing machine – a libidinal and discursive collaboration that might complicate the attribution of authorship to a single, heroic analyst or avant-garde writer.

However, while this collaborative assemblage is clearly a precondition for the text's production, a separation between the two ultimately occurs that allows Jones to compose the story of Insel. When the two meet again, their exchange is conditioned by a sense of loss and melancholy. Jones makes explicit the transformation and perhaps the transaction that occurred:

> I longed to get even with Insel, to say "I have absorbed all your *Strahlen*. *Now* what are you going to do?" [...] for one thing one feared as above all else menacing Insel was some climax in which his depredatory radioactivity must inevitably give out.[47]

The writing of Insel's story has bought Jones a new lease on a flagging literary career, but these lines suggest that it has been paid for with Insel's very being, transmitted to her in the form of his *Strahlen*. The text seems to express doubts over the ethical status of its own conditions of production. These doubts extend to the question of whether Jones's encounter with Insel has ultimately improved his condition. Jones seems to share Insel's concern that the miraculous singularity of Insel's psychic life might finally give out – that his transmissions might stop. Jones implies that she has "stolen his rays" in order to write her book.

That such violence is figured as the condition of possibility for her book haunts its final pages, transforming the ethical status of the text that we read. Further, this ethical self-reflection sends us back to the tradition of psychiatric and psychoanalytic case studies that shadow the novel. It anticipates the rise of antipsychiatry, which would pose similar ethical questions regarding the treatment of the mentally ill and the telling of their stories. In the 1950s and 1960s, in England, France, and the United States, alternative ways of understanding and relating to persons suffering from psychosis emerged, many of which would reconfigure the asymmetrical relation between doctor and patient in ways that *Insel* anticipates.

It is therefore tempting to find in *Insel* a compressed, novelistic history of psychotherapies – from the suggestion treatments of mesmerism and hypnotism, to the quasievolutionary fantasies of Myers, to the talking cure of Freud, to the ethical reconsiderations and revisions that would emerge with antipsychiatry. If such a historical narrative haunts Loy's novel, the text also uses the resources of the novel to make those modes of treatment copresent to one another. However, *Insel* also restages those treatments in order to rediscover their forgotten or ignored possibilities for unlikely intersubjective relations with patients that Freud and others notoriously regarded as impossible. Through its surreal experiments, *Insel* therefore proposes alternative and perhaps impossible visions of the treatment and writing of madness. These visions do not constitute a complete program

or doctrine but function as thought experiments or counterfactual sce-
narios – operations that could be achieved only through the subjunctive
resources of fiction. The novel subjects those competing aims to ethical
scrutiny while multiplying the kinds of voices through which madness
may be spoken, heard, and written. The novel asks not only whether alternative treatments of madness might be possible but also whether such
treatments, however hypothetical, are finally desirable.

A Portrait of the Artist as a Paranoiac

Loy was not alone in developing a highly technological representation
of mental illness in the late-modernist era, nor were such constructions
restricted to the work of writers closely associated with the avant-garde.
Few might expect to find points of resemblance between the work of Mina
Loy and that of Evelyn Waugh – the former is rightly associated with continental, avant-garde movements such as Futurism and Surrealism while the
latter is best known for his mannered social satires of upper-class England.
However, in his underexamined novel *The Ordeal of Gilbert Pinfold* (1957),
Waugh attempts to render a surreal novelization of his own experiences
in 1954 of technological thought broadcasting, paranoia, and feelings of
unreality. During a cruise to Ceylon, Waugh began to feel that he was
persecuted by agents of the BBC and that his thoughts were observed
and transmitted to him via radio waves. These experiences became source
material for the central drama of *The Ordeal of Gilbert Pinfold* – a novel
that rivals *Insel* in offering the most vivid, representation in fiction of the
"Influencing Machine Delusion."

Pinfold's auditory hallucinations and paranoid delusions are ultimately
explained by his self-medication with chromal bromide and alcohol.
Given this organic explanation, the narrative hesitates between framing
Pinfold's experiences as the meaningless epiphenomena of a drugged nervous system and exploring his symptoms as psychologically and culturally
meaningful – the hesitations that often recur between psychiatric and psychoanalytic accounts of psychosis. More than merely a record of Waugh's
experiences, the text reflects upon the phenomenological structure of acute
mental illness, its management through the production of a delusional
narrative, and the distinctly modern qualities of this form of paranoia.

Whereas *Insel* often draws upon generic conventions of clinical case
studies, *Pinfold* occupies an ambiguous space between memoir and fiction.
Although written in the 1950s by an author whose oeuvre is hardly known
for extravagant formal experimentation, it conspicuously reactivates the

narrative techniques most commonly associated with high modernism – with particular gestures toward Joyce and Kafka – in order to represent a hermetic, interior world shaped by paranoid delusion. The novel represents a form of paranoia that foregrounds its late-modernist status through a synthesis of the influencing machine delusion, concerns over the mass-cultural effects and taste-making authority of the BBC, and anxieties over the forms of psychological influence and cultural authority developed by psychoanalysis and psychiatry.

The novel's opening chapter introduces Gilbert Pinfold under the title "Portrait of the Artist in Middle Age" – a gesture toward Joyce that reflects the character's waning literary talents and perhaps the aging condition of modernist aesthetics. Having established his reputation with a series of well-received novels, Pinfold enjoys a country estate where he cautiously guards his privacy from inquiring reporters and readers who seek insights into his life and works. His desire for privacy presumes that he is worthy of such attention and discloses a growing anxiety that he might be exposed as a fraud whose best works are behind him. From the beginning, Pinfold's world is structured by fantasies that vacillate abruptly between megalomania and persecution.

Pinfold's withdrawal is often interrupted by the unwelcome visits of his eccentric neighbor, Reginald "The Bruiser" Graves-Upton, whose topics of conversation are restricted to "the wireless programmes he had heard during the preceding week," and "an object which he reverently referred to as 'The Box.'"[48] If these two technological obsessions initially share a superficial resemblance and metonymic relation, they are later condensed in the auditory hallucinations and paranoid delusions that plague Pinfold. The description of The Box is perhaps the clearest articulation in modern fiction of the "influencing machine."[49]

> This Box was one of many operating in various parts of the country. It was installed under the sceptical noses of Reginald Graves-Upton's nephew and niece at Upper Mewling. Mrs. Pinfold, who had been taken to see it, said it looked like a makeshift wireless set. According to the Bruiser and other devotees The Box exercised diagnostic and therapeutic powers. Some part of a sick man or animal – a hair, a drop of blood preferably – was brought to The Box, whose guardian would then "tune in" to the "Life-Waves" of the patient, discern the origin of the malady and prescribe treatment.[50]

As in Tausk's case study, The Box hypostasizes a synthesis in the popular imagination of information technology and modern therapeutic techniques that render the human manipulable via obscure forces. Like a religious fetish, the power of "The Box" is evidently underwritten by the belief of its faithful "devotees" and by the suspicions of those – such as Pinfold – who distrust all artifacts of both modernism and modernity: "His strongest tastes were negative. He abhorred plastics, Picasso, sunbathing and jazz – everything in fact that had happened in his own lifetime."[51]

The Box's resemblance to a wireless set compounds Pinfold's unease over a BBC interview to which he has ambivalently assented. His description of the interview process combines technophobia with growing concerns over his privacy. "Electricians would come to him with their apparatus."[52] "They were attempting to emulate a series that had been cleverly done in Paris with various French celebrities, in which informal, spontaneous discussion had seduced the objects of inquiry into self-revelation."[53] Following the discussion of "The Bruiser's" Box, the recording and broadcasting devices installed in Pinfold's home by the BBC's technicians seem charged with an obscure psychic influence, and the interviewer, Mr. Angel, is described as well practiced in modern interrogation strategies.

> The questions were civil enough in form but Mr. Pinfold thought he could detect an underlying malice. Angel seemed to believe that anyone sufficiently eminent to be interviewed by him must have something to hide, must be an impostor whom it was his business to trap and expose, and to direct his questions from some basic, previous knowledge of something discreditable.[54]

Pinfold's status anxiety ostensibly derives from his recent lack of literary success, but it is exacerbated by concerns over whether he can convincingly play the role of the country gentleman. This question of class has been compounded by a recent dispute over the Pinfolds' claim to their estate, which his wife inherited but which had been occupied by a local farmer during the war. The anxiety over his precarious position within a social or symbolic order – as celebrated author, as country gentleman, and perhaps even as a man – is drawn out by the BBC interviewer, whose probing questions embody the voice and judgment of a diffuse general public or Other. In Lacanian accounts of paranoia, the psychotic feels the symbolic order operating upon him in obscure ways. It is a distributed, unlocatable informatic system – homologous to the invisible, spatial reach of radio – which give order to the social field; for Pinfold, these effects manifest through both the taste-making authority and the obscure omnipresence of the BBC.

Following the interview, "He brooded. It seemed to him that an attempt had been made against his privacy and he was not sure how effectively he had defended it. He strained to remember his precise words and his memory supplied various distorted versions."[55] These minor distortions of memory escalate into more dramatic delusions of persecution that incorporate the unknown capacities of "The Box" and suspicions that his mind has been tampered with or assessed. Pinfold insists that his wife conceal these lapses, particularly from his neighbor, Graves-Upton.

> "...if you say I'm ill, he'll get his damned Box to work on me. [...] You've been giving him my hair for his Box."
> "Nonsense, Gilbert."
> "I could tell by the way he looked at me that he was measuring my Life-Waves."[56]

In order to recover his health and to escape the pernicious influences of both the BBC and Graves-Upton's Box, Pinfold books passage aboard a ship to Ceylon. However, his symptoms only grow more acute as he begins to suffer auditory hallucinations that he attributes to a secret or dysfunctional communications system aboard the ship.

> He was able to hear quite distinctly not only what was said in his immediate vicinity, but elsewhere. He had the light on, now, in his cabin, and as he gazed at the complex of tubes and wires which ran across his ceiling, he realised that they must form some kind of general junction in the system of communication. Through some trick or fault or war-time survival everything spoken in the executive quarters of the ship was transmitted to him.[57]

It is not just any voice that Pinfold hears, but the voices of authority and law, "the executive quarters of the ship," and the captain becomes a central figure within his expanding delusion. The apparatus of wires and tubes and Pinfold's lack of technical understanding afford the necessary conditions for his rationalization of the voices he hears: "Mr. Pinfold wished he knew more of the mechanics of the thing."[58]

The contents of these illicit transmissions include gossip about Pinfold, suggestions that he is under surveillance by agents aboard the ship, and a surreal trial over which the ship's captain presides in which an unknown man is being prosecuted for unspeakable sexual crimes.

> "Guilty," said the Captain and at the word Goneril vented a hiss of satisfaction and anticipation. Slowly and deliberately, as the ship steamed south with its commonplace load of passengers, the Captain and his leman with undisguised erotic enjoyment settled down to torture their prisoner.[59]

As in many of Kafka's works, the Law does not merely function as a force of prohibition but displays its own forms of obscene and perverse enjoyment. Slavoj Zizek writes, "The public Law 'between the lines' silently tolerates – incites, even – what its explicit text prohibits (say, adultery), while the superego injunction which ordains *jouissance,* through the very directness of its order, hinders the subject's access to it much more efficiently than any prohibition."[60] Within surrealist fiction and delusion, this obscene quality is no longer hidden "between the lines" but becomes nightmarishly manifest as in Pinfold's world, where the scene of trial and judgment is endowed with an excessive, perverse valence. The moment recalls sequences in Kafka's *The Trial,* in which punishment takes the highly sexualized and ritualized form of flogging.[61] In Pinfold's delusion, a similar, perverse force of judgment is directed toward his works of fiction through the ubiquitous cultural authority of the BBC. Closely following the logic of the hallucinated trial for sexual misconduct, the auditory hallucinations abruptly take the form of a BBC literary program "on Aspects of Orthodoxy in Contemporary Letters," in which Pinfold's work is evaluated by a reviewer who takes excessive enjoyment in his condemnation. The radio personality declares Pinfold's work perverse: "if one is asked – and one *is* often asked – to give one name which typifies all that is decadent in contemporary literature, one can answer without hesitation – Gilbert Pinfold."[62] That the voice of an abstract and diffuse Other takes the form of the BBC for Pinfold is confirmed by his suspicion that, "Other people in the ship were listening to the wireless. Other people, probably, had heard Clutton-Cornforth's diatribe."[63] In a delirious sequence that closely resembles the obscene and exaggerated logic of judgment and humiliation of Leopold Bloom in the "Circe" episode of *Ulysses,* Pinfold is quickly condemned as an "old queer,"[64] a decadent Oxford undergraduate, a German Jew named "Peinfeld,"[65] a "sodomite,"[66] and a bad neighbor.[67] If Pinfold suspected that the BBC might uncover something discreditable about him during the dreaded interview, it appears that the paranoid anxiety – or fantasy – has been realized. Pinfold becomes a ritualistic scapegoat whose expulsion from the social order for virtually every violation of proper behavior places him in the exceptional positions of both sacrificial lamb and messianic redeemer.

Consulting the ship's passenger manifest, Pinfold finds a name that enables him to explain the persecuting transmissions that have plagued him throughout the voyage. "And suddenly Mr. Pinfold understood, not everything, but the heart of the mystery. Angel, the quizzical man from the B.B.C. ' – *not wires, darling. Wireless*' – Angel, the man with the technical skill to use the defects of the *Caliban's* communications, perhaps to cause them."[68] The suspected presence of the BBC – which, for Pinfold, has meant intrusive judgments and obscure psychotechnical capabilities – becomes the key by which he is able to produce an explanatory narrative of his ordeals. "Mr. Pinfold felt as though he had come to the end of an ingenious, old-fashioned detective novel which he had read rather inattentively. He knew the villain now and began turning back the pages to observe the clues he had missed."[69] His story, or case, becomes rewritten not as a case study of mental illness but as a detective novel that has been solved. Pinfold adopts the closure promised by detective fiction so as to give his baffling experiences retrospective order under a single, monological, generic logic. Drawing upon these narrative resources for their explanatory and ordering powers provides some consolation, but even this story form is strained by increasingly unaccountable experiences. "Pinfold listened and spoke only to his enemies and hour by hour, day by day, night by night, carefully assembled the intricate pieces of a plot altogether more modern and horrific than anything in the classic fictions of murder."[70] Eventually, nearly half of the ship's passengers seem to have been recruited by Angel for the surveillance of Pinfold, and "The inquisitors, it seemed, possessed a huge but incomplete and wildly inaccurate dossier covering the whole of Mr. Pinfold's private life."[71] These fictionalized gaps in the conspirators' knowledge seem to be as disturbing to Pinfold as the conspiracy itself. He suspects that he has become a figure whose character is being fictionalized by some pernicious authority, and this fiction has displaced reality – an anxiety that becomes central in the work of Muriel Spark, as I demonstrate in the following chapter.

Pinfold discovers that a psychological form of surveillance conducted by the BBC's agents is accomplished through a device that grants its users access to Pinfold's mental state in ways that resemble his neighbor's Box.

> Angel had in his headquarters an electric instrument which showed Mr. Pinfold's precise state of consciousness. It consisted, Mr. Pinfold surmised, of a glass tube containing two parallel lines of red light which continually drew together or moved apart like telegraph wires seen from a train. They approached one another as he grew drowsy and, when he fell asleep, crossed. A duty officer followed their fluctuations.[72]

The device grants access at a distance to Pinfold's internal states. That his states of consciousness are instrumentally monitored by a duty officer suggests that the campaign against him has extended to the military, and the psychological warfare and interrogation techniques developed during World War II are integrated into his delusion, which now assumes international scale and importance. Through the dysfunctional communications system, he is forced to listen to a form of music developed by the Nazis in order to torture and extract information. "It's the three-eight rhythm. The

Gestapo discovered it independently, you know. They used to play it in the cells. It drove the prisoners mad."[73] In a Chaplinesque moment, a discordant soundtrack is transmitted as a purportedly therapeutic technique.

> One night they tried to soothe him by playing a record specially made by Swiss scientists for the purpose. These savants had decided from experiments made in a sanatorium for neurotic industrial workers that the most soporific noises were those of a factory. Mr. Pinfold's cabin resounded to the roar and clang of machinery.
>
> "You bloody fools," he cried in exasperation, "*I'm* not a factory worker. You're driving me mad."
>
> "No, no, Gilbert, you *are* mad already,' said the duty officer. 'We're driving you sane."[74]

Pinfold's delusion locates him within a perverse modernity in which disturbing, mechanical noises have soporific effects for demented industrial workers. The satirical sequence inverts therapy into a form of persecution. That Pinfold's delusional experiences of observation and treatment incorporate recognizable features of radio – and more specifically, the BBC – gives his experience of madness not only historical specificity but a dimension of cultural critique.

In a desperate letter to his wife, Pinfold summarizes his conspiracy theory and explains the BBC's role in his persecution.

> These B.B.C. people have made themselves a great nuisance to me on board. They have got a lot of apparatus with them, most of it new and experimental. They have something which is really a glorified form of Reggie Graves-Upton's Box. I shall never laugh at the poor Bruiser again. There is a great deal in it. More in fact than he imagines. Angel's Box is able to speak and to hear. In fact I spend most of my days and nights carrying on conversations with people I never see. They are trying to psychoanalyse me. I know this sounds absurd. The Germans at the end of the war were developing this Box for the examination of prisoners. The Russians have perfected it. They don't need any of the old physical means of persuasion. They can see into the minds of the most obdurate.[75]

The Box, the BBC, and the half-understood techniques of psychoanalysis are synthesized into a delusion of technological influence and observation at a distance that corresponds precisely to the terms of Tausk's case study.

Pinfold makes two attempts to redress and resist the ordeals to which he has been subjected. Initially, he tries to send private messages by radio to his wife detailing his experiences and asking for help, but he subsequently hears these private messages being read aloud over the ship's communications system to the others aboard the ship. Upon inquiring into this violation of his privacy with the captain, he learns that he has had no private messages broadcast. The mechanisms of communications either render him fully disclosed or entirely silent. "It seemed to him that he had said too much or too little."[76] The experience is consonant with many psychotics' feelings that they are not in control of their communication and that they occupy a world that is either entirely lacking or saturated with meaning.

The concern that he is not a master of his own discourse but rather subject to a larger, obscure system of communication leaves nonsense as Pinfold's only remaining form of resistance.

> Mr. Pinfold fought back with the enemy's weapons. He was obliged to hear all they said. They were obliged to hear him. They could not measure his emotions but every thought which took verbal shape in his mind was audible in Angel's headquarters and they were unable, it seemed, to disconnect their Box.[77]

Subject to transmissions that he cannot switch off and a constant stream of language that becomes overwhelming, Pinfold drowns out his voices with a counterdiscourse. "Mr. Pinfold tormented them in his turn by making gibberish of the text, reading alternate lines, alternate words, reading backwards, until they pleaded for respite. Hour after hour Mr. Pinfold remorselessly read on."[78] If sense itself – hypostatized as the machinery of communication – has become a persecutory system, his solution is the production of nonsense.

Pinfold discovers that any interruption of conventional language and communication becomes a relief from his persecutions. He enjoys a rare moment of reprieve from the communications system when he finally leaves the ship – a moment that recalls a similar peace experienced by Pinfold as a paratrooper in training during the war:

> there was an instructor on the ground bawling advice through a loudspeaker; but *Mr. Pinfold felt himself free of all human communication, the sole inhabitant of a private, delicious universe.* The rapture was brief [...] But in that moment of solitude prosaic, earthbound Mr. Pinfold had been one with hashish-eaters and Corybantes and Californian gurus, high on the back-stairs of mysticism. His mood on the road to Cairo was barely less ecstatic.[79]

The sources of Pinfold's suffering are both particular – Angel and the technologies of the BBC – and abstract – communication itself. A silent, private world devoid of language and, perhaps in Cairo, a place imagined as beyond the reach of modernity is Pinfold's fantasized oasis from persecution. "I thought I should get out of range of those psychoanalysts and their infernal Box. But not at all."[80]

When the hallucinations return, the voice of Angel pleads not to expose their treatment of him. " 'It was a serious scientific experiment. Then I let personal malice interfere. I'm sorry, Mr. Pinfold.' ... 'I'll switch off the apparatus. I promise on my honour we'll none of us ever worry you again.'"[81] Either Pinfold was subject to the impersonal, objective process of technoscientific research or he was the target of "personal malice." It is unclear which explanation is more disturbing for Pinfold.

When he finally returns, Pinfold's doctor identifies the chloral bromide pills with which Pinfold had been self-medicating as the cause of his auditory hallucinations. The doctor's diagnosis has the effect of both universalizing his experiences and normalizing them:

> "Lots of people hear voices from time to time – nearly always offensive."
> "You don't think he ought to see a psychologist?" asked Mrs. Pinfold.
> "He can if he likes, of course, but it sounds like a perfectly simple case of poisoning to me."[82]

The somatic diagnosis of an overdose could function as a way to disavow any psychological or psychoanalytic content that may have been revealed during Pinfold's ordeal. R. Neill Johnson argues that, "By informing readers from the beginning that the voices Pinfold hears are the result of bad medicine, the novel's narrator creates a stable plot that circumvents Pinfold's desire, and perhaps even his own."[83] However, even within the text, the psychiatrist's diagnosis is not the final word on the matter, as even it becomes folded into Pinfold's delusion when he hears Angel's voice advising him, "Tell your wife you had noises in the head through taking those grey pills."[84] Several competing accounts of Pinfold's voices therefore remain in competition. Pinfold is not moved from the view that he has been the subject of a technoscientific experiment, and his distrust toward the occult powers of media technologies persists: "I can't face the Bruiser. It will be several weeks before I can talk to him about his Box."[85]

The novel's balancing of these competing explanations has the effect of staging the distinct and contradictory approaches to psychosis proposed by psychiatry and psychoanalysis. If delusional explanations of hallucinatory experiences have often been dismissed as nonsensical epiphenomena of unspecified neurological problems by biological psychiatry, the often technological discourses in which those delusions manifest are generally passed over by psychoanalytic accounts that often "discover" the same latent sexual contents. This is perhaps nowhere more evident than in Tausk's insistence that the influencing machine is generally a figure for the subject's repressed libido or genitalia.

Others, such as Ivan Leudar and Philip Thomas, have adopted a phenomenological approach that considers the pragmatic functions that may be afforded by the particular metaphors and discourses adopted by a patient in a delusional system.

> Most psychiatrists see the "voices" as symptoms to be suppressed – like coughs, aches and measles spots – and many users of psychiatric services do indeed want to be rid of voices. Other voice hearers, however, may want to be able to talk about their exceptional experiences in public. Perhaps the best way to talk about different perspectives on "voices" is to say that each is an account of the experience and that each categorizes it differently. This should allow us to consider both the metaphors implicit in the accounts and their pragmatics: who administers them, for what purpose and with what outcomes. The question about what is the right concept for voices is possibly not the best one – a better one is: Which concept of voices is useful for this purpose?[86]

Leudar and Thomas share with psychoanalysis the view that delusional explanations may perform reparative work in which symptoms such as auditory hallucinations are not simply suppressed or treated but are integrated into a coherent world. Beyond a recognition of this general, reparative function of delusion, an attention to the "metaphors implicit in the accounts and their pragmatics" entails a form of listening that attends to the cultural and historical embeddedness of the delusional narrative and does not give immediate priority to a priori explanatory frameworks such as the libido theory.

Through its formal reproduction of the techniques of Joyce and Kafka and its protagonist's abhorrence of radio, psychoanalysis, "plastics, Picasso, sunbathing and jazz – everything in fact that had happened in his own lifetime,"[87] Pinfold's paranoid delusion is fashioned from conspicuously modernist elements. Waugh's novel therefore reflexively marks itself – like the fiction and treatises of Wyndham Lewis – as not merely a record of his own psychotic experiences but also as a critical response to the imperatives and techniques of modernism. The kind of world that is shaped by these imperatives and techniques is one in which Pinfold is increasingly unable to locate himself – perhaps the central concern animating this "Portrait of an Artist in Middle Age" whose work has begun to wane in relevance and whose place in the world has become uncertain. The expectations of psychological disclosure are, for Waugh, promoted by critics who "write about the author rather than the book" and assume "a personal intimacy with him which in fact they do not enjoy."[88] Waugh's ambivalence toward radio stems from the kind of personal access that its listeners come to expect. James Lynch notes that Waugh wrote "in a letter to John Betjeman on 11 June 1946 that, although the lower classes do not read books, 'they do listen to the wireless and when they have heard anyone speak they think this constitutes an introduction.'"[89] Pinfold expresses an uncanny sense that his is never speaking the proper discourse of the moment or that to speak the language of modernity requires an increasingly full disclosure of one's private thoughts. These uncertainties over what is permissible, what may remain private, and what must be expressed are anxieties pertaining to the boundaries of subjectivity that are notoriously elusive in moments of psychosis but, the novel suggests, may also have cultural-historical etiologies. In a 1956 CBC interview, Waugh complains that there is "no normal or proper society or code of behaviour."[90] Jacques Lacan refers to these protocols that often elude psychotics as the "symbolic order," while disability studies scholar Margaret Price theorizes them under the category of "rhetoric": "Rhetoric is not simply the words we speak or write or sign, nor is it simply what we look like or sound like. It is who we are, and beyond that, it is who we are allowed to be."[91] The modernism that Pinfold – and perhaps Waugh – seems to abhor may name a shift in the rhetorical protocols that make self-disclosure not only permissible but imperative, and this expectation to "see into the minds of the most obdurate" is the central anxiety that the novel stages.[92]

If Pinfold expresses anxieties about saying "too much or too little" and about the unstable condition of subjectivity that results from these evolving protocols, the publication of *The Ordeal of Gilbert Pinfold* triggered similar concerns for Waugh himself. In a prefatory note, Waugh acknowledges the novel's semiautobiographical status while also emphasizing the reparative role that narrative may perform in the construction of an epistemic framework within which hallucinations may be given meaning and perhaps made tolerable – a view that closely resembles the pragmatic approach proposed by Leudar and Thomas.

> Three years ago Mr. Waugh suffered a brief bout of hallucination closely resembling what is here described. It was an interesting experience for a man whose business is storytelling. Hallucination is far removed from loss of reason. The reason works with enhanced power, while the materials for it to work on, presented by the senses, are delusions. A story-teller naturally tried to find a plot into which his observations can be fitted.[93]

The subsequent text and its delusional content are therefore simultaneously presented as a work of fiction, a potential psychiatric case history, and an act of self-repair through narrative. If the generic status of the novel, like that of *Insel,* is somewhat ambiguous, so is the psychiatric status of the subject who suffers the ordeals that it represents. The note underscores the persistence of "reason" during these experiences and emphasizes that "a great number of sane people suffer in this way from time to time," implying that, despite the symptoms of paranoia, auditory hallucination, and feelings of unreality that are represented, Pinfold (and Waugh) should not be regarded as insane.[94] Pamela White Hadas observes a similar attempt to mitigate the scandal of the autobiographical disclosure in the fact that "Waugh subtitles his book *A Conversation Piece,* as if to make light of its harrowing subjects."[95]

The prefatory note therefore functions as a disclaimer that attempts to anticipate and defuse the diagnostic stigma that might delegitimize both text and author as mad. Waugh asserts his membership in the group of "sane people," insisting that his symptoms were merely temporary aberrations. The language of the preface implies that such experiences may not only define a minor set of individuals who suffer from chronic psychosis but that acute psychosis may afflict even the "sane" – an observation that transforms mental illness from a minority identity to a more universal concern. The extent to which Waugh's experiences were acute rather than chronic is unclear. While the psychiatrist Eric Strauss diagnosed his symptoms as the result of an overdose of phenobarbitone, which Waugh self-administered in order to manage insomnia, there is evidence that what he would describe as "an odd attack of Pinfold" continued to recur later in life.[96]

Despite its prefatory note, the novel exposed Waugh to armchair diagnosis in a review entitled, "What Was Wrong with Pinfold," by J. B. Priestley, who regarded the novel as autobiographical evidence of a "central self that he is trying to deny," and predicted that he "will crack again if it is walled up again within a false style of life."[97] The language of the review may suggest that, in keeping with Freud's famous study of Schreber's memoirs, Pinfold's/Waugh's paranoia and hallucinations were the results of repressed homosexual desires. This treatment of the novel repeats quite closely the moments in the novel that stage similar judgments and condemnations of Pinfold as an "old queer"[98] and a "sodomite"[99] as well as Pinfold's anxieties about being exposed and psychoanalyzed by critics. If these are the secrets that Pinfold or Waugh are hiding, they are not very well hidden. Instead, the novel had already anticipated the kind of "analysis" that Priestley produces. The text may be described as postpsychoanalytic in the sense that Pinfold's voices make manifest what, in most texts, might remain latent. Stephen L. Post argues that, "*Pinfold,* indeed, is like a diagnostic detective story: fascinating but lacking in depth – or, more accurately, disavowing depth."[100] For Post, such depth of interpretation is foreclosed, because Pinfold's drug use accounts for his symptoms – "that diagnosis is sufficient" – but this does not do justice to the ways that the novel reflects upon the interpretive desire for depth and disclosure.[101] Instead, the novel has a feeling of depthlessness because the conventional topology of concealment and disclosure that is often assumed by psychoanalysis is flattened, and the desire for exposure is frustrated. As in many psychotic delusions, what would be concealed is already brought to the surface. This textual effect, coupled with the prefatory note, makes attempts on the part of Priestley and more recent critics to use the novel as an occasion to psychoanalyze Waugh appear redundant.[102]

What is perhaps more interesting is the way that the logic of disclosure, diagnosis, stigma, and paranoia play out in the reception of a novel that overtly explores these same topoi. In response to Priestley's pseudopsychoanalytic review, Waugh published an aggressive rejoinder in which he returns pathologizing fire.

> I say, Priestley old man, are you sure you are feeling all right? Any Voices? I mean to say! No narcotics or brandy in your case, I know, but when a chap starts talking about "the enemy" and believing, for one, that he is singled out for unjust treatment, isn't it time he consulted his Jungian about his *anima*? Who is persecuting poor Mr. Priestley?[103]

The exchange indicates the ways that diagnosis is often experienced – perhaps with cause – as a form of delegitimation that threatens to undermine the status of a text and a person. Further, it extends the drama of persecution, paranoia, and diagnosis from the world of the novel into the actual world of author, reviewer, and reading public.

This movement in and out of delusional (and fictional) worlds comprises much of the dramatic and ontological tension that motivates late-modernist representations of mental illness. In Loy's novel, Mrs. Jones is able to enter into the surreal, technopsychic ecology of Insel while struggling to maintain a view toward the actual world in order to write his narrative, and the text that she produces becomes a reflection upon its own conditions of production. Similarly, in Waugh's novel, Pinfold becomes both character and author, and the final pages describe his composition of his delusional story as an element of his recovery. With this metafictional gesture, the novel marks an ontological difference between the world of Pinfold's delusion and a frame world of the novel within which it is nested. Waugh's semiautobiographical identification with the character in the prefatory note gestures toward a further ramification of such worlds that include his own delusional experiences, the novel that he composed (and its nested worlds), and the world of public opinion that would include the embattled, paranoid exchange with Priestley. The homologous capacities of both paranoid delusion and fiction to construct such worlds become the central concerns animating the work of other midcentury writers – particularly Muriel Spark and Anna Kavan, who, like Waugh, experienced periods of psychosis that became inspiration for the form and content of their fiction. The convergence of such fictional and delusional worlds and the reparative work that they may perform are the subjects of the following chapter.

CHAPTER 3

On Worlding and Unworlding in Fiction and Delusion
Muriel Spark and Anna Kavan

If Loy's surrealist novel is built upon the generic structure of the clinical case study, this chapter examines the fiction of two late-modernist writers, Muriel Spark and Anna Kavan, whose works more closely resemble the phenomenological and discursive modes of memoirs of mental illness. Rather than imaginative attempts to assume the perspective of the mentally ill, these texts draw upon the authors' lived experiences of hallucination, depersonalization, and paranoia. The results are novels and short stories that not only represent psychotic symptoms but that conspicuously foreground laborious acts of delusional world construction. In many of these works, this worlding is metafictionally marked as a point of convergence between paranoid delusion and fiction. Rather than merely demonstrating the failure of reality testing that is evident in delusional systems, the fictions of Spark and Kavan instead demonstrate the pragmatic necessity as well as the fragile precarity of such delusional worlds.

In addition to foregrounding the world-building operations performed by both fiction and delusion, this chapter also explores the meanings of the technical delusions that recur in the works of late-modernist writers, memoirs of mental illness, and in key psychiatric texts. Muriel Spark's early fiction shows continuities with Mina Loy's *Insel* and Evelyn Waugh's *The Ordeal of Gilbert Pinfold* in its representations of thought insertion as both a function of uncanny, technological influence and as a distinctly writerly problem. Her fictions pose ontological questions for both character and reader in ways that suggest homologies between mental illness and fiction. In Kavan's work, patients' feelings of mechanized depersonalization reflect their doctors' strictly mechanistic conception of the mind – a framework that was first critically evaluated by Karl Jaspers through the epistemic distinction between causal "explanation" and phenomenological "understanding." While Kavan's work registers the depersonalizing consequences of certain forms of psychiatry, Bruno Bettelheim's important case study of his patient, "Joey," demonstrates the ways that patients may pragmatically deploy the same mechanistic discourses in order to mediate their relations to the world. Collectively, the works of Kavan and Spark neither sensationalize nor idealize experiences of psychosis through fictionalization; instead, these works invite meditations on their own uncanny ontological status as precarious worlds that are phenomenologically necessary and always on the brink of unworlding.

The Fictional-Delusional Worlds of Muriel Spark

Shortly after the publication of *The Ordeal of Gilbert Pinfold*, Evelyn Waugh wrote an admiring review of Muriel Spark's first novel, *The Comforters*: "It so happens that *The Comforters* came to me just as I had finished a story on a similar theme and I was struck by how much more ambitious was Miss Spark's essay and how much better she had accomplished it."[1] Spark's novel shares much with *Pinfold* but goes further in posing metafictional comparisons between paranoid delusion and fiction. Waugh acknowledges that Spark succeeds in achieving the categorical convergence that was implied in his novel: "The first theme is the mechanics of story-telling, the second a case-history of insanity. The result is not easy to describe."[2]

While the plot and network of characters defy easy description, *The Comforters* clearly presents the symptoms of psychosis that recur in *Insel*, *Pinfold*, and other late-modernist novels of mental illness: a character hears voices that appear to narrate her thoughts and actions; she suspects that she is under constant surveillance; and she is plagued by the uncertain ontological status of herself, her fellow characters, and her world. As in *Insel* and *The Ordeal of Gilbert Pinfold*, the novel's central character, Caroline Rose, is an aspiring writer who is struggling with her current project. While visiting a Catholic retreat, she begins to hear the sounds of a typewriter and a voice that reproduces the diegetic narration of the novel. Caroline initially proposes the kinds of technological explanations that often recur in many schizophrenic delusions.

> She suspected everything, however improbable; even that the sound might be contained in some quite small object – *a box with a machine inside, operated from a distance*. She acted upon these suspicions, examining everything closely in case she should find something strange.[3]

The novel invokes the modern paranoia of obscure black boxes, a suspicion that is compounded by the presence of Caroline's boyfriend, Laurence, whose career at the BBC entails knowledge of broadcasting and audio technology that remains mysterious to Caroline: "He was fiddling about with a black box-like object which at first she took to be a large typewriter."[4] The "black box" proves to be a recording device that Laurence introduces in order to determine whether the voices Caroline hears are real. However, in a novel that establishes a thorough suspicion of pernicious influences, Laurence's presentation of the device is not entirely innocuous.

> He pressed a key. There was a whirring sound and the box began to talk with a male voice pitched on a peculiarly forced husky note. It said, "Caroline darling, I have a suggestion to make." Then it went on to say something funny but unprintable.[5]

The device appears to conform to the "influencing machine" in Tausk's case study: it operates by suggestion, and its suggestions are erotic in nature. The moment invokes the familiar form of technological delusion while also introducing one of several ontological debates staged in the novel over what may be regarded as "real."

> "If the sound has objective existence it will be recorded."
> "This sound might have another sort of existence and still be real."
> "Well, let's first exhaust the possibilities of the natural order – "
> "But we don't know all the possibilities of the natural order."[6]

Such ontological ambiguities, common in cases of schizophrenia, are converted into metafictional meditations when Caroline comes to suspect that the influencing device that shapes her thoughts and behavior is not a black-box but rather the novel itself: she believes that the sound of typing and the voice that she hears are those of the author of a novel in which she is a character. What follows from this are anxieties over the ontological status of not only the voice but of herself and the world that she occupies.

Her objections to this predicament are both ethical and aesthetic; defending her free will, she insists, "I refuse to have my thoughts and actions controlled by some unknown, possibly sinister being."[7] Given her literary-critical training and perhaps modernist aesthetic tastes, she objects to being a part of what appears to be a work of low, genre fiction. When Laurence shares his suspicions that his own grandmother is the ringleader of a gang of diamond smugglers, she dismisses his theory as the mechanistic plot of an implausible mystery novel:

> From my point of view it's clear that you are getting these ideas into your head through the influence of a novelist who is contriving some phoney plot. I can see clearly that your mind is working under the pressure of someone else's necessity, and under the suggestive power of some irresponsible writer you are allowing yourself to become an amateur sleuth in a cheap mystery piece.[8]

From the perspective of a metafictionally aware character, a mediocre novel is a thought-influencing device that subordinates the free will of its characters to the requirements of its schematic and predictable plot. "Her sense of being written into the novel was painful,"[9] and Caroline announces, "I intend to stand aside and see if the novel has any real form apart from this artificial plot."[10] The implication is that she is disturbed not simply because she subsists within a fictional world; rather, it is that the form of the work is so manifestly artificial that the illusion of reality cannot be sufficiently achieved. John Lanchester observes that "Spark satisfies our hunger for plot, and at the same time shows us the shortcomings of such things as plots – the extent of the human stuff that they ignore, and the troubling persistence of the questions they leave unasked."[11] The reality effect fails, and Caroline experiences the diminished ontological status of her world, her fellow characters, and herself.

This may explain the abrupt and bizarre disappearances of Georgina Hogg at several points in the narrative. Hogg is constructed as a rather flat character cast in the conventional role of a religious zealot and moralist whose presence causes unease for Caroline and others. One character admits he "was frightened of the damage she could do to body and soul by her fanatical moral intrusiveness, so near to utterly primitive mania."[12] As a child, Hogg would tell others, "I can know the thoughts in your head."[13] Lacking dimension and psychological complexity, Hogg merely embodies a tyrannical voice of moral censure; at times, she even appears to lack stable embodiment, leading Caroline to suspect that Hogg is her own hallucination or perhaps the source of the voices in her head. As in *The Ordeal of Gilbert Pinfold*, Caroline's strategy for combating these suspicions is to drown out the voices by speaking endlessly and aimlessly:

> And so Caroline rattled on, overtaken by an impulse to talk, to repeat and repeat any assertion as an alternative to absolute silence. For in such silence Caroline kept her deepest madness, a fear void of evidence, a suspicion altogether to be distrusted. It struck within her like something which would go neither up nor down, the shapeless notion that Mrs. Hogg was somehow in league with her invisible persecutor.[14]

This suspected link between Hogg and Caroline's "invisible persecutor" gains support as Hogg inexplicably vanishes from the world of the novel whenever she is not performing the role of moralistic scourge to her fellow characters. Several characters suggest that "She's not all there,"[15] an observation that can be understood as both a reference to her psychological instability as well as a metafictional remark upon her incompleteness as a fictional character. The novel conspicuously and humorously admits its own failure to convincingly construct and maintain this character when, "as soon as Mrs. Hogg stepped into her room she disappeared, she simply disappeared. She had no private life whatsoever. God knows where she went in her privacy."[16] This strange event is repeated when she vanishes during a car ride with two other characters.

> "She simply wasn't there," Helena declared. "I said to Willi, "Heavens, where's Georgina?" and Willi said, "My God! She's gone!" Well, just as he said this, we saw Georgina again. She suddenly appeared before our eyes at the back of the car, sitting in the same position and blinking, as if she'd just then woken up. It was as if there's been a black-out at the films. I would have thought I'd been dreaming the incident, but Willi apparently had the same experience.[17]

The malfunction of a medium is invoked – "a black-out at the films" – to describe the failure of fiction to maintain the precarious existence of its weakest character.

In this way, *The Comforters* often compares the medium of the novel to other media technologies – as instruments of influence, as devices that can produce artificial subjects, objects, and worlds. In perhaps its most metafictionally delirious moment, the narrator insists upon the fictional status of the novel's characters – an extradiegetic remark that Caroline hears and transcribes across several other media:

> At this point in the narrative, it might be as well to state that the characters in this novel are all fictitious, and do not refer to any living persons whatsoever.
>   *Tap-tappity-tap. At this point in the narrative . . .* Caroline sprang up and pressed the lever on the dictaphone. Then she snatched the notebook and pencil which she had placed ready, and took down in shorthand the paragraph above . . .[18]

In an illustration of Friedrich Kittler's conception of the modern "discourse network" defined by the "transposition of media," the sequence creates a heterogeneous assemblage that includes hallucination, delusion, electronic recording, transcription, and fiction.[19] The effect is a vertiginous circulation of a self-reflexive statement that marks its transmission across those media while calling into question its own ontological status. The novel's metafictional moments and their explicit links to experiences of madness imply that fiction prompts us to hallucinate characters into and out of existence, and, in reflecting upon these processes, the novel induces its own failure to maintain the reality effect. Like a film blackout or a broken record, the novel's moments of breakdown and malfunction make the medium's mechanisms conspicuous. It is not simply that the mind of Caroline exhibits symptoms of mental illness; a breakdown of the medium within which that mind works is also staged. In this sense, Spark's novel pursues a Beckettian ethos, forging better, more interesting forms of failure and disclosing the ways in which the mechanisms of narrative fiction may be understood through their dysfunctions.

The Comforters is a text that erodes the ontological difference between the world of the protagonist and the world of the (fictional) author. The effect is a meditation on the ontology of fiction. This becomes explicit in the ways that Caroline reflects upon the status of her social, fictional, and delusional "worlds" – a signifier that begins to recur with increasing frequency within the text. When she returns to an old bar that she once frequented, she considers, "That word 'bourgeois' had a dispiriting effect on her evening – it was part of that dreary imprecise language of this *half-world* she had left behind her more than two years since."[20] The literary circle in which she used to travel constitutes a sphere that she has escaped. Similarly, "The West End was another half-world of Caroline's past."[21]

This strange, recurring category of the "half-world" takes on a psycho-pathological valence when it is used to describe the space of delusion. As she explains to Laurence her theory that she is hearing the voice of the author of a novel in which she is a character, she asks him to join her within the world of her delusion:

> "Will you be able to make an occasional concession to the logic of my madness?" she asked him. "Because that will be necessary between us. Otherwise, we shall be really separated." She was terrified of being entirely separated from Laurence.
> "Haven't I always tried to enter your world?"
> "Yes, but this is a very remote world I'm in now."[22]

This discourse of "worlds" and "half-worlds" makes manifest the variety of social, psychological, and fictional systems that the novel creates.

Such fundamental questions regarding the ontology of fiction and its status in relation to the actual world are often passed over in literary criticism. However, these concerns have been productively addressed by a strain of narratology that draws upon the discourses of modal logic and possible worlds theory developed by David Lewis, Saul Kripke, Jaakko Hintikka, and others.[23] Narratologists such as Thomas Pavel, Lubomír Doležel, Marie-Laure Ryan, and Ruth Ronen have adapted this framework in order to address questions concerning the strange ontology of fictional worlds.[24] Summarizing the two principal contributions that this framework makes to the study of literature, Ryan invokes, "the metaphor of 'world' to describe the semantic domain projected by the text; and the concept of modality to describe and classify the various ways of existing of the objects, states, and events that make up the semantic domain."[25] Similarly, Ruth Ronen promotes the adoption by narratology of "the concepts of necessity and possibility, that of world, world-set and transworld relations, concepts referring to world constituents, and to modes of existence (nonexistence, incomplete being, and so on)."[26] Such categories enable us to examine the strange ways that characters and their worlds could be said to exist without being actual and in what sense one could say something about those non-actual worlds and their inhabitants that could be regarded as true. Ronen points out that these concepts "proceed in the direction of relaxing philo-sophical notions of *truth, existence,* and *world-language relations,* notions that traditionally received rigid delimitations."[27] Such rigid delimitations are evident in the work of earlier logicians who regarded fiction as simple falsehood – a position that does not adequately address the ways in which fiction has reality for its readers and the ways that, in some instances, read-ers may feel a heightened form of intimacy with fictional characters that they may rarely experience with actual persons. Such concerns fall under the category of "trans-world relations" (the ontological difference between, for example, a fictional world and the actual world) as well as the notion of "accessibility" (the epistemological access that an actual reader may have to a fictional world). Ronen writes, "Accessibility has to do with the posi-tion of the reader relative to the fictional world: propositions about fiction reflect the fact that while not being part of the fictional world, the under-stander of fiction is affected by that world."[28]

The same categories may be adapted to forms of discourse that generate nonactual worlds other than fiction, including the language of delusion. As with fiction, an understanding of delusion benefits from precisely what Ronen calls "a relaxing philosophical notions of *truth, existence,* and *world-language relations*" in order to consider the pragmatic work that delusional and fictional worlds might perform. David Herman articulates the ways that narrative acts of world formation are cognitive operations that are not restricted to the work of fiction: "storyworlds are mental models of the situations and events being recounted – of who did what to and with whom, when, why, and in what manner. Reciprocally, narrative artifacts (texts, films, etc.) provide blueprints for the creation and modification of such mentally configured storyworlds."[29] Delusions are often internally and externally marked as kinds of worlds that, for certain subjects, take ontological priority over the actual or normatively structured social world, which may be experienced as comparatively lifeless, mechanical, or unreal.

This inversion of ontological priority is analogous to the act that fiction performs. Marie-Laure Ryan argues that "Fiction is characterized by the open gesture of recentering, through which an APW [alternative possible world] is placed at the center of the conceptual universe. This APW becomes the world of reference."[30] Delusion, like fiction, populates a world with nonactual objects and establishes an idiosyncratic system of relations among those objects that internally structures that world in ways that may diverge from the relations that govern normative social worlds. It is because fiction and delusion both perform gestures of "narrative recentering" that paranoid delusion has so often become not only the subject matter of fiction but also a trope for metafictional reflections upon the act of worlding that fiction performs.

In this way, works such as *The Comforters* foreground the worlding operations that are performed in both fiction and delusion, at times suggesting points of indiscernibility between the two. Defining what constitutes the fictionality of fiction has proven to be embarrassingly difficult even for narratologists. Ronen notes that any effort to isolate internal textual features as reliable signals of fictionality tends to founder against counterexamples in which the same features manifest in putatively nonfictional forms of discourse. For Ronen, the basic differences between the kind of worlds that are called fiction and other kinds of worlds – such as delusion – may simply be reduced to a matter of cultural competence. Identification of these differences is often contingent upon their presentation within particular sociological and institutional contexts.

Marie-Laure Ryan usefully points out the ways that fiction could be said to generate not only one world; instead, "the semantic domain of the narrative text contains a number of subworlds, created by the mental activity of characters. The semantic domain of the text is thus a collection of concatenated or embedded possible worlds."[31] The accessibility of such an embedded, mental "subworld" is precisely what is foregrounded in *The Comforters* when Laurence insists that he has tried and perhaps failed to enter Caroline's "world." This exchange poses the problem of the accessibility of others' psychological and especially delusional worlds and thereby stages what Karl Jaspers identified as the "un-understandability" of psychosis.

However, given the novel's striking metafictional maneuvers, such as announcing the fictionality of its characters to a character who happens to be studying narrative form, Caroline may be understood as directly addressing not only Laurence but also the reader when she encourages entrance into her "remote world." This would suggest that the problem of accessibility is staged in order to compare what she calls "the logic of my madness" with that of fiction. Ronen observes the strange double logic of accessibility that defines fictional worlds and what Ryan calls their mental "subworlds."

> The psychological accessibility of fiction is also problematic in that it involves mixing ordinary emotions of admiration or distress with aesthetic desires and interests. That is, when alluding to Anna [Karenina]'s unfortunate fate we mingle our psychological response with an aesthetic detachment, a kind of duality which the notion of *catharsis* so adroitly expresses . . .[32]

Fiction renders epistemic access to a distinct world and its subworlds at an aesthetic and ontological remove. In certain forms of fiction, readers often have rare access to the thoughts and worlds that are generated by other minds. Lyndsey Stonebridge observes that "Literature too, it is often claimed, is one place where you can hear the voices of others without actually going mad: in some ways it is the consciousness of this fact that makes fiction fiction."[33] Spark's work pursues these potential links between access to the thoughts of others and mental illness by considering their effects upon a character who exists at a point of convergence between delusion and fiction. Caroline seems to recognize that readers have access to her thoughts and that an author has influence over her thoughts at some distance – forms of access and influence that are the central concerns of many paranoid delusions. The anxieties that follow from Caroline's suspicion that she is a fictional character within a fictional world are rendered as the anxieties that appear in so many psychotic delusions such as thought insertion, thought surveillance, and feelings of unreality.

Caroline's awareness of her own fictional status is further complicated by the suggestion in the final pages of the novel that she goes on to write the text that we have read, making her both interior and exterior to the fictive world that she has occupied. "Of her constant influence on its course she remained unaware and now she was impatient for the story to come to an end, knowing that the narrative could never become coherent to her until she was at last outside it, and at the same time consummately inside it."[34] The paradoxes of self-narration that the novel confronts through such metafictional tropes also have psychological implications when translated back into the discourse of mental illness: the subject experiencing auditory hallucination is often conceptualized as both a subject narrated and the subject who is narrating. In his review of *The Comforters*, Evelyn Waugh writes: "The area of [Caroline's] mind which is composing the novel becomes separated from the area which is participating in it, so that, hallucinated, she believes that she is observant of, and observed by, and in some degree under the control of, an unknown second person."[35]

Despite this evident convergence of delusion and fiction writing in *The Comforters*, critics have most often approached Spark's work through her religious commitments. For example, John Lanchester argues that, "The need to gesture at the fictionality of her fictions is, I would suggest, rooted in Spark's Catholicism, and particularly in her wish not to compete with God."[36] As a result, the links that Spark's work often draws between the ontologies of fiction and delusion have often been passed over. However, Patricia Waugh offers an incisive exception to this critical tendency when she writes that "Her metafictional explorations of the relations between art and delusion, creativity and psychosis, also open up deeper questions about the existential and ontological sources of our world-making activities."[37] Yoking fiction's capacity for world-making to that of delusion has paradoxical effects: such delusional worlds are more urgently asserted as phenomenologically necessary while at the same time gaining a sense of artificiality. We see this in the ways that Caroline attempts to maintain her sense of worldedness while remarking upon its unconvincing, generic qualities. Patricia Waugh suggests that Spark's work exhibits a form of hyperreflexivity that Louis Sass associates with schizophrenia in which one's phenomenological world is undermined by reflections on the tacit processes that normally produce it. "This mode of intellectualized hyperawareness converts the body into an object for contemplation rather than a place in which to dwell, and the ensuing disconnection requires that the world be brought into being from nothing, built painstakingly out of words and ideas, in effect, like the fictional worlds of a novelist."[38] This hyperreflexivity can be attributed to the pathological splitting of processes commonly observed in cases of schizophrenia, but it may also be a function of Caroline's vocational splitting between the roles of author and critic. Here, it is important to note that her voice hearing begins when she struggles to complete her book about form in the twentieth-century novel. Specifically, she admits, "I'm having difficulty with the chapter on realism."[39] It is the reality effect in fiction that seems to elude her, and she casts a critic's eye on the "artificial plot" in which she finds herself.[40] Caroline is therefore split among the roles of character, author, and critic – these competing voices allow for reflections upon the world-building functions of the novel as well as interruptions of those operations.

If *The Comforters* shares with the work of Mina Loy and Evelyn Waugh a formal synthesis of fiction and delusion, it also shares with those works certain autobiographical sources. Prior to the composition of *The*

Comforters, Spark experienced paranoid delusions and hallucinations of a distinctly literary sort. She describes her symptoms in a 1954 letter to the Ministry of National Insurance, which had denied her claim for psychiatric treatment: "It was due to overwork and insufficient rest; I am a literary critic and had been working very hard on a book [...] Briefly, the trouble was that I began to imagine secret codes in everything I read, even in the press."[41] The trigger for these experiences seemed to be a work of late-modernist drama: after attending a production of T. S. Eliot's play, *The Confidential Clerk,* she began to develop paranoid delusions. Biographer Martin Stannard writes,

> around 15–20 January 1954, something went badly wrong. Her friends noticed the trouble before she did: T.S. Eliot, she insisted, was sending her threatening messages. His play was full of them. Some were in the theatre programme. Obsessively she began to seek them out, covering sheet after sheet of paper with anagrams and cryptographic experiments.[42]

It would seem that Spark's relation to modernism – here in the person and work of T. S. Eliot – was shaped by a rather literal anxiety of influence. If Eliot could be said to embody high modernism, he was also – like Spark and her character Caroline Rose – a figure divided between the roles of creator and critic, and his works were also riven by the impulses toward totality and disintegration. While Eliot and his play seemed to torment Spark, her friends suspected that her paranoid interpretation performed a work of self-repair that may have prevented even more radical psychological disintegration. "The text [of the play] kept her mind somehow together [...] This was another part of her mind [...] the sense of structure [... and] the idea of prying, of being watched."[43] Such experiences would shape the subject and form of her fiction. After her recovery, Spark wrote, "Now I feel released from a very real bondage & can make use of the experience. The real deliverance is the feeling that I can discover things about myself independent of the 'code'."[44] Her symptoms subsided, but the experience evidently left a durable influence on her work.

As in the case of Evelyn Waugh, Spark's psychotic experiences may have been related to drug use. During an especially difficult period of writing as an aspiring critic, Spark began taking Dexedrine – an amphetamine that has been shown to cause paranoia and hallucination. She was eventually treated with Largactil (chlorpromazine), a new psychiatric drug that was often used to treat psychosis. Traces of Spark's experiences along with the pharmacological agents appear in several of her works. Characters exhibit signs of paranoia when they are administered Dexedrine in *Loitering with*

Intent (1981), a later novel that is focalized through an aspiring novelist, Fleur Talbot, who takes a position as a ghost writer for an "Autobiographical Association." The group has been convinced by a charismatic figure to compose their memoirs in ways that only loosely relate to their actual lives. While augmenting these memoirs with fictional, dramatic events, Talbot also composes her first novel, and the strange relations among these texts becomes the central mystery of the narrative: the members of Autobiographical Association begin to act out the events that occur in Talbot's manuscript, renewing questions that Spark had raised in her first novel about the ontological relations between fictional and actual worlds.

Talbot appears to have some obscure influence over the members of the group, and her experiences also appear to be strangely mediated by the fictional world that she creates. When a member of the Association says of their influential leader, "Well, I can't explain, but I do believe in Quentin. I'm sure you do too, Fleur," her response is, "Oh, yes. I almost feel I invented him."[45] Conversely, she comes to feel that she is herself a character who suffers from incomplete characterization. "For a moment I felt like a grey figment, the 'I' of a novel whose physical description the author had decided not to set forth."[46] She is prompted into this feeling of unreality by a discussion of Cardinal Newman's *Apologia Pro Vita Sua*, a text that leads her to reflect on the consequences of radical self- and world construction through narrative. In response to a passage from Newman's work, Talbot says, " 'I think it awful [...] to contemplate a world in which there are only two luminous and self-evident beings, your creator and your-self. You shouldn't read Newman in that way [...] It's a beautiful piece of poetic paranoia.' "[47] What stands behind Talbot's objection may be the recognition that, like Caroline in *The Comforters*, she is both the creator and character of her story; in light of this recognition, Newman's claim entails a form of solipsism in which she is the only "luminous and self-evident being" – a feeling that seems to be confirmed when the actions of others seem to be determined by her narrative. Frank Kermode's discussion of *The Comforters* extends to *Loitering with Intent*: "*The Comforters* is always conscious of the fact that to make up fictive narratives is, in a way, a presumptuous activity, because the characters of a novelist, unlike those created by God, are not endowed with free will; she enjoys power at the expense of her characters."[48] In *The Comforters*, Caroline experiences this condition from the perspective of a character whose thoughts and actions are determined by an obscure authorial voice; in *Loitering with Intent*, Fleur Talbot comes to regard herself as the author of her fellow characters and perhaps of herself as well. This vacillation between narrating and narrated subject may account for her alternating feelings of megalomania and paranoia. "I was in a flutter, feeling partly that I had in fact some delusions of grandeur or of persecution or some other symptom of paranoia."[49] She often describes a division of her mind into parallel processes, and she compares her experience of writing to auditory hallucination. "I have the impression that I was tuning into voices without really hearing them as one does when moving from programme to programme on a wireless set."[50]

Audio technology and madness converge in much of Spark's work. In addition to Caroline's suspicion that the voices she hears emanate from "a box with a machine inside, operated from a distance,"[51] and Fleur Talbot's comparison of her fictional characters to voices heard on a "wireless set," elderly characters in *Memento Mori* are persecuted by an anonymous and potentially hallucinated voice on the telephone that reminds them they must die. The shared experience is dismissed by police as group hysteria or dementia, while the telephone itself becomes metonymically charged with a persecutory valence for its victims. One insists, "I must be protected from the sight of the telephone."[52] Radio in particular is often associated with paranoid suspicions of thought-insertion and thought-broadcasting in Spark's oeuvre, and Stonebridge notes that such paranoid associations with wireless may have been related to her experiences working "in 'Black' propaganda in the war as part of Sefton Delmer's unit broadcasting the sham German radio station, Radio Atlantic (Deutscher Kurzwellensender Atlantik), an experience she later drew on for her 1973 novel, *The Hothouse by the East River*."[53]

The convergence of madness and media technology becomes especially charged in the radio dramas that Spark composed for the BBC, such as *The Danger Zone*, a play that explores generational differences through the language of psychopathology.[54] Adolescents and their parents find themselves unable to communicate, as each generation is convinced that the other occupies a delusional, unreachable world. The play works by maintaining ambiguity over which world is actual. The effect forces the listener to perform the work of "double-bookkeeping," occupying two worlds at once in a way that simulates one of the symptoms that Eugen Bleuler originally identified with schizophrenia.[55] This ambiguity is repeated in Spark's radio play, *The Party through the Wall*, in which the narrator, Dr. Fell, presents himself as a retired psychiatrist who relates the case of Miss Carson, a neighbor who seems to experience auditory hallucinations.[56] Over the course of the play, this narrative role shifts to Miss Carson, who is warned that it is Fell who is mad. As in *The Danger Zone*, the play's dramatic tension depends upon the parallactic movements between the distinct worlds of mentally ill characters. In many ways, the formal resources and limitations of radio make such sustained epistemological and ontological problems possible – a convergence between madness and radio that Samuel Beckett would pursue in his writing for the BBC, as I demonstrate in Chapter 5. Spark underscores the phenomenological convergence of radio and modern paranoia when, like her character Fleur Talbot, she writes her preface to the collection *Voices at Play,* "I turned my mind into a wireless set and let the characters play on my ear."[57]

Across multiple works, then, Spark renders both the felt mechanization of the mind that had become a recurring feature of many experiences of twentieth-century psychosis and a reflection of the mechanistic psychiatric discourses through which such experiences were "explained." Those machine metaphors became the discursive materials from which delusional experiences of self and world could be fashioned. Further, the works of Muriel Spark make manifest the simultaneous necessity and difficulty of constructing those precarious worlds. In *The Comforters* and *Loitering with Intent,* the ad hoc phenomenological environments that narrative worlds afford are always threatened by the recognition of alternative possible worlds. Given its hyperreflexive and metafictional features, Spark's work may sensibly be regarded as postmodern, but I suggest that it comes into new focus when read in light of late-modernist fictions such as *Insel, The Ordeal of Gilbert Pinfold,* and the little known work of Anna Kavan, with whom Spark shares a great deal. If acts of worlding and unworlding are repeatedly staged by these writers as central problems that motivate their fiction, they are also revealed to be the key problems of delusion, and by staging homologies between these modes of discourse, these works announce their kinship with limit experiences that have long been marked as beyond the limits of understanding.

Asylum Pieces

"Anna Kavan" was the name assumed by British-born novelist Helen Woods (1902–1968) after she underwent a period of treatment in a Swiss psychiatric hospital. The name was taken from that of a recurring character in her earlier novels and reflects a technique of narrative self-construction that she foregrounds in much of her fiction. Along with the new identity came a darker and sparer form of writing that shares much with the paranoid worlds of Franz Kafka, whom she identified as a key influence on her later work. Her fiction is marked by formally experimental representations of radical mental illness and addiction, and it was admired by many of her late-modernist contemporaries. Kavan's biographer, D. A. Callard writes:

> She was one of the first English writers, and certainly the first woman writer, to have absorbed and transmuted the methods of Kafka: his depersonalization, despair, and the constant struggle against anonymous, mysterious powers. The review that would have given her most pleasure was praise from Kafka's translator Edwin Muir, who described her as a writer of "unusual imaginative power".[58]

In an early review of her novel *Eagle's Nest*, Duncan Fallowell described her as "the best English woman writer since Virginia Woolf."[59] Jean Rhys wrote with admiration,

> I've never read a long novel about a mad mind or an unusual mind or anybody's mind at all. Yet it is the only thing that matters and so difficult to put over without being dull.
>   Anna Kavan's stories I like, and I have her novel *Who Are You?* Very short, but what a splendid title. If only I'd thought of it . . .[60]

Anais Nin strikes a similar note of admiration for the short-story collection *Asylum Piece* (1940), which she describes as "a classic equal to the work of Kafka [. . .] in which non-rational human beings caught in a web of unreality still struggle to maintain a dialogue with those who cannot understand them. In later books the waking dreamers no longer try: they simply tell of their adventures. They live in solitude with their shadows, hallucinations, prophecies."[61] Despite the evident admiration of her contemporaries, Anna Kavan has been almost entirely forgotten by scholars of modernist and twentieth-century literature.

Kavan struggled with addiction and severe mental illness through much of her life and was a patient in numerous mental institutions and sanatoria. In her diary, she complains of "a feeling of unreality and of memory lapses: she seems to be suffering bouts of literal paranoia in which the world and inanimate objects appear threatening."[62] Elsewhere, she recounts these feelings of hallucinatory unreality in ways that are consistent with many first-person accounts of psychosis, and these experiences would become the psychological terrain that she would mine in her subsequent fiction. She writes in 1926:

> I am much more abnormal; indeed, at times, I am really afraid of going mad [. . .] This afternoon a curious thing happened to me. The reality of everything began to recede. I felt lonely and inaccessible and forgotten, and had a number of illusions, sometimes vivid and sometimes unreal.[63]

Seeking treatment on the continent, Kavan eventually developed a close relationship with the German psychiatrist Karl Theodore Bluth whose acquaintances included Brecht, Heidegger (whom Kavan would briefly encounter), and the eminent Swiss psychiatrist Ludwig Binswanger, to whom Kavan was eventually referred. On Bluth's recommendation, Kavan worked in a psychiatric clinic for traumatized soldiers during the Second World War. Her clinical experiences as both psychiatric patient and care-taker would become the source material for much of her later work.

Her short story "The Case of Bill Williams" appeared in the journal *Horizon* in 1944, along with responses by several psychiatrists. She would go on to write book reviews for *Horizon*, one of which reads like a mani-festo that indicates her modernist influences and the psychological ambi-tions of her work:

> [C]haracters come fully alive only through the elucidation of subconscious tensions which determine the basic patterns of human behaviour. A writer must speak, as it were, the language of the subconscious before he can pro-duce his best work. And this is true, not only of such writers as Kafka and James Joyce, who communicate by means of a dream or fantasy medium, but also of those who describe the external happenings of the outer world.[64]

The 1940 collection of short stories *Asylum Piece*, perhaps her most com-pelling work, was published shortly after her stay in a Swiss sanatorium and offers an intimate account of radical mental illness as it evolves from early experiences of depression, anxiety, and paranoia toward institutional-ization. *Asylum Piece* occupies an ambiguous generic space between fiction and memoir of mental illness that Mina Loy, Evelyn Waugh, and Muriel Spark would also explore. Jane Garrity, one of the few critical interpreters of Kavan, expresses concern that references to Kavan's mental illness might reduce appreciation of its avant-garde artistry, arguing that "within this con-text her disjointed narratives – a salient characteristic of much of her work – are assumed to result from her unstable psyche, rather than interpreted as a radical challenge to realist notions of language and style."[65] Garrity's insis-tence on the complexity and aesthetic challenges posed by Kavan's work is important, particularly given the lack of attention that her oeuvre has received within literary studies. However, much of the force of that artistry is explicitly directed toward a critical evaluation of psychiatric constructions of madness, and Kavan's "challenge to realist notions of language and style" is posed in order to represent experiences that have long been regarded as beyond comprehension – constructions and experiences with which Kavan was intimately familiar. While Garrity does not address *Asylum Piece* or *I*

Am Lazarus – the texts in which Kavan most explicitly explores institutions of psychiatry and experiences of psychosis – she acknowledges that "much of Kavan's writing interrogates the issue of what constitutes 'psychic normalcy' specifically for women within an increasingly alienating and fragmented social context."[66] I argue that Kavan's work shares with that of Muriel Spark a performative examination of the continuities between the world-making operations of paranoid delusion and fiction. To pass too quickly over the problem of mental illness at the center of Kavan's work would miss her fiction's singular investigations into these points of convergence and her representation of a mechanistic psychiatric regime.

The ambiguous interconnection of the short stories in *Asylum Piece* compounds the uncanny impressions produced by their form and content: the stories share a similar narrative style, but there is little conclusive evidence that the collection represents a single storyworld as experienced by the same, consistent subject. This uncertainty over the status of the world or worlds that one occupies as a reader formally reproduces the ontological ambiguities that schizophrenic patients often describe. Edwin Muir wrote of a similar collection of stories by Kavan, *I Am Lazarus* (1945), "we do not know the world in which these things are happening, and yet we feel their truth, and feel that they are telling us something which could be told in no other way."[67]

Asylum Piece is therefore comprised of a series of semiautonomous vignettes that render experiences of persecution delusions: one or more first-person narrators suspect that "Somewhere in the world I have an implacable enemy although I do not know his name."[68] It appears that this enemy has complete access to the narrator's movements and thoughts, and this persecution expands to a vaguely defined bureaucratic authority that threatens incarceration. An undefined "case" has been brought against the narrator, who knows little about the law, the nature of her infraction, or what forms of defense may be available to her. "Sometimes I think that some secret court must have tried and condemned me, unheard, to this heavy sentence."[69] Elsewhere, she thinks, "If only one knew of what and by whom one were accused, when, where, and by what laws one were to be judged, it would be possible to prepare one's defence systematically and to set about things in a sensible fashion."[70] The narrative logic that is set in motion by such suspicions shares much with the worlds of paranoid delusions and those developed by Kafka in *The Trial* and *The Castle*. The pernicious, bureaucratic system is at once omnipresent and only knowable through inscrutable, blue telegrams through which its obscure medico-legal determinations are intimated:

He took a pale blue form out of his pocket and held it towards me. But in the uncertain light from the street lamp and the cars I only had time to make out some unintelligible legal phrases, and my own name embellished with elaborate scrolls and flourishes in the old-fashioned style, before he hastily put the stiff paper away again.[71]

As in Kafka's fiction, an abstract and obscure sense of the Law is both omnipresent and unintelligible. Without a clear understanding of the protocols enforced by this system, virtually all behavior is felt to be saturated with latent, pernicious meaning that remains undisclosed to the narrator. The result is a delusion of reference in which she feels herself to be in constant violation of this obscure system until all external phenomena become charged signs for interpretation that eludes her. Subjects and objects seem directed toward her as mechanisms of surveillance and judgment.

No sooner had I discovered this than a change seemed to come over everything. It was as though, in some mysterious way, I had become the central point around which the night scene revolved. People walking on the pavement looked at me as they passed; some with pity, some with detached interest, some with more morbid curiosity. Some appeared to make small, concealed signs, but whether these were intended for warning or encouragement I could not be sure. The windows lighted or unlighted, were like eyes more or less piercing, but all focused upon me. The houses, the traffic, everything in sight, seemed to be watching to see what I would do.[72]

A rigidly structured world takes shape that locates the narrator at its center as a source of disturbance of an undisclosed protocol. In her attempts to rationalize this suspicion of a latent system, the narrator imagines possible social orders from which she has been excluded.

Perhaps I am the victim of some mysterious political, religious or financial machination – some vast and shadowy plot, whose ramifications are so obscure as to appear to the uninitiated to be quite outside reason, requiring, for instance, something as apparently senseless as the destruction of everybody with red hair or with a mole on his left leg.[73]

What begins as a metaphor – conspiratorial "machinations" – is made literal and internalized when the narrator reflects upon her own mental operations. As in many memoirs and fictions of mental illness, the narrator generates a technological delusion that reflects the modernity of her madness.

A sequence entitled "Machines in the Head" describes the narrator's painful experience of her own thought and behavior as a system of automatisms over which she has little control. Her cognitive and emotional functions operate without volition or warning, and she is subject to these implacable mechanisms in the same way that she is subject to the apparent conspiracy against her. Whereas many delusions forge a clear distinction between self and persecutory Other, this sequence suggests that the narrator's psychic interiority has become incorporated within a larger assemblage of machinations. "I am awake now for good, or rather, for bad; the wheels, my masters, are already vibrating with incipient motion; the whole mechanism is preparing to begin the monotonous, hateful functioning of which I am the dispirited slave."[74] The antecedents of these mechanical figures are ambiguously internal and external to the narrator. Her consciousness is epiphenomenal to their work, passively observing their results without a clear sense of what these psychic machines are for, even as they perform the routine tasks of everyday life. "What's the good of appealing to senseless machinery? The cogs are moving, the engines are slowly gathering momentum, a low humming noise is perceptible even now. How well I recognize every sound, every tremor of the laborious start."[75] The machines are characterized as "senseless" and deaf to any appeals for mercy or reprieve. The tacit, human ecology of purposes and desires that would normally render a sensible world are not available to her; yet, the work of the mind and body continue in an uncanny, senseless fashion. Between the bureaucratic conspiracy and the machines in her head, the narrator is subject to inscrutable forces that are both above and below the scale of the human.

This delusion of depersonalization is presented as both a consequence and a compensation for a lack of tacit understanding that would make her at home in a world. Without access to a symbolic order that tacitly organizes and structures her environment, her behavior is experienced as unmotivated and automatic. When she is confronted with a choice, the narrator is unable to act, as is evident in meetings with her "advisor," whose euphemistic title obscures his psychiatric function while indicating that she requires clear direction for her behavior.

> "Why won't you tell me what I ought to do?" I asked him indignantly at the end of our interview. "Why can't you give me a definite line of conduct and save me from all this suffering and uncertainty?"
> "That's exactly what I don't intend to do," he answered me. "The trouble with you is that you're always avoiding responsibility. This is a case where you must act on your own initiative."[76]

In her state of epiphenomenal passivity, initiative – or the conventional illusion of initiative – is no longer possible. To the extent that she acts, she feels that her actions are motivated by unconscious operations that are now disclosed to observation as automatic, mechanical systems – an awareness that reveals conventional feelings of initiative to be illusions.

Such an inability to choose is evident in the story of another patient – perhaps the same narrator at a different moment in time – who finds herself in an asylum struggling with quotidian decisions such as what to wear. "I never could decide what to put on." [...] "it was really awful. You can't think how this silly affair used to worry me. So at last I thought of a plan to avoid making a choice. I just put on the same suit every day."[77] The narrator's delusion of persecution and "machines in the head" may be understood as another "plan" or adaptation to account for this inability to decide properly. If a task is performed by the narrator, it appears to be performed without her will.

> I implore, with my hands already, in automatic obedience, starting to perform their detested task.
> What does a machine care about green woodpeckers? The wheels revolve faster, the pistons slide smoothly in their cylinders, the noise of machinery fills the whole world. Long since cowed into slavish submission, I still draw from some inexorable source the strength to continue my hard labour although I am scarcely able to stand on my feet.[78]

The narrator reflects upon the operations of her mind and body without identifying with them or experiencing them as her own. In this respect, her discourse reflects those of psychiatry and neurology that attempt to identify the dysfunctional mechanisms that give rise to schizophrenia.

In his *General Psychopathology* (1913), Karl Jaspers critiqued the tendency toward mechanistic approaches to mental illness by introducing an epistemological distinction between "explaining" and "understanding" the experiences of patients. Explanation operates through objective, third-person observations of symptoms and issues hypotheses about their underlying, physiological causes. By contrast, understanding demands a phenomenological inquiry into the structure of pathological experiences – the feeling of what it is like to suffer particular symptoms such as hallucinations, paranoia, and depersonalization. Jaspers writes that, "[p]sychological understanding cannot be used mechanically as a sort of generalized knowledge but a fresh, personal intuition is needed on every occasion."[79] Understanding pathological experience avoids reductions to hypothetical, mechanistic causes and attends to the singularity of the individual patient and the meanings of her experiences within the context of her life story and the cultural materials from which her world is constructed. With regard to Jaspers's distinction, Kenneth Kendler observes, "Understanding is particular and unique rather than general, linked to the first-person perspectives, and is 'story-focused.'"[80]

Schizophrenia, in Jaspers's view, lies beyond the realm of understandable, meaningful relations and can only be explained through reference to biological causes (although he acknowledges that no satisfactory biological explanation has been accomplished). This skepticism toward the possibility of understanding schizophrenia has become the dominant psychiatric attitude and has two major consequences: (1) the meaning-making processes that comprise a patient's delusional system are often disregarded by psychiatrists as the epiphenomenal effects of biological dysfunctions, and (2) the patient is reduced to a dysfunctioning mechanical system rather than a person whose experiences can be either imagined or understood.

In "Machines in the Head," Kavan describes a self-experience of this reduction – one that reflects the discourse of mechanistic "explanation" that Jaspers distinguishes from phenomenological understanding in which the doctor might inquire more fully into the first-person experiences of the patient. In Kavan's account, the subject experiences herself as driven by an alienating mechanism, but she often continues to perform basic, everyday functions. Jaspers finds that schizophrenia differs from other neurological disorders such as general paralysis in that the schizophrenic patient may continue to be "peculiarly productive" in a way that resembles Kavan's narrator's self-experience.

> In the one case, it is as if an axe had demolished a piece of clockwork – and crude destructions are of relatively little interest. In the other it is as if the clockwork keeps going wrong, stops and then runs again. In such a case we can look for specific, selective disturbances. But there is more than that; the schizophrenic life is peculiarly productive.[81]

What is of particular interest about schizophrenia for Jaspers is that its cognitive and affective operations cannot be so easily dismissed as those of other neurological disorders. He suggests that there is something intriguing about the meaning that is produced through the "selective disturbances" of schizophrenia – elements that he sometimes regards as "un-understandable" but that may remain uncannily "productive." This functionalist, mechanistic language also is consistent with the metaphors adopted by so many modern writers and mental patients to describe and "explain" these experiences, suggesting a mirroring or looping effect between the discourses of the mind sciences and their patients.

If some delusions appear to be especially productive of sense and submit to interpretation, Jaspers finds that the recurrent expressions of depersonalization and unreality remain beyond the scope of phenomenological understanding. In his view, it is impossible for a subject to empathize with an experience that is defined by a loss of subjectivity and a reduction to objective, mechanistic causation. To do so would be for subjectivity to imagine the experience of objectivity. Christoph Hoerl develops the epistemic limit on psychiatric understanding that Jaspers first articulated:

> And this may be seen to make any attempt at understanding them a particularly paradoxical endeavour. On the one hand, to attempt to understand them, in the way envisaged by Jaspers, means that we must suppose that the patient's attitude towards their own thoughts somehow emerges from other, prior, aspects of their psychic life. Yet, actually "sinking ourselves into the psychic situation" of the patient in fact means giving up, within the project of trying to understand the patient, on this very conception of psychic states as emerging from within in a meaningful way. Thus, in schizophrenia, the content of the delusion that we are trying to understand – *the idea of a "made" mental life* – conflicts with the very conception of the mental that governs the project of empathetic understanding.[82]

This notion of a "'made' mental life" describes well what Kavan and so many modern psychotic patients and writers represent. It is what Jaspers's epistemic framework of "explanation" entails: one's psychic experiences are not meaningful results of other psychic experiences but are merely the senseless consequences of neurobiology gone awry – what Nancy Andreasen has called "the broken brain" hypothesis of biological psychiatry.[83] The mechanical delusions that recur in memoirs and fictions of schizophrenia are uncanny reflections of the psychiatric discourse through which the patient is only "explained" as a broken neurological machine and never understood. In this way, the patient's experiences are doubly reduced to something less than the status of subjectivity: through the feeling of being "made" to feel by some obscure machinery and through the mechanistic discourse of explanation deployed by a biological psychiatry that finds such experiences "un-understandable."

However, while, in this view, only neurobiological damage can explain those experiences, Jaspers admits, "we do not know a single physical event in the brain which could be considered the identical counterpart of any morbid psychic event."[84] Despite this conspicuous absence of neurological evidence, the hypothesis that "mental illness is cerebral illness" remains a dominant assumption into the twenty-first century.[85] Even while reducing schizophrenia to hypothetical physiological "explanations," Jaspers also critiques the "brain mythologies" that had been promoted on the basis of specious evidence – especially claims to localize particular functions and dysfunctions that followed the early correlations of certain forms of aphasia with particular neurological regions that had been accomplished by Broca and Wernicke. Such belief that a simple biological-mechanical cause would be found – in the absence of any real evidence – attests to a desire to establish the discipline of psychiatry in a legitimate, scientific foundation of technophysical causal explanations: "in physics and chemistry we have to a certain extent reached the ideal, which is the expression of causal laws in mathematical equations. We pursue a similar aim in psychopathology."[86]

While frankly acknowledging psychiatry's disciplinary ambitions to ground itself in the causal, objective, and empirical methods that the natural sciences had achieved, Jaspers also articulates the potential limits of these efforts with regard to the human mind and its disorders.

> Unwittingly many a psychiatrist has been overcome by the feeling that if only we had an exact knowledge of the brain, we would then know the psychic life and its disturbances. This has led psychiatrists to abandon psychopathological studies as unscientific, so that they have lost whatever psychopathological knowledge had been gained up to then.[87]

Here, "psychopathological knowledge" refers to phenomenological *understanding* of the experiences of psychiatric patients. The methods by which such understanding may be achieved are not, Jaspers admits, strictly scientific but are closer to the training one can only acquire through other means, including literary study – training that might enable the psychiatrist to interpret and understand the discourse and writings of psychotics. Jaspers writes, "But patients do not often offer us anything empirically objective to investigate. There have been certain important historical phenomena and by a lucky chance we may get something from our patients. *The methods for knowledge in this field are only acquired through a training in the humanities.*"[88] In support of this view, Jaspers makes frequent references to the poetry of Hölderlin and others whose writings occupy an ambiguous discursive space between literature and psychosis. We might add to this category writers like Anna Kavan, whose works often enlist the experimental methods of earlier modernists such as Kafka and Joyce in order to represent subjective experiences that might otherwise seem "un-understandable."

While psychoanalysts developed their own hermeneutic methods for the treatment of neurotics, few psychiatrists followed Jaspers's recommendations that training in the humanities might be useful in understanding the experiences of schizophrenic patients, and efforts to develop phenomenological understanding gave way to biological forms of psychiatry that pursued a primarily mechanistic, causal "explanation."[89] Perhaps in response, psychotic delusions often assume the same mechanistic language with an uncanny, "peculiar production" of their own elaborate "brain mythologies."

One exception to this tendency in psychiatry may be found in the work of Bruno Bettelheim, who attempted to understand the potential meanings of the commonly recurring technological delusions as are evident in his case history of "Joey" – a patient who is presented as "autistic" at a moment when the nosological distinctions between autism and schizophrenia were not clearly defined. Joey conceived of himself as an assemblage of electronic components that were powered by electrical cables. Bettelheim writes, "If he did anything at all, he seemed to function by remote control – a 'mechanical man,' run by machines that were both created by him and beyond his control."[90] This equivocal matter of control shares much with the ambiguities described by Kavan's narrator, who feels herself motivated either by the delusional machines in her head or by obscure, external machinations. Bettelheim continues, "There was nothing he could do unless powered by machines. Before beginning to read, even before he could sit down, he had to connect up his desk to a source of energy. Then he had to plug himself in, plug his book or pencils into the desk, and then tune himself in."[91] Energetic and informatic machinery was not avoided by Joey but was embraced as the condition of possibility for his behavior.

Working within a psychoanalytic framework, Bettelheim contributed to the controversial view that severe disorders such as autism and schizophrenia could be traced to frigid mothers. Bettelheim states that Joey's mother showed little interest in him. "At birth, his mother 'thought of him as a thing rather than a person.' But even before that he made little impression. 'I never knew I was pregnant,' she said, meaning that consciously the pregnancy did not alter her life. His birth, too, 'did not make any difference.'"[92] The suggestion is that there was no position or role for Joey's subjectivity within the symbolic order of his mother's world – his personhood was not recognized from the start. As a consequence, Joey fashioned a world that was devoid of the kind of relationship that would conventionally be called human, and attempts at emotional intimacy and care would prove disruptive. "If the world of human warmth was closed to him so that to feel was to be hurt, he would create one where feelings had no place. But since things do happen, it had to be a world where they can happen without feelings being involved. It had to be a world of machines."[93] Rather than a deficit, the affectless, automatic operation of machines was a consolation – the delusional world of mechanical devices within which he imbricated himself was preferable to the alternative possible worlds that he found painfully uninhabitable. In his theory and clinical practice, Bettelheim affirmed and supported the development of the delusion as a necessary procedure of world building. "We had created a situation that made him indeed *homo faber*, man the tool maker. It started him on the long trek of transforming, first material things, to fit them to the needs of his life, and later himself too, so that he could not only have the things but also the life that he wanted."[94] Bettelheim's etiological claims aside, he recognizes the procedure of world building as not simply a symptom but as a pragmatic process of self-management.

The nonnormative semantic and syntactic qualities of Joey's discourse render a more clear picture of the shape that his world would take. He developed linguistic procedures that reflected his flattened ontological system, which recognized no fundamental difference between persons and machines, and he avoided the use of names or personal pronouns, including "I." Bettelheim writes, "If one has twice struggled to see oneself as a person and had to give up, it does not come easy to try again. But not feeling himself a distinct person, no one else seemed a distinct person either."[95] To recognize the other as a person when one cannot recognize one's own personhood could entail a subordination of oneself to others as a tool or instrument of their will. Bettelheim proposes that Joey's world system and linguistic idiosyncrasies can be understood as compensations for a felt lack of autonomy. The machines or "preventions," as Joey sometimes called them, were systems that ran on his own terms and by his own designs.

> After all, his elaborate preventions around eating at the table had originated in the parochial school where he felt he had to guard against his very life (his body) being run by mortal enemies. If he was now run by machines they were at least partly in his control, since they work only if he plugged them in.[96]

The capacity to cut power to these machines enabled him to interrupt any interaction or behavior that became threatening. Joey's preference for recognizing only machines rather than people within his world enabled him to mediate his social relationships and reestablish some sense of control.

The mechanical world also afforded Joey a repertoire of controls for modulating his own psychic states that were regulated and systematic – even if they bore little resemblance to the social rules of proper behavior that he, like the narrator of *Asylum Piece*, could not intuitively access. "He had to obey unfathomable, if not plainly capricious laws."[97] Rather than conforming to conventional social and ethical protocols that are tacitly obeyed by most normative subjects, Joey's behavior and world were governed by laws that more closely resembled the laws of physics. This would leave him vulnerable to disruptive events when an actual device failed to conform to his expectations.

Once, for example, when a night light in his dormitory (small blue bulbs of low wattage) burned out it threw him into a panic. He was convinced that his body was falling apart. He insisted that the School was "against the law" because the bulb had burned out, that its inner connections had given way, that the ceiling was caving in on him, and so forth. It jeopardized his life when machines went awry.[98]

The consistency and predictability of machines were the source of their consolation to Joey, including his ability to manage their presence or absence: his capacity to turn them on and off. Unlike Joey, the narrator of *Asylum Piece* is unable to turn off the machines in and out of her head – a problem that also manifests in a later novel by Kavan, *Who Are You?* (1963), in which a narrator hears a voice repeating, "Who-are-you? Who-are-you? Who-are-you? Loud, flat, hard and piercing, the repetitive cry bores its way through the ear-drums with the exasperating *persistence of a machine that can't be switched off*."[99]

Despite Bettelheim's attempts to understand the pragmatic work that Joey's world performed, he also follows Jaspers in acknowledging an irreducible limit in his capacity to empathize and fully understand the experiences of the patient. He repeatedly describes the uncanny effect that Joey's performance had upon members of the clinical staff who sometimes struggled to recognize his personhood:

Joey was a child devoid of all that we see as essentially human and childish, as if he did not move arms or legs but had extensors that were shifted by gears.[100]

This boy-machine was only with us when working; it had no existence when at rest. Though just an instant ago not "there," in the next Joey seemed a machine, the wheels busily cranking and turning, and as such held us rapt, whether we liked it or not.[101]

The best I can do is to say that watching him interfered to a serious degree with our ability to experience and relate to him as human beings.[102]

Bettelheim adopts a distinctly phenomenological form of discourse when he addresses Joey's uncanny status as either "there" or not; Joey's "being there," what Heidegger would call *dasein*, is not simply given but is erratic and intermittent. "It," as Bettelheim curiously describes the patient, often only appears as an uncanny level of animated objectivity that does not give the impression that a subject is present. Jaspers elucidates the uncanny feeling that Bettelheim reports:

It is easier to describe the common factor in subjective terms, that is, in terms of the effect on the observer, rather than try to do so objectively. All these personalities have something baffling about them, which baffles our understanding in a peculiar way; there is something queer, cold, inaccessible, rigid, and petrified there, even when the patients are quite sensible and can be addressed and even when they are eager to talk about themselves. We may think we can understand dispositions furthest from our own but when faced with such people we feel a gulf which defies description.[103]

This experience of irreducible alienation from such a patient is the reason why, for Jaspers, schizophrenics remain ultimately un-understandable. Beyond the often internally coherent logic and historically specific discourses of many delusions, there remains in his view a form of life that cannot be imagined. This recurs in the descriptions provided by Joey's caregivers and renders a prevailing impression of the boy as all but inhuman.

It is this impression that is rendered by the writing of Anna Kavan. If one power of fiction is to produce a "reality effect" in which characters are experienced by readers as virtually real personalities, an obverse power may be described as an "unreality effect." This does not indicate a deficit in a narrative's capacity to persuade the reader; instead, it is a capacity to represent a felt lack of personhood and the experience of unworlding. In this way, it is not simply that a work such as *Asylum Piece* superficially shares with certain memoirs and case studies the subject of mental illness or certain metaphorical tropes; instead, it shares with such writing the formal capacity to report and even to reproduce for its readers the phenomenology of mental illness.

The ambition of making such experiences understandable and legible is evident in the ways that *Asylum Piece* and subsequent works such as *I Am Lazarus* locate feelings of unreality, depersonalization, objectification, and hallucination within an explicitly psychiatric institutional context. The latter collection of short stories, which may be read as a companion to *Asylum Piece,* clearly establishes looping effects between the mechanistic delusions experienced by certain mental patients and the mechanistic discourses of the brain – the "brain mythologies" – through which those experiences are explained. Thomas Fuchs accounts for the technical delusion as a consequence of the mechanization of the psyche.

> The decisive reason for the affinity between schizophrenia and technology is thereby made clear: the machine is an appropriate metaphor for a subjectivity that has turned inside out, as it were, and has indeed become a synthetic object or piece of machinery to itself. *The mechanisation of the psyche precedes the development of the technical delusion*: what is reflected in the influencing-machine, is nothing else but the alienation and objectification of subjectivity itself.[104]

This mechanization of the psyche can be understood as both a function of the psychotic's scrutiny of cognitive and emotional processes as if they were "machines in the head" and as an effect of the historical discourses of psychiatry and neurology that attempt to describe those processes in the same objective and mechanistic fashion. The stories collected in *I Am Lazarus* represent the links between this disciplinary mechanization of the psyche and mental patients' lived experiences of such objectification. The collection appeared shortly after Kavan's experience in 1943 working at the Mill Hill Emergency Hospital in London, a psychiatric clinic for soldiers. Whereas her earlier stories primarily maintain the first-person perspective of a psychiatric patient, the works that comprise *I Am Lazarus* vacillate between the perspectives of the clinic's patients and staff, a strategy that enables the work to measure the kinds of alienation that the clinicians feel during encounters with profound mental illness while also indicating the dialectical, discursive loops that often occur between the discourses of doctors and patients.

The collection's title story is initially focalized through an English doctor who visits his former patient at a continental mental asylum. The doctor doubts the ethics and therapeutic effects of the somatic treatments to which the man has been subjected:

> In particular he distrusted this insulin shock treatment there had been such a fuss about. Why should putting imbeciles into a coma make them sane? It didn't make any sense. He did not think and never had thought that there was a cure for an advanced dementia praecox case like young Thomas Bow.[105]

By the 1940s, insulin shock had become a popular treatment for schizophrenia, or "dementia praecox" as it was initially taxonomized by Emil Kraepelin, even in the absence of any clear neurological explanation. The English doctor once regarded Thomas Bow as "hopelessly insane," and he is surprised to find him comparatively docile. However, the patient's current condition only provokes greater unease.

> He felt disapproving and indignant and uncomfortable without quite knowing why. Of course, the boy looks normal enough, he said to himself. He seems quiet and self-controlled. But there must be a catch in it somewhere. You can't go against nature like that. It just isn't possible. He thought uneasily of the young inexpressive face and the curious flat look of the eyes.[106]

The impression is that Bow poses no threat, but this lack of animation is not the same as a cure, in the doctor's view. If there is something unnatural or perhaps inhuman about Thomas Bow, the narrative goes beyond outward impressions of the doctor by shifting focalization to the patient's view of the same scene. Bow is incapable of responding to the doctor's questions, and his experiences of the visiting doctor, his fellow patients, and nurses devolve into sense data devoid of coherence or meaning.

> What had he to do with talking? All around the table were different coloured shapes whose mouths opened and closed and emitted sounds that meant nothing to him. He did not mind either the shapes or the sounds. They were part of the familiar atmosphere of the workroom where he felt comfortable and at ease.[107]

Bow's view only acknowledges nonhuman objects – a condition that enables him to operate without disturbance within the space of the workroom. If at one level he registers that "talk" is going on around him, he cannot engage in the protocol. When he is led out of the workroom for lunch, he is displaced from his flattened ontology of shapes, colors, and sounds, and he struggles to refashion a working relationship to a socially dense environment. "The young man laboriously assembled words in his head."[108] He moves as if blind into a space that he is unable to map cognitively and that he experiences as unpredictable, precarious, and threatening. "At any moment something might pounce on him, something for which he did not have the formula. He waited tensely, on enemy ground."[109]

Bow's inability or refusal to recognize and engage in conversation with others is compounded by the clinicians' refusal to recognize any efforts to communicate. "The gym mistress did not listen to what he was trying to say. It was not the fashion at the clinic to listen to what patients said. There was not enough time."[110] This refusal to acknowledge the discourse of the patient along with the insulin shock treatments to which Bow has been subjected (treatments that historically preceded even more brutal methods such as frontal lobotomies and electric shock) are evidence that "the fashion of the clinic" is a form of biological psychiatry in which the patient's history and laborious acts of world construction are not regarded as relevant. Given these mechanistic and arguably inhumane forms of treatment, it is perhaps not surprising that patients who were subjected to this neurological reductionism would regard themselves as mere mechanisms. Ironically, the kind of depersonalizing experience that these patients have of themselves and of others is consistent with the mechanistic framework that clinicians would often apply to those patients.

I Am Lazarus represents this effect in the narrative of a patient who hallucinates and identifies with a clock that is encased in glass – its internal mechanisms are at once separated from the external world yet exposed to view.

> A picture of a clock drifted in front of him. It was an electric clock that had belonged to one of his aunts, it was made of brass with all its work showing, a skeleton of a clock inside a glass dome, and it never required winding. When he was a small boy there had seemed to him to be something horrific and fascinating and pathetic about the sight of the pendulum frantically swinging, swinging, swinging, perpetually exposed and driven in that transparent tomb.[111]

His relation to the uncanny, inhuman movement becomes ambiguous. "Pictures and confusion crowded inside the glass."[112] His thoughts are experienced as an acephalous, undirected form of motion that he can neither identify with nor stop – a recurring motif in Kavan's work. "And now suddenly there was nothing but the skeleton in the transparent cell, brass midriff and spine, wheels and frangible springs, the hollow man, bloodless, heartless, headless; only the crazy pendulum swinging in place of head."[113] The image performs an explanatory function for the patient, but it is a private explanation that he is unable to translate to his incurious doctors or even to his weeping fiancée: "he thought that he ought to try to explain something, but it was impossible because *there was nothing but the swinging pendulum with which to explain*."[114] This failure can be ascribed to the impoverished explanatory resources that mechanistic accounts offer to those who would attempt to communicate their experiences. As we are led through the psychiatric institution, we encounter patients whose worlds are in various stages of construction, totality, and disintegration.

As in the case of Thomas Bow, experiences of unworlding and failures to distinguish between humans and objects disturb nearly all of the narrators of *I Am Lazarus*. One character finds herself fixated on objects and unable to engage with other persons at a cocktail party.

> What exactly is it that's wrong with me? What is the thing about me that people never can take? her thoughts wandered, although she knew the answer perfectly well. It was the woolgathering, of course, the preoccupation with non-human things, the interest in the wrong place, that was so unacceptable.[115]

She feels herself organizing her environment in a nonnormative way by not giving priority to persons over objects or, like many of Kavan's narrators, by not observing this ontological distinction. While she shares Bow's faint awareness of the pathological status of her own indifference to people, this awareness does not redirect her attention. "There was nothing to be done anyway. The woolgathering was far stronger than she was."[116] This splitting of awareness is evident in the short story "Who Has Desired the Sea," in which a patient struggles with social obligations that he cannot carry out. "He knew this was what he should do. But the knowledge had no relevance. It did not seem to apply directly to him."[117] The passage describes a division in which awareness persists but cannot be related to oneself and one's behavior.

In "Face of My People," a soldier suffers a similar alienation from tacit social protocols that govern one's relations to persons and things. Standing in the yard of the hospital, he is invited to participate in a game with his fellow patients and caretakers. His altered sense of the world is evident in his failure to recognize the use of particular objects within simple practices and protocols such as the game. "He picked up the big ball and held it in both hands as though he did not know what to do with it, as though he could conceive of no possible connection between himself and this hard spherical object."[118] Later, he experiences a similar alienation and bewilderment facing other patients. "Far from the reaches of his non-being Kling looked at the faces round him. They were all looking at him but they had no meaning."[119] As in many memoirs of schizophrenia, *I Am Lazarus* renders the phenomenology of altered or shattered worlds in which persons are experienced as strangely animated part-objects whose gestures no longer carry significance. David Herman writes that, in addition to constructing worlds,

> stories place an accent on unexpected or noncanonical events – events that disrupt the normal order of things for human or human-like agents engaged in goal-directed activities and projects within a given world, and that are experienced as such by those agents.[120]

Herman's language captures the homologies between a phenomenological and narrative sense of "world," both of which are given structure by "goal-directed activities and projects." The disruption of this structure by unexpected events is precisely what is staged in Kavan's stories, and this disruption is taken to the limit point of unworlding. When figures like Kling and Bow have lost all sense of "the normal order of things," they also experience themselves as something other than "human or human-like agents." If, as in the case of Joey, a similar feeling of radical disruption often extends to patients' caretakers, this feeling is also reproduced for readers of Kavan's fiction, who may feel a conspicuous loss of "the normal order of things." This crisis differs from the kind of unworlding that is staged in *The Comforters* when Caroline feels that events fit all-too-neatly within the "phoney plot" of a fiction novel. Instead, Kling is unable to organize his experiences within any narrative trajectory.

Formally, Kavan's minimalistic vignettes are unresolved fragments that evoke unreality effects and render scenes of unworlding rather than conventional narratives as defined by Herman. As the title *I Am Lazarus* suggests, the collection elicits a sense that we have entered a modernist world of the undead – a kind of space in which personhood is no longer given that recurs in other late-modernist texts such as Wyndham Lewis's *The Childermass* and, as I will discuss in Chapter 4, Flann O'Brien's *The Third Policeman*. Within the early, psychiatric pieces, this manifests through nurses and doctors who cannot recognize a living person in their patients. In later stories, the uncanny feeling is generalized from individual minds and distributed into diffuse environments and fragmented half-worlds. One narrator describes her home as an uncanny space of the undead and as a locus of madness: "Yes, it's just as if one were forced to live with someone out of his mind, or, worse still, with the actual physical corpse of a loved person which a diabolical chemistry had rendered immune from the process of dissolution."[121] Kavan's work often invokes this feeling of unreality as an unresolved ontological status that may be rendered by both delusion and fiction.

If Kavan's work aspires to a discursive representation of the worlding and unworlding that shape experiences of mental illness, it shares this aspiration with other works of late-modernist fiction and with the memoirs of patients. Further, this formal convergence of experimental fiction with memoir of mental illness occurred from both directions. One memoir, entitled *Operators and Things: The Inner Life of a Schizophrenic* (1958), gives a singular account of the kind of mechanistic self-experiences that recur in the fiction of Kavan, Spark, Waugh, Loy, and others. The text is framed by an introduction and prefatory note written by psychologists whose recommendations of the text equivocate only over its genre: "I believe that not only will professionals regard this work as an outstanding contribution to studies on the etiology, treatment and sociology of mental illness, but that all readers will view this work as brilliant literature and see in it the emergence of an artist."[122] While *The Ordeal of Gilbert Pinfold, The Comforters, Asylum Piece,* and *I Am Lazarus* circulate as works of fiction, they draw equally upon their authors' experiences of mental illness and the formal legacy of experimental modernist fiction. Such texts challenge simple appeals to "cultural competence" as criteria for rigidly distinguishing the narrative worlds of fiction from those of delusion.

The erosion of such distinctions are at the core of many ontological confusions that define the textual worlds in question. Psychotic discourse often articulates an absence of tacit understanding of social and institutional protocols. This is evident in Kavan's patients, who are unable to recognize a ball as part of a game with others; the blue telegrams that seem to be inscrutable pronouncements of a Law that cannot be understood; or the case of Joey, who "had to obey unfathomable, if not plainly capricious laws."[123] Beyond these explicit articulations of confusion, psychotic discourse often formally demonstrates a limited capacity to organize the objects and events of experience into their conventional phenomenological places and relations. That is, these narratives fail or refuse to render the internal structure of a world that is often simply given for normative subjects or to recognize the priority of the "actual worlds" of consensus. Recognizing the distinctions among the worlds of reality, fiction, and delusion is precisely the form of metacognition with which psychotics conspicuously struggle and that this strain of late-modernist fiction dramatically resists.

CHAPTER 4

Flann O'Brien and Authorship as a Practice of "Sane Madness"

In Flann O'Brien's novel *The Third Policeman*, characters fear that they have merged physically and mentally with the bicycles that they ride, a machine captures loud noises and transforms them into a source of energy, and all material objects can be reduced to a single infinitely versatile element called "omnium." If twentieth-century science could sleep, it would dream this world. It is an uncanny space located between the familiar and the impossible constructed by an author whom one critic has aptly labeled "the literalist of the imagination."[1] The fantastic extremes of *The Third Policeman* only narrowly outstrip the disorientating scientific changes to which the novel responds with the complaint that "Anything can be said in this place and it will be true and have to be believed."[2]

Flann O'Brien's novels satirically represent a historical moment when the possible and the impossible, reality and delusion, science and scientism mix in the popular imagination as uncontrollably as the molecules of the bicycle and those of its rider. The absurdities of *The Third Policeman* (written in 1939, published in 1967) and *The Dalkey Archive* (1964) are nearly as plausible as the inscrutable breakthroughs of quantum physics, relativity theory, and atomic warfare that they are barely able to satirize. More accurately, it is not science itself but rather the inscrutability of its discoveries for a broad population and the confusion of categories that those breakthroughs often render that are the objects of O'Brien's satirical gaze. Lacking the means to safely distinguish science from scientism or to integrate the claims of these new forms of materialism within a phenomenological world, the Everyman of O'Brien's fiction undergoes a virtual "loss of reality" that is frequently coded as a form of madness in which fundamental assumptions about "the human" and its ontological status are no longer secure. Under such conditions, the truth values of twentieth-century science can only be accepted on faith, with gaps in the popular understanding of these theories being supplemented by fantasy and delusion.

O'Brien's novels therefore suggest that a twentieth-century culture that identifies itself as rational, secular, and scientific rests upon the supposedly antimodern foundations of belief, desire, and fantasy. The dream worlds of *The Third Policeman* and *The Dalkey Archive* lay bare the unconscious of this purportedly rational culture by making legible the unacknowledged desires that motivate such distinctions. The subject of Flann O'Brien's work is not, as in Mina Loy's *Insel*, the developing science of psychology but rather a psychology of science: the unarticulated fantasies and anxieties through which new accounts of matter, mind, and temporality are culturally absorbed.

O'Brien's career renews the Irish satirical tradition of Sterne, Swift, and Joyce that rewrites the novel as a counterencyclopedia – a literary form well suited for checking the ambitious projects of knowledge production, organization, and legitimation that have been the purported engines of modernity. If, as Bruno Latour has argued, "modernity" announces itself as a "work of purification" by which rational inquiry is cleansed of irrational belief, O'Brien's novels suggest that belief in the possibility of such purification is the deluded work of fools and madmen.[3] As we have seen, such resistance to ontological confusion and contamination structures the delusions of many paranoid psychotics. Their self-narratives are attempts to restore failing distinctions between the human and the inhuman, self and other, the meaningful and the meaningless even at the cost of persecution anxiety and delusions of grandeur. O'Brien's satirical project stages attempts and failures to redraw such ontological distinctions. If, as Latour argues, modernity defines itself by such "work of purification," then it may also be shown to exhibit a desperate, paranoid logic. This is the deluded conception of modernity that O'Brien's work represents and satirizes.

Paranoid delusion, hallucination, identity loss, and unreality effects recur in *The Third Policeman* and *The Dalkey Archive* as not only psychological symptoms but as cultural anxieties that had become historically urgent for a wide population. At the same time, the delirious excesses of madness are reconstructed as resources for O'Brien's idiosyncratic procedures of authorship. As Anne Clissmann suggestively puts it, "his vision, which at times appears to be darkly insane, is a way to sanity and to balance; it is what O'Brien himself called 'sane madness.'"[4] Clissmann attempts to reduce the ambiguity of this notion, suggesting that homeopathic doses of madness are for O'Brien the path to some notion of sanity. I argue that this hasty reduction passes over the uncomfortable ambiguity that O'Brien's work poses; his strategy is to thematize those moments in which the rational and the irrational become indiscernible. As in Hamlet's equivocal performance of derangement, it becomes unclear whether O'Brien's work tactically inhabits the condition of madness or whether madness finally inhabits his work.

Any inquiry into the problems of madness in the work of Flann O'Brien inevitably leads to his idiosyncratic practice of authorship. Whereas the paranoiac fashions a delusional narrative in order to restore a fragile and fragmenting self-identity, the effect of O'Brien's literary production is to destabilize and multiply his persona. Over the course of his career, O'Brien would construct a series of pseudonymous alter egos through which he could ventriloquize his literary provocations. Public identity was a peril of authorship for Brian O'Nolan, the man behind Flann O'Brien, Myles na gCopaleen, John James Doe, George Knowall, Brother Barnabas, and the other untraceable pseudonyms under which he published.⁵ The authors of *At Swim-Two-Birds*, *The Third Policeman*, *The Hard Life*, *The Dalkey Archive* (Flann O'Brien), and of *The Poor Mouth* and the *Irish Times* column "Cruiskeen Lawn" (Myles na gCopaleen) were invented characters, avatars, masks, and mouthpieces. The anonymous narrator of *The Third Policeman* articulates a strategy that is in keeping with the author's own methods, "I considered it desirable that he should know nothing about me, but it was even better if he knew several things which were quite wrong."⁶ Such dissembling provokes a desire to discover the true man behind the pseudonymous creations. However, as I will argue, O'Brien's work often suggests that this series of identities is an infinite regression that does not end with a final, authentic, private person (even "Brian O'Nolan" proves to be an Anglicized deformation of his given Irish name Brian Ó Nualláin). As O'Brien's authorship reserves no sense of authentic purity that he must maintain and defend, the threats of hybridity and contamination that provoke paranoia seem always, already defused. His protean procedures of authorship do not resist but rather promote the dislocations of self-identity that the paranoiac fears.

Explaining the Fantastic

The Third Policeman was for many years a lost treasure of late modernism that was published only after its author's death. Written shortly after O'Brien's celebrated metafiction, *At Swim-Two-Birds* (1939), the manuscript was rejected by Longmans Publishers and declared lost by its discouraged author only to be discovered by his widow and published in 1967. The novel is a modernist book of the undead in which personhood collapses within an environment of physical and metaphysical confusions. The story's unnamed narrator devotes his time to studying the work of a fictional scientist, inventor, and philosopher named "de Selby." As Ondrej Pilny and others have suggested, the savant's bizarre theories and inventions recall Alfred Jarry's impossible science of pataphysics: de Selby postulates that the world is not spherical but shaped like a sausage; he claims that one may see a younger image of oneself by arranging a series of mirrors on the principle that light travels at a finite speed; a cinematograph convinces him that movement is the result of a series of static states arranged in serial succession.[7] This scientism attracts an equally absurd community of scholars whose territorial debates over de Selby's life and work become an obsession of our narrator, who has authored a work of de Selbian scholarship.

In order to fund his book's publication, the narrator hatches a scheme with his friend John Divney to rob a wealthy neighbor named Mathers. The robbery ends in the murder of Mathers with Divney hiding the cash box in a safe place to be collected and divided between them at a later date. After a lengthy and suspicious delay, Divney finally reveals that he has hidden the box in the floor of Mathers's house. When the narrator is about to lay hold of this long-delayed reward, an ambiguous "event" occurs that launches him into a bizarre world of hallucinatory experiences and de Selbian inventions. For a time, it appears that the crackpot theories that our narrator has studied so faithfully have been born out in this uncanny environment. Principles of physics, chemistry, and psychology seem to be fundamentally altered, and yet the narrator remains surprisingly credulous, prepared as he is for such fantastic experiences by his study of de Selby's work.

However, as many of his experiences challenge the explanatory power of even de Selbian scientism, the narrator is increasingly plagued by radical epistemic doubt, and motifs of madness begin to disturb the novel. These epistemological and ontological uncertainties begin with the fateful moment of transformation as he reaches for the cash box.

> It was some change which came upon me or upon the room, indescribably subtle, yet momentous, ineffable. It was as if the daylight had changed with unnatural suddenness, as if the temperature of the evening had altered greatly in an instant or as if the air had become twice as rare or twice as dense as it had been in the winking of an eye.[8]

This "unnatural" sensation signals an experience of "unreality" of which psychotics often complain, and it is consistent with what psychologist Louis Sass identifies as a signature symptom of schizophrenia: "the truth-taking stare."[9] In this despondent state, the schizophrenic senses that some fundamental change has occurred in which his environment discloses itself in a new, terrifying, and uncanny way. This ambivalent experience is marked by a combination of wonder and radical anxiety in which the subject feels that the unspeakable "truth" of the epiphanic moment threatens to overwhelm him. In Sass's account of this schizoid state, the familiar experience of a practically organized environment recedes and is replaced by impressions of authentic revelation or the disturbing feeling of "unreality."

> Generally the person has a sense of having lost contact with things, or of everything having undergone some subtle, all-encompassing change. Reality seems to be unveiled as never before, and the visual world looks peculiar and eerie – weirdly beautiful, tantalizingly significant, or perhaps horrifying in some insidious but ineffable way.[10]

This prodromal experience often precedes the onset of hallucinations in the progression of schizophrenic symptoms. In keeping with this progression, the narrator of *The Third Policeman* often describes such a "truth-taking stare" just prior to some unaccountable experience: after the initial "unnatural" feeling, he begins to hear voices and appears to enter into a conversation with his own dissociated soul, whom he familiarly calls "Joe."

In the novel's conclusion, it is revealed that the transformative event that launched his fantastic narrative was an explosion in which the narrator was killed. In place of the hidden cash box, John Divney planted a bomb in order to eliminate his partner in crime and keep for himself the full amount contained in Mathers's cash box. The bizarre phenomena that follow that moment are ultimately revealed to be features of a strange afterworld that the deceased narrator has unknowingly entered. His recognition of his own death is disavowed or deferred until the end of the narrative when he again meets Divney, who finally admits his duplicitous scheme and joins the narrator in his delirious purgatory.

It is the deferral of this knowledge for both the narrator and his audience that launches this text onto the generic terrain of the fantastic. Tzvetan Todorov has argued that this genre is marked by not only bizarre events and delirious logics but by an epistemic hesitation between competing explanatory frameworks.[11] The narrator of *The Third Policeman* struggles to determine whether the phenomena he experiences are to be understood as natural, supernatural, or psychological in nature. By maintaining this ambiguity, the fantastic also forces its reader to adjudicate among these explanatory accounts, and it is through this comparison that the novel's satirical effect is achieved. The unsatisfactory ambiguity provokes a desire to define these phenomena as rational or irrational. It is a desire to effect the "work of purification" by which these categories and explanatory accounts may be distinguished and the disorienting experiences may be resolved. The novel's prolonged deferral of such a decision not only makes that unsatisfied desire felt, but also suggests that these explanatory possibilities are mutually imbricated in ways that defy any facile "work of purification."

The narrator's effort to determine the status of his experience is complicated by the curious influence of de Selby, whose work also conspicuously collapses distinctions between delusion and reality, science and scientism in ways that may reflect the confusions that arise at the intersections of twentieth-century science and culture. The first epigraph, presented as an excerpt from de Selby's writings, declares that hallucination is not a rare psychological symptom but rather the basis upon which fundamental distinctions between life and death are based.

> Human existence being an hallucination containing in itself the secondary hallucinations of day and night (the latter an insanitary condition of the atmosphere due to accretions of black air) it ill becomes any man of sense to be concerned at the illusory approach of the supreme hallucination known as death. – de Selby[12]

Death and life are equally hallucinatory phenomena that warrant no concern or further inquiry, in de Selby's account. The name "de Selby" may be understood as a distorted signifier for "of the self," and the theories that are attributed to him often have the effect of deforming conventional models of subjectivity. To the extent that the narrator's world appears to be shaped by "de Selbian" motifs, it renders any sense of self as similarly distorted and illusory.

A passage that closely resembles the novel's epigraph would later appear in a "Cruiskeen Lawn" column in which Myles na gCopaleen writes,

> man is merely an objective phenomenon, a private hallucination of my own, not so much my faithful subject as my priceless object, my personal anonymentity (*sic*), my household inanimity. Yet this inert and homemade ... being, albeit incapable of initiating any meritorious action, can sometimes, by sole virtue of my approval, please.[13]

Myles anticipates the logical consequences of a radical physicalism that has come to dominate neuroscience and that reduces the subject to an epiphenomenal illusion arising from material substrates. Personhood is stripped of agency, identity, and reality – reduced to hallucinated "anonymentity." This passage appeared roughly one year after the eminent physicist Erwin

Schrödinger delivered his lectures "What Is Life?" at the Dublin Institute for Advanced Studies at Trinity College, where he had been in residence for several years. Schrödinger demonstrates the ways that life might be understood as arising from laws of physics and concludes by demonstrating the contradiction between this physicalism and "the unpleasant feeling about 'declaring oneself to be a pure mechanism'. For it is deemed to contradict Free Will as is warranted by direct introspection."[14] The laws of physics cannot be integrated with the phenomenology of experience; this proves to be one of the fundamental problems that O'Brien's fiction addresses. The self-experience of subjectivity, Schrödinger concludes, is an illusion whose ontological status may be compared to that of a fictional character.

> The youth that was "I," you may come to speak of him in the third person, indeed the protagonist of the novel you are reading is probably nearer to your heart, certainly more intensely alive and better known to you. Yet there has been no intermediate break, no death. And even if a skilled hypnotist succeeded in blotting out entirely all your earlier reminiscences, you would not find that he had killed you. In no case is there a loss of personal existence to deplore. Nor will there ever be.[15]

As in the de Selby epigraph of *The Third Policeman,* the life and death of the "I" are equally illusory. Subjectivity is a fiction – a modal claim that O'Brien would underscore in his metafictional novels repeatedly. The de Selbian worlds of *The Third Policeman* and *The Dalkey Archive* may be seen as attempts to envision the uncanny consequences of Einstein's theory of relativity and Schrödinger's uncertainty principle – both of which draw epistemic limits on human observation. These theories seemed to trouble Myles deeply as he would frequently reference Schrödinger in his satirical "Cruiskeen Lawn" columns in which he described modern physics as "a department of speculation" – a description that could also be applied to the form of work that de Selby seems to conduct.[16]

Beyond modern physics, Keith Hopper has suggested that another likely source of the bizarre de Selbian doctrines is J. W. Dunne, whose cult work of parapsychology, *An Experiment with Time* (1927), O'Brien read with interest. Dunne's speculative writing presents itself as a scientific investigation into the relations between consciousness and time and attempts to explain the author's purported precognitive experiences. In Dunne's theory, the directional flow of time is an illusion – or delusion – produced by consciousness, and dreams grant access to other moments in time.

Dunne's theories gained the attention of numerous modernist writers, including James Joyce, T. S. Eliot, Aldous Huxley, and J. B. Priestley.

Versions of his claims appear within the space of *The Third Policeman* alongside oblique and overt references to contemporaneous and perhaps equally counterintuitive doctrines of psychoanalysis, subatomic physics, and relativity theory. The effect is a vertiginous world in which science and scientism are not easily distinguished even by a self-styled scholar such as the narrator, who thinks to himself, "anything can be said in this place and it will have to be believed."[17] With the figure and theories of de Selby, O'Brien only mildly exaggerates the confusion that these scientific and pseudoscientific developments presented to the lay person who was told in a variety of ways that his intuitive experience was somehow an illusion or a delusion. The novel suggests that, in such a vertiginous cultural environment, the criteria by which the rational may be distinguished from the irrational have become uncertain.

The epigraph's denial that life and death constitute distinct states of being anticipates the narrator's disavowal of his own unliving, uncanny status after the obliquely narrated explosion. Only by refusing to acknowledge this unsatisfactory truth about his ontological status is the narrator able to continue. His self-understanding is founded on this refusal, and the narrative that follows reflects his failing efforts to maintain that delusion. Like patients suffering paranoid schizophrenia, the narrator labors to confirm his own distinct being through the narrative that he tells. When he is confronted with evidence of the unbearable truth, his narrative breaks down and he once again lapses into the despondent "truth-taking stare." In the strange moment when he reaches for the cash box and finds it missing, he is confronted by this unsatisfactory truth. The "cash box," which becomes the object of his fantastic quest, is a placeholder for this impossible recognition. It is what Lacan calls the Thing – the inhuman and even monstrous kernel of the subject's nonbeing which has been disavowed and projected outward.[18] To confront this Thing is to face the fact of one's lack of self-consistency as a subject, an unacceptable truth that induces feelings of unreality, as in the moment of the "truth-taking stare." In such a confrontation, one's symbolic organization of the world – according to which one is an independent and autonomous human subject within a community of similar subjects – collapses. Psychosis is often marked by a failure to maintain this illusion. The paranoid narratives that psychotics construct function to recover some fugitive horizon of meaning and phenomenological order according to which phenomena may be experienced as significant and functional.

These are the structural characteristics of the narrator's tale in *The Third Policeman*. If the anxious, epiphanic moment that the narrator undergoes when he reaches for the cash box may be understood as precisely such a confrontation with the Thing, then the fantastic events that follow constitute a narrative whose function is to restore some sense of order and meaning in the face of otherwise inexplicable, hallucinatory phenomena. Like the paranoid delusions of many psychotics, the narrator's story adheres to a rigorous if deluded logic that often seems to parody conventional or scientific explanations.

Following this anxious confrontation with the Thing, the narrator and his environment take on an uncanny quality that intimates his unacknowledged, unliving status. The narrator recalls, "I remember that I noticed several things in a cold mechanical way"; this state of passivity, in which his thoughts, perceptions, and actions seem induced from some prior agency, signals both the deterministic materialism represented by Schrödinger and the thought insertion that defines many modern delusions.[19] His first uncanny observation is a corpselike figure gazing at him from a rocking chair in the corner of the room where he had been searching for the cash box. The narrator feels himself fixed in the intense gaze of this figure, whom he ultimately recognizes as Mathers, the man whom he murdered and robbed. More than just a look of accusation and a source of guilt for the narrator, this gaze seems to further disturb his sense of being. "The light of morning vanished from my sight, the dusty floor was like nothingness beneath me and my whole body dissolved away, leaving me existing only in the stupid spellbound gaze that went steadily from where I was to the other corner."[20] This "spellbound gaze" cannot easily be attributed to the narrator or the corpse seated opposite him but appears to be an ambiguous force that unites and identifies the two uncanny figures in their condition. Like all figures within the novel, they appear as animated automata. Searching the corpse's lifeless eyes for any sense of a responsive interiority, the narrator speculates that there is only an infinite regress of nested homunculi:

> Looking at them I got the feeling that they were not genuine eyes at all but mechanical dummies animated by electricity or the like, with a tiny pinhole in the centre of the "pupil" through which the real eye gazed out secretively and with great coldness. Such a conception, possibly with no foundation at all in fact, disturbed me agonizingly and gave rise in my mind to interminable speculations as to the colour and quality of the real eye and as to whether, indeed, it was real at all or merely another dummy with its pinhole on the same plane as the first one so that the real eye, possibly behind thousands of these absurd disguises, gazed out through a barrel of serried peep-holes.[21]

This moment constitutes the first of several instances in which personhood dissolves into a series of impossible infinite regressions – precisely the critique of the Cartesian model of the mind as an interior space that Daniel Dennett poses in order to establish a materialist framework.[22] Julian Murphet observes that "In what will become a recurrent trope, the figure of recursion introduces a conspicuous anxiety about the multiple residing inside the One – an apt illustration of the crisis of character in modernity, which we have posited in terms of an overwhelming of the singular by the multiple."[23] This "conspicuous anxiety about the multiple residing inside the One" could serve as a succinct account of many experiences of schizophrenia in which the mind is experienced as divided against itself and reduced to constituent functions and is at the same time the thesis of neurological and psychoanalytic models of the mind.

The disturbance of any psychological unity by internal division and multiplication becomes a recurrent motif throughout the novel. Elsewhere, the narrator describes himself, "thinking my own thoughts with the front part of my brain and at the same time taking pleasure with the back part in the great and widespread finery of the morning."[24] After his encounter with the uncanny figure of Mathers, the narrator hears a voice whose source is ambiguously internal and external to him.

> But who had uttered these words? They had not frightened me. They were clearly audible to me yet I knew they did not ring out across the air like the chilling cough of the old man in the chair. They came from deep inside me, from my soul. Never before had I believed or suspected that I had a soul but just then I knew I had.[25]

The narrator names this auditory hallucination "Joe." Through the strange interventions of this voice, we suspect that Joe may know more than the narrator and may harbor an agenda of his own. Confronted with this auditory hallucination and the ambiguously animated corpse's gaze, the narrator attempts to explain away these ontological and epistemological mysteries as simply the elements of a dream, but Joe insists upon their reality. He recalls killing Mathers – a memory that is incompatible with the figure before him. Unable to reduce this contradiction, he chooses the path of empirical evidence.

> I decided in some crooked way that the best thing to do was to believe what my eyes were looking at rather than to place my trust in a memory. I decided to show unconcern, to talk to the old man and to test his own reality by asking about the black box which was responsible, if anything could be, for each of us being the way we were.[26]

In trusting his vision, and in being seduced by the voice he hears, the narrator begins a journey down "a crooked way" – a path toward increasingly

uncanny experiences. He interacts with the figure of Mathers in a procedure of reality testing with the suspicion that the ontological uncertainty
that afflicts him is indeed attributable to his encounter with the black
box. The failure of such "reality testing" has long been regarded as a signal
symptom of psychosis. Confronted with these impossible conditions and
doubting his own rationality, the narrator is reduced to a form of empty
mimicry of normal behavior: "I knew that I would go mad unless I got up
from the floor and moved and talked and behaved in as ordinary a way as
possible."[27]

Speech and narration become the means by which some stability may
be maintained in the face of this delirium, but his language is never
entirely under control. "Words spilled out of me as if they were produced
by machinery."[28] He experiences himself as an informatic machine that is
unable to fully reflect upon the meaning of his own discourse. The frantic
narrative that follows might be understood as an effort to explain or even
obscure the narrator's flickering existence. He must talk himself away from
the brink of nonbeing. At the same time, the mechanical, uncontrollable
form of speech bears the trace of the inhuman condition it is meant to
conceal.

> While speaking inwardly or outwardly or thinking of what to say I felt brave
> and normal enough. But every time a silence came the horror of my situa-
> tion descended upon me like a heavy blanket flung upon my head, envelop-
> ing and smothering me and making me afraid of death.[29]

The narrator must recreate and maintain himself from discourse – akin
to a fictional character whose existence is narratively generated and to
Daniel Paul Schreber, who describes the urgent need to speak in order
to maintain his own existence. Even a nightmarish narrative is preferable
to acknowledging one's precarious ontological status. This subjective precarity is underscored by the narrator's loss of identity.

> I did not know my name, did not remember who I was. I was not certain
> where I had come from or what my business was in that room. I found I was
> sure of nothing save my search for the black box [...] I had no name.[30]

The narrator can only identify with the drive toward the Thing that set this
fantastic delirium in motion. Confrontation with it has proven to be catastrophic and yet he can do nothing but pursue it. "I began to think that
I would never be happy until I had that box again in my grip."[31] Through
a bizarre conversation with Mathers and Joe, the narrator decides to seek
out the counsel of the local policemen of this strange country who may
help him locate his missing object of desire and anxiety. If the narrator's

effort to orient himself to his surroundings entails learning the rules and laws that govern his environment, then the police station is the logical place to begin. As in psychosis, he must reconstruct the rules and laws of his baffling environment and forge some sense of identity by determining his place within this world.

Enforcing Ontology

The narrator finds it difficult to engage the policemen, who speak a strange discourse of bicycles. He learns that bicycle-related crimes plague this strange country at epidemic proportions. Stolen and misplaced bicycles constitute the vast majority of cases these policemen must investigate, and one of the sergeants finds it unbelievable that the narrator's business is not bicycle-related: "never in my puff did I hear of any man stealing anything but a bicycle when he was in his sane senses."[32] That the narrator's behavior does not comply with what is expected and reasonable in this country is made evident to him, "he thought I was in delicate mental health."[33] In order to understand the laws that govern this community, the narrator accompanies Sergeant Pluck on a search for one citizen's stolen bicycle. He is amazed when the sergeant is able to quickly find the machine in a cluster of bushes. When pressed to disclose the secret to his prodigious investigative skills, the sergeant admits that he was able to locate the bicycle because he was the one who stole it and that the rash of bicycle-related crimes is the result of such thefts on the part of the police. The narrator learns that this is not simply a case of simple police corruption; rather, the policemen are fighting a peculiar form of *ontological* corruption that plagues the community. This ontological corruption is a consequence of what Sergeant Pluck calls the "Atomic Theory": " 'It is doing untold destruction,' he continued, 'half of the people are suffering from it, it is worse than the smallpox.' "[34] Pluck blames the County Council for allowing the propagation of this dangerous theory that has corrupted the community like a disease. Belief in this new scientific theory, according to Pluck, has had the deleterious effect of transforming their sense of being. After asking the narrator if he has studied modern physics, the sergeant explains:

> Everything is composed of small particles of itself and they are flying around in concentric circles and arcs and segments and innumerable other geometrical figures too numerous to mention collectively, never standing still or resting but spinning away and darting hither and thither and back again, all the time on the go. These diminutive gentlemen are called atoms.[35]

Pluck compares these "diminutive gentlemen" to dancing leprechauns – a metaphor suggesting that modern science functions as a folk mythology with its own inscrutable mysteries, priests, and rituals. In Pluck's view, this modern mythology of science constitutes a dangerous account of the world evident in its strange effects on its believers. According to this Atomic Theory, when a person comes into contact with another object his particles are exchanged with those of the object. Over time, such prolonged exchange can lead to the hybridization of a person with whatever it has encountered.

> "The gross and net result of it is that people who spend most of their natural lives riding iron bicycles over the rocky roadsteads of this parish get their personalities mixed up with the personalities of their bicycle as a result of the interchanging of the atoms of each of them and you would be surprised at the number of people in these parts who nearly are half people and half bicycles."
> I let go a gasp of astonishment that made a sound in the air like a bad puncture.
> "And you would be flabbergasted at the number of bicycles that are half-human almost half-man, half-partaking of humanity."[36]

What these policemen appear to enforce is the ontological purity of their fellow citizens – their status as human. They are metaphysical policemen, maintaining older ontological laws and categories that are threatened by the doctrine of modern physics. The contagion of the Atomic Theory with its power to transform the world of the parishioners is marked by the narrator's mechanical expression of disbelief as he gasps like a punctured tire. The gap between experience and modern physics is evident when the narrator searches for empirical evidence of this Atomic Theory.

> The scene was real and incontrovertible and at variance with the talk of the Sergeant, but I knew that the Sergeant was talking the truth, and if it was a question of taking my choice, it was possible that I would have to forgo the reality of all the simple things my eyes were looking at.[37]

The narrator suggests that the counterintuitive world postulated by modern science must be accepted on faith even against the evidence of his senses. The narrator finds himself in a hallucinatory world where distinctions between the human and the inhuman, the animate and the inanimate, are no longer secure. As the narrator begins to experience anxiously the implications of this materialism, his sense of place in the world grows precarious: "I would like to be far away from here"; "My head was packed tight with fears and miscellaneous apprehensions."[38]

This anxiety increases when Sergeant MacCruiskeen describes the momentous discovery of the basic element of matter to which all things may be reduced. This element, called "omnium," is an infinitely versatile substance that behaves in mysterious ways.

> "You are omnium and I am omnium and so is the mangle and my boots and so is the wind in the chimney."
> "Some people," he said, "call it energy but the right name is omnium because there is far more than energy inside of it, whatever it is. Omnium is the essential inherent interior essence which is hidden inside the root kernel of everything and it is always the same."
> I nodded wisely.
> "It never changes. But it shows itself in a million ways and it always comes in waves."[39]

Julian Murphet proposes a Marxist analysis of the crucial passage, arguing that "Omnium is the spurious infinity of exchange value as such, a neutral network of market equivalences, in which everything is finally the same."[40] However, the ontological anxieties of the narrator that are rooted in his obsessions with de Selby suggest that the passage describes the monistic materialism of modern physics that, as Schrödinger observes, eliminates the "I" and prompts "the unpleasant feeling about 'declaring oneself to be a pure mechanism.'" Omnium names the same form of monism that troubled both Wyndham Lewis and Martin Heidegger, according to which all being is reducible to a single material principle. In *The Art of Being Ruled*, Wyndham Lewis writes, "There are, on the market today, patterns of belief extending from the extreme position, on the one hand, that there is in fact no traceable psyche, but only *one stuff*, out of which our mind is composed."[41] As in Lewis's *The Childermass*, we find in this nightmarish afterworld the ontological flattening of all differences into something approaching Heidegger's notion of "standing reserve." Ontological differences are reduced to a single order of being in which qualitative difference is translated into quantities of resources that may be spent.

As he drifts to sleep in the police station, the narrator feels himself lost within this monistic ontology, where differences between subject and object, human and inhuman, are reduced. Having lost his leg in an accident at an early age, he now hobbles on a wooden prosthetic. Under the influence of the policemen's extreme materialism, he fears that the lifeless leg is contaminating him, compromising his ontological integrity.

> I had a curious feeling about my left leg. I thought that it was, so to speak, spreading – that its woodenness was slowly extending throughout my whole

body, a dry timber poison killing me inch by inch. Soon my brain would be changed to wood completely and I would then be dead. Even the bed was made of wood, not metal. If I were to lie in it – [42]

His great fear is that his mental processes will soon be compromised by this prosthetic, and he feels himself taking on its wooden features. Unable to convince himself of his ontological distinction, he merges with his bed.

Robbing me of the reassurance of my eyesight, it was disintegrating my bodily personality into a flux of colour, smell, recollection, desire – all the strange uncounted essences of terrestrial and spiritual existence. I was deprived of definition, position and magnitude and my significance was considerably diminished.[43]

The narrator describes the loss of form and unity that Mrs. Jones suffers in Loy's *Insel*. He feels himself merging with his environment as his own qualities drift apart in confusion. When the narrator wakes to learn that this horrific experience was only a nightmare, he hears the voice of Joe articulating his relief, "*Thank goodness to be back to sanity.*"[44] This assertion of rational order is belied by its source – an internal, hallucinated voice that the narrator hears throughout his journey that appears to have an agenda of its own.

Fears of contamination by a noxious alien substance are defining symptoms of paranoia. The condition is marked by the desperate need to draw and redraw the boundary between self and other through the work of narration. The interpretative procedures of paranoia are defenses against any encroaching outside force. Through these feelings of persecution, the paranoiac is able to achieve a sense of identity – a feeling of distinction and a unique sense of being. Following Lacan, Leo Bersani has argued that paranoid thought processes are not restricted to the pathological conditions of psychosis but constitute the foundation of all personal identity.

We must therefore begin to suspect the paranoid structure itself as a device by which consciousness maintains the polarity of self and nonself, thus preserving the concept of identity. In paranoia, two Real Texts confront one another: subjective being and a world of monolithic otherness. This opposition can be broken down only if we renounce the comforting (if also dangerous) faith in locatable identities.[45]

In both his fiction and his pseudonymous practices of authorship, O'Brien's project is to satirically stage the paranoid logic that grounds identity and to suggest alternative ways of being in the world that are not founded on the conditions of aggression and persecution.

This paranoid logic is not restricted to physical or metaphysical forms of identity. In Sergeant Pluck's view, his losing battle against the hybridization of his citizens and their bicycles has not only dire ontological consequences but political ones as well. He tells the narrator, "Many a grey hair it has put into my head, trying to regulate the people of this parish. If you let it go too far it would be the end of everything. You would have bicycles wanting votes and they would get seats on the County Council."[46] The sergeant's fantastic anxiety over people and bicycles uncontrollably mixing synthesizes and coordinates several concerns that share the same structure and logic of paranoia. The narrator's nightmare exhibits the fear of being *physically* contaminated and losing all personal individuation within a materialist monism. However, Sergeant Pluck's language suggests that this fear functions as a metaphorical vehicle for the transgression of gender and political categories. Through Pluck's reactionary complaint, the novel only slightly exaggerates and satirizes concerns over the transformation of gender roles that occurred with the rise of the New Woman and universal suffrage. Several historians and literary scholars have argued that the great "bicycle craze" at the turn of the twentieth century was intimately connected with the New Woman movement and with women's suffrage in England, Ireland, and America. As the bicycle became a popular new form of transportation, concerns over its effects on women were articulated in acerbic newspaper cartoons and satirical pieces. Patricia Marks has written that women on bicycles were for a time perceived as not only improper (concerns over the sexual stimulation caused by the bicycle seat were common) but also exceedingly masculine: female riders often wore "bloomers," gained greater independence and a wider social sphere, and even developed basic mechanical skills – all of which had been closely guarded privileges of men.[47] In the view of many, the technology contributed to a shift in gender constructions that was closely followed by a transformation of the voting population. Sergeant Pluck's fantastic concern over the political effects of the bicycle therefore has some historical precedent in the women's movement through which gender distinctions began to erode. Paranoid anxieties of contamination and category confusion therefore manifest not simply at the level of the individual subject's body and mind; as in Pluck's reactionary politics, it also guards against perceived threats to the stability and purity of the civic body.

The animated bicycle also encodes anxieties over sexual impulses that are disavowed and displaced onto other agents. Pluck tells a story of a bicycle that engaged in illicit acts, the responsibility for which could not easily be assigned.

Whatever way Gilhaney's bicycle managed it, it left itself leaning at a place where the young teacher would rush out to go away somewhere on her bicycle in a hurry. Her bicycle was gone but here was Gilhaney's leaning there conveniently and trying to look very small and comfortable and attractive. Need I inform you what the result was or what happened?

Indeed he need not, Joe said urgently. *I have never heard of anything so shameless and abandoned. Of course the teacher was blameless, she did not take pleasure and did not know.*[48]

The narrative satirically suggests that this paranoid work of purification is a fool's errand that can never be achieved. The intolerable truth that Sergeant Pluck cannot admit is that states of hybridity and "contamination" always already afflict the citizenry that he would protect. The bicycle, which has duped the school teacher, is only animated by the substance and personality of the local citizen, Gilhaney. The dangerous "other" that posed the contaminating threat from the outside is therefore internal to the community itself. In spite of Pluck's characterization, the animated bicycle embodies not a noxious, foreign element but rather a disavowed and socially unacceptable drive that is at the core of the community and its citizens. It is the unacceptable, inhuman Thing that must be negated and projected outward as a foreign threat. Because the source of this contaminating foreign substance is internal to the community, the work of purification with which Sergeant Pluck is charged can never be complete.

This paranoid logic of purification and projection is most evident in the narrator's nightmare. After he feels himself merging with his prosthetic leg and with the bed on which he rests, he is plagued by the sense that "Joe," the voice that has accompanied him on his journey, is at once an intimate friend and an alien, threatening creature. The voice has been a source of comfort to him during the confusion of his journey, and he now experiences it as an embodied substance lying beside him. In a moment of homosexual panic, this intimacy is transformed into revulsion and persecution as the narrator is unable to acknowledge this object of desire.[49]

His voice was near me, yet did not seem to come from the accustomed place within. I thought that he must be lying beside me in the bed and I kept my hands carefully at my sides in case I should accidentally touch him. I felt, for no reason, that his diminutive body would be horrible to the human touch – scaly or slimy like an eel or with a repelling roughness like a cat's tongue.[50]

The part-object of the intimate, male voice has been transformed into an abject source of disgust that terrorizes the narrator. The narrator had initially interpreted it as the voice of his soul – the thing that constitutes the core of his being. While the narrator's prosthetic wooden leg threatened him with a foreign contamination, the repellant characterization of Joe suggests that the narrator is always already "contaminated" from within. Slavoj Žižek's elucidation of this paradoxical state of self-contamination in terms of the Lacanian Thing recalls Freud's analysis of Schreberian projection:

> In monsters, the subject encounters the Thing which is his impossible equivalent – *the monster is the subject himself, conceived as Thing* ... what we have here is not the relationship of two entities but rather the two sides, the two "slopes," of one and the same entity.[51]

The Thing, for Žižek, stands in for the independent and indefatigable operation of the unconscious drive that refuses to be subordinated to conscious control but instead serves its own obscure agenda. To acknowledge this extimate relation is to recognize one's irreducible hybridity and incoherence – a recognition that catastrophically threatens one's sense of self-identity. Žižek compares this radical subjective destitution to a state of psychosis in which one is unable to locate one's place within the world. *The Third Policeman* is precisely such a confrontation with this ontological confusion. With each fantastic sequence, the novel stages the paranoid work of purification by which identity would be maintained, and with each failure of that work it suggests that such an impossible demand for self-identity may finally be the problem. This will be the subject of O'Brien's last novel, *The Dalkey Archive*, in which the perils that must be avoided are not threats to one's identity but rather the snares of identity itself.

Making a Mess of Identity

The *deus absconditus* of *The Third Policeman* – the eccentric De Selby – finally appears in *The Dalkey Archive*. O'Brien's last novel has often been regarded as a messy, unsuccessful reprise of his earlier manuscript in which O'Brien recycles his most memorably bizarre inventions. The epigraph to *The Third Policeman* that announces the hallucinatory quality of that world could equally describe the disorienting space of *The Dalkey Archive*: James Joyce is secretly still alive, now tending bar in a small town outside of Dublin and aspiring to become a Jesuit priest; St. Augustine appears and offers a critique of Cartesian metaphysics; and a plot to destroy all life on earth is narrowly averted. It would appear that such an absurdist novel refuses our desire for any tidy suture of these disparate threads. Yet, as in a dream or a delusion, a series of strangely interlocking motifs suggest a rigorous if hidden logic that organizes the constellation of fantastic tangents.

As the novel opens, two friends – Mick and Hackett – stumble upon De Selby during a stroll down Vico Road near Dalkey. The elderly gentleman is slightly injured and the two lads help him back to his secluded home. This chance encounter launches a fantasy that, like *The Third Policeman*, anarchically mixes physics, theology, psychology, and metaphysics. At De Selby's home, Mick and Hackett learn that he is an eccentric polymath who claims to have discovered an explosive substance capable of destroying all oxygen on earth. De Selby's intention is to distribute this substance, "DMP," throughout the world and to detonate it in order to destroy all life. In De Selby's view, the world is morally fallen beyond repair, and the destruction of all life is the only ethical course of action that remains. Knowledge of De Selby's diabolical plot weighs heavily upon Mick, and it becomes his self-assigned duty to avert global extermination by stealing De Selby's supply of DMP.

If the parallels between DMP and atomic physics were not already apparent, the savant explains that his research into the structure of matter has also revealed some surprising truths about the nature of time. De Selby explains that "a deoxygenated atmosphere cancels the apparently serial nature of time and confronts us with true time and simultaneously with all the things and creatures which time has ever contained or will contain, provided we evoke them."[52] DMP allows De Selby to create windows into eternity in which he may encounter historical figures from the distant past, engaging in learned conversations with the great figures of history. During one such conversation, De Selby engages in a debate with Augustine over his place in the history of philosophy and over the limitations of Cartesian metaphysics.

While developing a plan to steal De Selby's supply of DMP, Mick learns of a rumor that his literary idol, James Joyce, staged his death and is living under a pseudonym in the small town of Skerries near Dublin. Mick believes that only a genius such as Joyce may be able to reason with De Selby, and he seeks out the recluse but is disappointed to find that the celebrated author has been reduced to an elderly bartender who has no memory of writing the majority of his work and that his only wish is to enter a Jesuit monastery. The reserved and suspicious Joyce disapproves of *Ulysses*, which he believes to be an immoral book written by a group of hacks and fraudulently published by Sylvia Beach under his name. The shame of this publication has forced him to assume a false identity and to retreat from the public eye. Mick finally satisfies Joyce's last wish by arranging a meeting between Joyce and a local Jesuit priest, which ends in disappointment and paralysis for Joyce. Meanwhile, Mick successfully steals the noxious DMP only to learn that De Selby has decided to abandon his apocalyptic plan, never to be seen again. The novel's hasty, melodramatic conclusion leaves the various narrative threads untied – a disappointing conclusion to the novel that is perhaps evidence of Flann O'Brien's failing health and exhausted literary powers.[53]

It is perhaps fitting that O'Brien's final novel invokes the figure of James Joyce in its inquiry into the limits and pathological perils of identity. Flann O'Brien shared with Beckett the task of finding a way to write in the wake of Joyce's encyclopedic books of the world that announced for many the culmination of the novel's intellectual ambitions. In the end, O'Brien's solution would be to satirically thematize that tendency for world building that made Joyce the *deus absconditus* of his works. It is this godlike megalomania that O'Brien's texts deflate with their recurring figures of mad scientists and delusional narrators whose fundamental desire is to mark for themselves a sense of ontological distinction through the world that they have projected. In *The Dalkey Archive*, the mad figure of De Selby is explicitly compared to Joyce – the author who constructed the books of day and night and who must now bear the burden of that responsibility. Mick wonders, "how would two exquisitely cultivated but distracted minds behave on impact with each other?"[54]

Like *The Third Policeman*, *The Dalkey Archive* often gestures toward the rigorous formal structures and geometric planning of *Ulysses* and *Finnegans Wake* only to leave the desire for such order unsatisfied. In this, O'Brien's final novel, a specter of madness haunts this desire to project such crystalline narrative order as that desire takes the darker forms of conspiracy theory and megalomaniacal delusions of grandeur. If Joyce fictionalized his life and world, the same could be said of Augustine, whose *Confessions* could be understood as a heretical act of self-authorship. Sean Pryor argues that such fictional world- and self-creations in which authors engage recur in O'Brien's work as godlike acts. "Augustine's real sin turns out not to be lust or heresy, but making, narrating"; "authorship would then mean falsity, the self-serving pretense of virtue and the vice of self-deluding fiction."[55] If Augustine's or Joyce's acts of world creation are cast as both godlike and delusional, then so must O'Brien's own fictional worlds be understood, and his first novel, *At Swim-Two-Birds*, signals this concern and metafictionally deflates it by telling the story of an author whose characters gain autonomy and revolt against him when he sleeps. "It was undemocratic to compel characters to be uniformly good or bad or poor or rich. Each should be allowed a private life, self-determination and a decent standard of living."[56]

The delusion of godlike autonomy is also raised in Schrödinger's lectures in which he pits the naïve intuition of free will against the determinism of the physical world. To insist upon one's autonomy, he argues, is to declare that "I – I in the widest meaning of the word, that is to say, every conscious mind that has ever said or felt 'I' – am the person, if any, who controls the 'motion of the atoms' according to the Laws of Nature." But this would entail that one has become god-like, and " 'Hence I am God Almighty' sounds both blasphemous and lunatic."[57] We have seen that in *The Third Policeman* O'Brien represents the dissolution of subjectivity within a material monism, or, in Schrödinger's words, the "unpleasant feeling about 'declaring oneself to be a pure mechanism.' " O'Brien's work also pursues the alternative delusion of godlike megalomania that accompanies the creation of worlds and selves through authorship – a delusion that becomes associated with the literary acts of Augustine and Joyce.

O'Brien is hardly the first or the last to suggest that a certain madness inheres in the Joycean text and family. Carl Jung famously diagnosed Joyce's daughter, Lucia, as a schizophrenic, and he determined that James Joyce showed the potential for a similar mental disorder but that he was able to manage his delirium through his experimental writing.[58] Many years later, Jacques Lacan devoted a seminar to Joyce's work in which he also found the potential for psychosis.[59] For Lacan, it was Joyce's ego as constructed and maintained through his acts of authorship that maintained his psychic order in a way that eludes most psychotics. Jean-Michel Rabaté similarly argues that Joyce's late writing was imagined as a solution to the thought disorder that may have plagued his daughter.[60]

The Dalkey Archive offers its own account of Joycean madness. The novel's protagonist, Mick, dismisses Joyce's insistence that the novels published in his name were the result of a collaboration among several charlatans who unethically hijacked his reputation.

> Yet the same Joyce must have been somehow connected with the writing of *Ulysses* and *Finnegans Wake*, certainly far more than the probably hallucinatory attributions of authorship by Sylvia Beach. There was a possibility that both books were the monumental labors of several uniquely gifted minds, but a central, unifying mind seemed inescapable.[61]

The theological need to posit some governing consciousness behind the world of the novels prompts Mick to reject Joyce's claim. Mick is gripped by a religious insistence upon a godlike figure whose plan is undeniably present in the text. Mick's attribution of literary divinity to Joyce seems to confirm Joyce's complaint that his identity has been taken over and reconstructed by others – whether those others are the fraudulent authors of his works or the audience that insists upon his genius. Mick ultimately speculates that it is the burden of this public identity as genius that has driven Joyce mad. The man has been crushed by the burden of an impossible public identity that he could never uphold. "It was not the false imputation of authorship which drove Joyce askew, but rather the lonely exertion of keeping pace with a contrived reputation was what finally put the delicate poise of his head out of balance."[62] Contrary to Lacan's analysis, the ego of the author is represented as the cause of his madness rather than its solution. Whether this sense of distinction is forced upon Joyce or is the product of his world-building writing, *The Dalkey Archive* suggests that this megalomania is the peril of authorship – a critique that may account for O'Brien's own pseudonymous practices.

The fictional Joyce is neither the only instance of such megalomania nor is he the only character who appears to have gone "queer in the head."[63] Between De Selby, who plans to annihilate all life on earth, and Mick, whose self-appointed task is to save mankind, megalomania becomes a contagion that spreads throughout the novel, with each character attempting to rewrite the narrative in which he is a character. Pryor similarly argues that "Mick sins against the truth that his motives are compromised and, more fundamentally, against the truth that he is not his own maker."[64] These competing megalomaniacal plots arrogate to their narrators the same ontological distinction that paranoia would grant, and as Freud writes, "most cases of paranoia display an element of megalomania and megalomania can itself constitute a paranoia."[65] Schreber's delusion was organized around the notion that he had been chosen by God as a mate through whom the world would be repopulated after an apocalyptic end to all life. De Selby believes that his discovery of the dangerous DMP substance can only be explained as the will of divine providence, making him the savior of a fallen world. "The Almighty had led De Selby to the DMP substance so that the Supreme Truth could be protected finally and irrevocably from all the Churches of today."[66] The content of this Supreme Truth remains obscure to all but de Selby, but the megalomaniacal structure of his delusion is fully apparent.

Hearing De Selby's delusional proclamations, Mick grows uneasy, "his mind felt sickeningly clouded by the modest claim of De Selby – for it was nothing less – that he was in fact a new Messiah."[67] In this messianic delusion through which De Selby understands his own role as "author" of the miraculous substance, a Catholic conspiracy is imagined which has made De Selby's apocalyptic intervention necessary. This symmetrical, paranoid logic appears to be borne out when Mick arranges for a Jesuit priest to meet with De Selby in the hopes that the church will interrupt the mad scientist's plot. "I thought there might be some parallel between the propagation of the faith and the worldwide dissemination of this substance."[68] The two share the homologous, global ambitions to remake the world, and the priest unwittingly assists De Selby. When the church fails to stop De Selby, it falls on Mick to thwart his insidious plot – a responsibility that he assumes with initial trepidation followed by his own growing sense of messianic, world-historical importance.

Even as he recognizes the "neuropsychotic aberrations" in De Selby's plot, the same delusional patterns are reflected in Mick's personal narrative.[69] His thoughts become disorganized as he confronts his responsibility for the fate of the world. "They made his head feel like a hive full of bees and he had to remind himself that his own reason must be kept on tight rein."[70] The chaotic, amorphous "swarm" of Mick's interiority indicates a weakened coherence, or what Julian Murphet describes as an "anxiety about the multiple residing inside the One."[71] In his effort to reconstitute himself, Mick crystallizes a totalizing, megalomaniacal delusion that mirrors the structure of De Selby's plot: "But his present situation was that he was on the point of rescuing everybody from obliteration, somewhat as it was claimed that Jesus had redeemed all mankind. Was he not himself a god-figure of some sort?"[72] "He thought a bit about his growing, if secret, importance in the world as he walked, his quiet command of the issues in a confrontation that was quite fabulous."[73] A feeling of order has been gained, but it has been underwritten by a megalomaniacal delusion that reflects that of De Selby. When Mick enlists his friend in his own plot to steal the dangerous DMP from De Selby, Hackett recognizes Mick's mimetic repetition of the scientist's delusion, "The position seems to be, he said, that De Selby can destroy the world with it. Your proposition is that De Selby's power should be transferred to yourself."[74] This is the oppositional structure of paranoid knowledge by which one monadic ego reflects and negates another. *The Dalkey Archive* is constituted by such a hall of mirrors in which the same pattern of megalomaniacal ambition and messianic delusion is repeated and inverted from character to character.

In these repetitions and inversions, megalomania rapidly transforms into its opposite. Mick's messianic delusion erratically empties out into a sense of diminished importance as he asks, "Was he losing sight of the increase and significance of his own personal majesty?"[75] Later, he feels that his hypertrophic ego is under duress and that he has been used by some unknown force. "He was conscious of a pervasive ambiguity: sometimes he seemed to be dictating events with deific authority, at other times he saw himself the plaything of implacable forces."[76] This vacillation between a feeling of omnipotence and the sense that one has been instrumentalized reflects the psychic terrain of O'Brien's entire oeuvre as well as that of psychosis.

In the novel's rapid conclusion, we learn that the savant has given up his plot and has disappeared: "he now admits that he had been under a bad influence, pretty well subject to an exterior power. But by a miracle – or a series of them – his mind was cleared."[77] It is tempting to read the hasty resolution via this deus ex machina to the apocalyptic crisis as an embarrassing defect of the narrative. However, it should be clear that this satirically abrupt and "miraculous" resolution is the only end that might satisfy the paranoid desire for order and self-distinction. O'Brien's absurdly abrupt conclusion may also be read as O'Brien's satire of his audience's demand for narrative closure, in effect retraining his readers to abandon such an impossible and absurd literary desire whose kinship with totalizing, paranoid plot construction he has made apparent.

If the novel's internal plots appear to be motivated by a desire for order and a central location for the character within that order, then the mimetic repetition of De Selby's megalomaniacal plot does not end with Mick's messianic delusion but extends to the character of James Joyce. Mick suspects that a certain pathological kinship unites De Selby and Joyce, and he fantasizes about bringing the two into dialogue across the two cultures of science and literature. However, while Mick suspects that Joyce's mental infirmity is caused by his godlike status as author, Joyce's understanding of his own significance seems to have little to do with the famous novels that carry his name. He explains to Mick that his mission, like De Selby's, is to combat the Jesuits' propagation of theological falsehood. Joyce fancies himself a private theologian whose work will correct this doctrinal error and restore a fundamental truth to church's teaching. In keeping with so many of the delusional psychotics who populate O'Brien's novels, Joyce's dispute is over the status of the human.

Mick learns of Joyce's position on this matter when he describes a local policeman's "Mollycule Theory" – a reprisal of the Atomic Theory that causes so much anxiety in O'Brien's earlier novel. As in the world of *The Third Policeman*, the local inhabitants interpret the radical materialism of modern physics as a threat to the ontological distinction of the human. Learning of this new theory, Joyce responds, "I never had any love for those machines."[78] Still, the aspiring theologian recognizes in this anxiety similarities to his own project, and he goes on to suggest that his inquiries similarly attempt to resolve the precarious place of the human. His claim is that the notion of the Holy Spirit was a spurious invention of the Catholic Church that threatens to disrupt the delicate theological order and humanity's place within it.

> There we have a choice. Psychical research or cycle research. I prefer the psychical. Ah, indeed ... my own little troubles are more complicated than the sergeant's. I have to get into the Jesuits, you might say, to clear the Holy Ghost out of the Godhead and out of the Catholic Church.[79]

He traces this problem to the theological doctrine of the Holy Trinity. In his view, the doctrine of the trinity, including the Holy Spirit, is the result of an error of translation perpetrated by the church fathers. Through this error, the creative power of God was substantialized and interpreted as a person.

> The Holy Spirit was the invention of the more reckless of the early Fathers. We have here a confusion of thought and language. Those poor ignorant men associated *pneuma* with what they called the working of the Holy Spirit, whereas it is merely an exudation of God the Father. It is an activity of the existing God, and it is a woeful and shameful error of identity to identify in it a hypostatic Third Person. Abominable nonsense![80]

The effect of the church's interpretive error is the construction of a person that, in Joyce's view, does not exist. This fallacy reflects the "error of identity" that he has suffered as the purported author of *Ulysses* and *Finnegans Wake*. He intends to disabuse the world of this notion of identity that has caused so much trouble for himself and, as we have seen, for characters such as De Selby, Mick, and the narrator of *The Third Policeman* who have succumbed to the delusional traps of identity. Through the figure of James Joyce, Flann O'Brien not only finds a way into the pathological problems of identity; he also imagines an alternative way of being in the world through the fictionalization of his master. If the megalomaniacal hazards of authorship are projected onto Joyce, the fictionalized Joyce also articulates the "error of identity" that *The Dalkey Archive* appears to critique.

This fictionalization of Joyce reflects the idiosyncratic practices of authorship of Brian O'Nolan, who refused to identify with the authors of his books. "Flann O'Brien" and "Myles na Gopaleen" named creative events rather than consistent and stable persons. The implications of this difference are made clear in *The Third Policeman* and *The Dalkey Archive,* where the delusions and fears that ground self-identity are made actual.

In his satirical representation of anxieties provoked by the misunderstood theories of modern physics, the transformation of gender roles, and disavowed homosexual desires, O'Brien uncovers the same paranoid need to locate one's place in the face of disorienting transformations. Each of these is experienced as a threat of contamination that dislocates the precarious and deluded sense of order by which the human and the inhuman, self and other, and the living and the dead may be distinguished. His fantastic worlds stage the inevitable breakdowns of these distinctions along with the failed, paranoid narratives by which they are desperately drawn and redrawn. O'Brien's novels abandon the work of purification that underwrites identity in favor of a self-conscious practice of "sane madness."

CHAPTER 5

"Prey to Communications"
Voice Hearing, Thought Transmission, and Samuel Beckett

After the death of his father in 1933, Samuel Beckett suffered a severe nervous breakdown and sought psychiatric treatment at the Tavistock Clinic in London with the psychotherapist in training, Wilfred Bion.[1] Through his friend Geoffrey Thompson, he gained access to the Bethlem Royal Hospital, where he could observe and interact with psychiatric patients and their caretakers.[2] A year earlier, Beckett's friendship with James Joyce famously suffered a break after he ended his romantic relationship with Joyce's daughter Lucia, whose psychological instability led her into brief treatment with Carl Jung and a diagnosis of schizophrenia. In addition to these encounters, and as a supplement to his own treatment, Beckett began a period of research into psychology and psychoanalysis that lasted several years and produced over twenty thousand words of typewritten notes.[3]

These experiences contributed to a durable fascination with mental illness that would shape Beckett's work formally and conceptually for several decades. That psychological disorders loom large in Beckett's early fiction has been observed by some readers as have the diminishing psychological references in his later, antiencyclopedic writing.[4] A common critical tendency has been to identify Beckett's work after *Watt* as a movement away from psychological problematics toward philosophical critiques of Cartesian metaphysics and epistemology that anticipate poststructuralist logics. While this approach has gone far in articulating tropes of linguistic instability that clearly structure his work, it often ignores evidence of Beckett's persistent engagements with mental illness and renders a degree of abstraction that overlooks the specificity of the symptoms and the unique phenomenological conditions that distinguish particular psychological disorders and disabilities such as schizophrenia. Recent critical turns toward problems of disability and literary culture's engagements with the mind sciences prompt a reassessment of these concerns in the trajectory of Beckett's work and across modernism more broadly. Critics such as

Ulrika Maude, Laura Salisbury, Peter Fifield, and Lois Oppenheimer have made compelling cases for reading Beckett's work in light of neurological disorders such as aphasia, Tourette's Syndrome, and Cotard Syndrome.[5]

In the service of this critical reassessment, I demonstrate the ways that Beckett conducted a protracted and formally experimental inquiry into the conditions of mental illness that shaped his early fiction and launched his later experiments with electronic media in ways that have not been fully recognized. Beckett's representations of psychic deterioration and cognitive disorder often manifest as uncanny mechanizations of the body and mind. Such forms of experience elude conventional narrative orientation but could be effectively transferred and transmitted to his audience via the unique formal resources of electronic media such as radio – a medium heavily entangled in modernist experiences of radical mental illness.

A trajectory can be traced through Beckett's career by following his persistent returns to the discursive and ontological problems posed by severe mental illnesses and the ways in which successive discursive techniques are tested by those psychological conditions. Such an account offers one rationale for his reduction and abandonment of the novel in favor of other media. While much has been made of Beckett's turn toward the stage following the formal impasse reached with *Texts For Nothing* (1952) and *The Unnamable* (1953), I will suggest that it is through his experimentation with electronic media such as radio that he found a way forward in his career-long exploration of cognitive disability and mental illness. In radio dramas such as *Embers* (1959) and *Rough For Radio I* (1961/1973), Beckett found the resources not only to represent but to make manifest for his audience the phenomenological structures of mental illness that had eluded his formal experiments with the novel. Through these innovative radio dramas, one experiences directly the erratic voices and thought transmissions that torment his characters, thereby circumventing the mediation of textuality that had restricted his earlier, novelistic investigations of psychosis. Further, these works make audible a phenomenological convergence between the technicity of radio and the symptoms of "thought transmission" and auditory hallucination suffered by psychotics – a convergence that puts pressure on Karl Jaspers's famous claim that the experiences of psychosis are fundamentally "un-understandable."[6] The ethical stakes of such a claim are high as it entails a limit on the reach of empathy, and it has effectively delimited those experiences that fall within the category of the "human." Disability theorist Margaret Price writes:

> The problem of naming has always preoccupied DS [disability studies] scholars, but acquires a particular urgency when considered in the context of disabilities of the mind, for often the very terms used to name persons with mental disabilities have explicitly *foreclosed our status as persons*.[7]

Beginning with *Murphy*, Beckett's work broaches these limits in order to simulate and perhaps make understandable what had been clinically defined as beyond the reach of human understanding and empathy.

In the work of the Surrealists, Beckett found an early model for the discursive simulation of madness that, I suggest, constitutes a significant, organizing thread within his oeuvre. In 1932, prior to his nervous breakdown, therapy, and research into psychoanalysis and psychology, Beckett translated several short texts by André Breton and Paul Eluard, including "Simulation of Mental Debility Essayed," "Simulation of General Paralysis Essayed," and "Simulation of the Delirium of Interpretation Essayed."[8] As their titles suggest, these short pieces attempt to reproduce the linguistic effects of a range of cognitive disabilities and mental illnesses, including paranoia and schizophrenia. James Knowlson observes that while Beckett had an ambivalent relationship with the Surrealists, his work was in many ways highly compatible with their program.[9] Daniel Albright is more forceful, arguing that "Beckett's early translations of the Surrealists were [...] as important to his artistic development as his critical studies of Proust and Joyce were."[10] While Beckett would develop his own techniques, I suggest that his engagement with the Surrealists' literary simulations of mental illness helped him to develop a project that would unfold for several decades.

In *Murphy* (1938), Beckett's inquiries into madness are perhaps so explicit as to make commentary unnecessary: the titular character is diagnosed as a "schizoidal spasmophile" and finds employment at an asylum where he attempts to befriend and even emulate a schizophrenic patient.[11] Before considering the formal transformations of his later works for radio, I will underscore the ways that Beckett's research into the psychiatric and psychological discourses of the 1920s and 1930s shaped this early novel and, of particular importance for his subsequent works for electronic media, the ways that modern mental illness is consistently rendered by doctors and patients as the mechanization of the body and mind.[12]

The Figures and Grounds of Madness

Composed prior to Beckett's antiencyclopedic turn, *Murphy* operates in the Joycean mode of conspicuous erudition and showcases the research that he had conducted into the histories of psychology, psychoanalysis, and philosophy. J. D. O'Hara has called the novel a "psychological love story" in which the title character discovers that he is a rival with his lover Celia for his own love – a dynamic that was most likely inspired by Freud's essay "On Narcissism."[13] In a similar vein, Phil Baker has persuasively established the "mythology of psychoanalysis" as fundamental to the architecture of the novel.[14] There is much that supports these lasting interpretations: Murphy's narcissism is introduced early when he rocks himself to a state of withdrawal from the outside world into a condition "where he could love himself," and Wylie theorizes that one's "quantum of wantum cannot vary."[15] It follows from this pithy summary of Freudian libido theory that the investment of desire in one object entails its withdrawal from another. O'Hara therefore argues that the ambivalent pattern of approach and withdrawal between Murphy and Celia can be reduced to the tension between Murphy's narcissism and object libido.

This synthesis of Freudian depth psychology with the classic love triangle narrative is a compelling structural explication of *Murphy*'s otherwise eccentric form, but it only accounts for the opening problematic that sets the novel in motion, and there may be a remainder of narrative energy that it fails to address. The Freudian essay is only one among many psychological sources that Beckett drew upon for the architecture of the novel, and it is hardly the only discourse that plays such a role. Just as frequently, the text invokes the "figure-ground" distinction of Gestalt psychology that Beckett discovered in texts such as Robert Woodworth's *Contemporary Schools of Psychology*.[16] The distinction was proposed by the Gestalt school as a way to account for the rapid pace of early psychological development and phenomenological orientation. Founders of Gestalt psychology such as Kurt Koffka argue that the infant's capacity to recognize the form of a parent's face against the chaotic field of sense data is a foundational moment for all subsequent interaction with the world and is a necessary condition for proper subject formation.[17] Neary, Murphy's therapist and guru, generalizes the Gestaltist position when he declares that "all life is figure and ground."[18] In this basic opposition, the novel condenses a series of fundamental distinctions between self and world, mind and body, objects of desire and the absence of desire, and stages the consequences of their radical failures.

This fascination with the possible failure or regression of subject formation brings Beckett to the phenomenology of psychosis. In 1936, Beckett attended a lecture by Carl Jung at the Tavistock Institute, where he heard the story of a psychotic girl who, in Jung's words, "had never been born entirely."[19] References to this experience recur in Beckett's work, most explicitly in the radio drama *All That Fall* (1957). Translating this case into the language of Gestalt psychology, Beckett may have found in the experience of this psychotic girl a model for the failure of the figure/ground distinction and its phenomenological consequences.

In *Murphy*, Neary diagnoses Murphy as a "schizoidal spasmophile."[20] The nosological category, "schizoid," was written about extensively by the British object relations analyst Harry Guntrip, a contemporary of Wilfred Bion who identified the condition with symptoms of narcissism, regression, and depersonalization.[21] While exhibiting many of the same features as schizophrenia, the condition was classified as less severe and more responsive to treatment. By regression, Guntrip indicates an impulse to return to the womb, the original ground from which the figure of the subject could be said to emerge. Such a condition, coupled with the uncontrollable behavior implied by the term "spasmophile," suggests that Murphy is often reduced to the kind of presubjective automatisms that afflict the narrators of Beckett's later novels. Elsewhere, Neary formulates Murphy's condition in Cartesian terms – "I should say your conarium has shrunk to nothing" – a reference to the mythic point of interaction between mind and body.[22] Its disappearance implies that Murphy's mental and physical aspects have lost their coordination. Hugh Kenner famously suggests that the Beckettian motif of a rider who awkwardly pedals a bicycle hypostatizes a Cartesian mind dysfunctionally joined up to the machinery of the Cartesian body.[23] C. J. Ackerley points to the work of the Flemish post-Cartesian philosopher Arnold Geulincx (1624–1669), another early source for Beckett, who writes, "I am therefore merely the spectator of this machine. In it I produce nothing, nor reproduce nothing; nor do I construct here, nor deconstruct; all that is the work of someone else."[24] These lines may be read as an articulation of the relation of the mind toward the physical world, subject to its mechanistic causal chains and merely a product and unreliable observer of their results. However, it may also be understood as an anticipation of later theories of the unconscious, in which the "someone else" that performs the work of production, reproduction, construction, and deconstruction is the unconscious subject that works autonomously and independently of consciousness. It is this tendency toward rapid syntheses of multiple psychological and philosophical discourses that is exhibited throughout *Murphy*. Much of what follows in the novel can be understood as a series of imperfect solutions to Murphy's painful, epiphenomenal experience of his own dysfunctional, unconscious machinery.

Rather than seeking to reestablish some functional dualism or conscious, executive control, Murphy pushes further the loss of his own subjective figure within the undifferentiated ground of acephalous, mechanistic automatism. This is most evident when he returns to his only reliable source of fugitive enjoyment: his infamous rocking chair. Tied to the chair, Murphy regresses to a fantasized, infantile stage prior to the fundamental division between self and world or figure and ground. Murphy and the chair are described as an "entire machine" that is eventually overturned in a moment of malfunction.[25] This malfunction is itself mechanical: Murphy's symptomatic heart irregularity causes him to flail his limbs desperately, overturning the apparatus and leaving him in a bloody heap, where his lover Celia finds him. This bloody state suggests that a mock birthing process has occurred that resembles Marinetti's famous account in the "Futurist Manifesto" of his own technological rebirth through an auto accident: despite his best efforts to achieve full regression, Murphy has been ejected into distinct being once again. As Celia cradles his head and wipes away the blood, he experiences the foundational distinction of figure and ground in which the maternal face comes into focus: "The beloved features emerging from chaos were the face against the big blooming buzzing confusion of which Neary had spoken so highly."[26] As Murphy emerges from his self-induced fetal state, the recognition of the other is accompanied by the distinction of himself from the unthinking, mechanical morass into which he had regressed.

This is neither his first nor his last attempt at such self-reduction to the most basic biological mechanism. Wylie recalls that Murphy "was saving up for a Drinking artificial respiration machine to get into when he was fed up with breathing."[27] Like the rocking chair, the iron lung is intended to function as a surrogate mother that would engulf Murphy. Nor is this impulse to mechanistic reduction limited to Murphy but manifests in several minor characters. Celia's uncle, Mr. Kelly, embodies a similar path of regression as he approaches mindless delirium in his old age: "a little while and his brain-body ratio would have sunk to that of a small bird."[28] When he lies back in his bed, his eyes close, "as though he were a doll."[29] Mr. Kelly's mind is described as little more than an automatic system to which Celia appeals for advice, "She knew that if by any means she could insert the problem into that immense cerebrum, the solution would be returned as though by clockwork."[30] Ulrika Maude and John Bolin attribute such moments of mindless mechanization to Beckett's extensive research into medicine and psychology.[31] Maude argues, "Beckett's writing captures a paradigm shift in our understanding of subjectivity, for since the second half of the nineteenth century, Darwinian thought, neurology, behaviourism and even some aspects of psychoanalysis had pointed to a biomechanical rather than conceptual understanding of the self."³²

While Murphy appears to delight in the reduction of the mind through automatic operations of the body, the novel also pursues his withdrawal away from embodied materiality into a mind that is all but bereft of body. His "shrunken conarium" means that he is unable to manage a moderate connection between mind and body, figure and ground. He therefore vacillates between the rarified positions of polymorphous body without mind, and mind disconnected from body. "As he lapsed in body he felt himself coming alive in mind."³³ The famous sixth chapter of the novel is comprised of an exploration of the tripartite structure of Murphy's mind. "There were the three zones, light, half light, dark, each with its specialty."³⁴ These zones are distinguished according to the mental "forms" or gestalts that he experiences and their relation to the external world. In the light zone, mental forms correspond directly to physical forms. Here, Murphy's interiority is brought into contact and agreement with the outside world. In the "half light zone," thought becomes increasingly abstract and detached from materiality. "Here the pleasure was contemplation."³⁵ However, the third state, "the dark zone," introduces an entirely different condition that foretells Murphy's later pursuit of madness.

> The third, the dark, was a flux of forms and perpetual coming together and falling asunder of forms. The light contained the docile elements of a new manifold, the world of the body broken up into the pieces of a toy; the half light, states of peace. But the dark neither elements nor states, nothing but forms becoming and crumbling into the fragments of a new becoming, without love or hate or any intelligible principle of change. Here was nothing but the commotion and the pure forms of commotion. Here he was not free, but a mote in the dark of absolute freedom.³⁶

In this chaotic mental space, the figure of the subject is diminished into a single, minimal point that is lost in a field of dissolving and appearing figures. Epistemological orientation breaks down in this confused flux of hallucinatory instability. To the extent that Murphy can be described in this condition, he is overwhelmed by the acephalous, automatic movements. If this passage recalls many accounts provided by psychotics of their thought disorder, it also shares much with philosophical attempts to describe a moment prior to subjectivity. In his description of "subjective destitution" and psychosis, Slavoj Žižek invokes a passage from Hegel's manuscript for the *Realphilosophie* of 1805–1806 that is remarkably resonant with the Murphy's "dark zone":

The human being is this night, this empty nothing, that contains everything in its simplicity – an unending wealth of many presentations, images, of which none happens to occur to him – or which are not present. This night, the inner of nature, that exists here – pure self – in phantasmagorical presentations, is night all around it, here shoots a bloody head – there another white shape, suddenly here before it, and just so disappears. One catches sight of this night when one looks human beings in the eye – into a night that becomes awful …[37]

For Hegel, this hallucinatory world is the state of being prior to its organization via negation. Žižek argues that this organizing force of negation grounds the subject – a cut that is not unlike the fundamental distinction between figure and ground that was proposed by the Gestalt psychologists. The psychotic break is here construed as a regression to a presubjective moment of confusion. These experiences can only be regarded as "intensities," since this dark zone appears to operate before any distinction between pleasure and pain, an excessive intensity that is described vividly in *Murphy*. "But how much more pleasant was the sensation of being a missile without provenance or target, caught up in a tumult of non-Newtonian motion. So pleasant that pleasant was not the word."[38] This account corresponds to Freud and Lacan's characterization of the death drive as operating beyond the pleasure principle, not regulated by homeostasis or the release of tension. This reckless self-destruction becomes evident as this programmatic chapter of *Murphy* concludes:

Thus as his body set him free more and more in his mind, he took to spending less and less time in the light, spitting at the breakers of the world; and less in the half light, where the choice of bliss introduced an element of effort; and more and more in the dark, in the will-lessness, a mote in its absolute freedom.[39]

The trajectory of Murphy's regression therefore takes him beyond the reality principle and the pleasure principle into a "dark zone" that signals psychosis. This last zone is succinctly described as a "Matrix of surds."[40] The mathematical term "surd" indicates an unresolved, irrational root.

Murphy's trajectory into this irrational, dark zone contrasts with the efforts to restore some fugitive sense of subjectivity that is evident in the work of Wyndham Lewis, Mina Loy, Evelyn Waugh, Anna Kavan, and others. I have argued that this effort to restore a sense of self often manifests as a paranoid narrative that reinscribes a fundamental difference between oneself and a malevolent outside world. Murphy's inclination toward the "dark zone" entails the refusal to recognize any fundamental difference or negation. Ackerley suggests that this movement – from the light toward the half-light and dark zones – constitutes the narrative order of Beckett's later trilogy of novels, *Molloy, Malone Dies,* and *The Unnamable.*[41] While this simple mapping may be too schematic, we may nevertheless read *Murphy* as a plan for Beckett's later work as he continues these literary approximations of madness. If Lewis's work exhibits a paranoid attempt to write one's way out of the loss of individuation, Beckett's writing constitutes a deeper descent into this "dark zone."

After Celia rescues him from his bloody rebirth in the rocking chair, she becomes determined to "make a man of Murphy," insisting that he search for gainful employment.[42] This demand to be "a man" is at odds with his desire for depersonalization – a state of unthinking, mechanized automatism that is compared to both a fetal state and to the dementia that accompanies old age. Murphy will find a third way to depersonalization in the form of dementia praecox.

This third way appears when Murphy encounters the inept poet Ticklepenny, who complains of his job as a nurse at the Magdalen Mental Mercyseat. "I cannot stand it [...] it is driving me mad."[43] The suggestion that prolonged exposure to psychotics may threaten one's sanity is precisely what appeals to Murphy, and he sees a way of resolving the apparent contradiction between Celia's demand that he get a job and his own desire to regress into unthinking automatism. "Ticklepenny was immeasurably inferior to Neary in every way, but they had certain points of contrast with Murphy in common. One was this pretentious fear of going mad."[44] Rather than fearing madness, Murphy makes it his goal. "To those in fear of losing it, reason stuck like a bur. And to those in hope ...?"[45] This is the question that brings Murphy to the Magdalen Mental Mercyseat asylum.

When Murphy finally assumes his new position as an orderly at the asylum, he is struck with admiration for the psychotics who appear to have achieved the regression toward a presubjective condition that has been his goal.

> They caused Murphy no horror. The most easily identifiable of his immediate feelings were respect and unworthiness ... The impression he received was of that self-immersed indifference to the contingencies of the contingent world which he had chosen for himself as the only felicity and achieved so seldom.[46]

The first sentence closely resembles the language of a 1935 letter to Tom McGreevy in which Beckett describes his experiences at the Bethlem Royal Hospital, the clear model for Magdalen Mental Mercyseat: "I was down at Bedlam this day week & went round the wards for the first time, *with scarcely any sense of horror,* though I saw everything, from mild depression to profound dementia."[47] For Murphy, the patients' "self-immersed indifference" constitutes a refusal to maintain the precarious dualisms that he finds himself unable to manage. If he idealizes the psychotics, he feels only disdain for the psychiatric regime that attempts to restore some connection between the patients and reality. "All this was revolting to Murphy, whose experience as a physical and rational being obliged him to call sanctuary what the psychiatrists called exile and to think of the patients not as banished from a system of benefits but as escaped from a colossal fiasco."[48] In Murphy's view, these psychotics have achieved the self-immersed regression to the "dark zone" that he only briefly visited in the novel's earlier episodes.

If Beckett demonstrates a fascination with the phenomenological conditions of mental illness, his work does not share Murphy's naïve idealization of psychosis. Beckett recalled a visit to the Bethlem Royal Hospital in which he approached a schizophrenic who remained unresponsive, "like a hunk of meat. There was no one there. He was absent."[49] The novel undermines Murphy's construction of the psychotics when it becomes clear that his interpretation of the patients' conditions is a projection of his own agenda.

> The frequent expressions apparently of pain, rage, despair and in fact all the usual, to which some patients gave vent, suggesting a fly somewhere in the ointment of Microcosmos, Murphy either disregarded or muted to mean what he wanted . . .
> [E]ven if the patients did sometimes feel as lousy as they sometimes looked, still no aspersion was necessarily cast on the little world where Murphy presupposed them, one and all, to be having a glorious time.[50]

The immense dysphoria that often accompanies psychosis is disavowed by Murphy in order to maintain the fantasy of a complete, endopsychic self-enjoyment. Persisting in this delusion, Murphy dismisses the psychiatric diagnosis of the patients as well as any evidence that does not conform to his fantasy. "The more his own system closed around him, the less he could tolerate its being subordinated to any other."[51] This projection expands to megalomaniacal proportions. Whereas earlier Murphy's faith in his horoscope indicated a belief that the outside, material world exerted some determining force on the "little world" of his mind, this causal relation is now reversed. "They were *his* stars, he was the prior system. He had been projected, larval and dark, on the sky of that regrettable hour as on a screen, magnified and clarified into his own meaning. But it was *his* meaning."[52] In these megalomaniacal delusions, Murphy becomes another of the asylum's paranoiacs.

In the psychotic patient Endon, Murphy finds the embodiment of his fantasized "dark zone" of the mind. As his name suggests, Endon seems to have lost the capacity to relate to the outside world or to recognize others. Murphy's interactions with Endon, such as they are, are mediated through chess. When he looks in on Endon during his nightly rounds, Murphy imagines that Endon recognizes the gaze of a friend, but even this minimal exchange proves to be a projection of Murphy's self-delusion. "Mr. Endon would have been less than Mr. Endon if he had known what it was to have a friend; and Murphy more than Murphy if he had not hoped against his better judgment that his feeling for Mr. Endon was in some small degree reciprocated."[53] It is this failure to find a foundation for some recognition of the other that brought Freud to the opinion that psychotics were virtually unreachable through his "talking cure" grounded in a transferential relationship between analysand and analyst. The asymmetry of the nonrelation between Murphy and Endon becomes manifest: "Whereas the sad truth was, that while Mr. Endon for Murphy was no less than bliss, Murphy for Mr. Endon was no more than chess. Murphy's eye? Say rather, the chessy eye. Mr. Endon had vibrated to the chessy eye upon him and made his preparation accordingly."[54] What Endon recognizes is only a subjectless part-object that is more closely associated with a mechanical procedure of moving chess pieces than with any person or subject.

Even in the "game" that proceeds, Murphy finds that Endon does not recognize the pressure or presence of an opponent but only proceeds to rearrange the pieces on the board according to his own internal schema, indecipherable to Murphy. As he comes to suspect that Endon does not recognize his opposition, Murphy attempts several attacks that fail to elicit any rational response. He finally comes to acknowledge that he is virtually alone in the game, unrecognized by his "friend." As this disturbing realization passes over him, Murphy looks up at Endon but sees only an incoherent field of part-objects with no organizing principle of subjectivity: "little by little his eyes were captured by the brilliant swallow-tail of Mr. Endon's arms and legs, purple, scarlet, black and glitter, till they saw nothing else, and that in a short time only as a vivid blur, Neary's big blooming buzzing confusion or ground, mercifully free of figure."[55] Endon is ground with no figure or a field of figures without organization against ground. At the same time, Murphy feels the imminent collapse of his own precarious, neurotic subjectivity that remains dependent upon the recognition of the other. "Then this also faded and Murphy began to see nothing, that colourlessness which is such a rare postnatal treat, being the absence (to abuse a nice distinction) not of *percipere* but of *percipi*."[56] If, as Berkeley asserted, "to be is to be perceived," then it is Endon's failure to recognize Murphy that launches him into the psychic disintegration that he had searched for.[57] He hears and repeats a voice in his head, "The last Mr. Murphy saw of Mr. Endon was Mr. Murphy unseen by Mr. Endon. This was also the last Murphy saw of Murphy."[58]

Murphy's moment of subjective crisis continues as he leaves the asylum, strips naked, and lies upon the grass, merging once again with the ground. He tries to summon the faces or figures of Celia, his father, his mother, "In vain."[59] It appears that he has lapsed into the Endon's state, incapable of recognition, and he is left in the "dark zone" of part objects and hallucinated sense data. "Scraps of bodies, of landscapes, hands, eyes, lines and colours evoking nothing, rose and climbed out of sight before him, as though reeled upward off a spool level with his throat. It was his experience that this should be stopped, whenever possible, before the deeper coils were reached."[60] Murphy is in danger of becoming unspooled. He curiously recognizes the danger of this schizoidal experience and draws back from the psychotic break that he has been approaching throughout the novel.

Yet, in a more literal sense, he is finally given over to the fragmentation of part objects and "scraps of bodies." Murphy abruptly dies in a conflagration when his poorly constructed gas heater explodes. Suicide appears to be unlikely as the pull-chain that ignites the system is located a floor below his garret. This pull-chain is described as a mechanism similar to the flusher of a toilet, suggesting that Murphy's end is comparable to the disposal of human waste. In this morbid sense, he may have finally gotten what he wanted, satisfying the ethical maxim of Geulincx: *Ubi nihil vales, ibi nihil velis* ["where you are worth nothing, there you should want nothing"].[61] Murphy is finally reduced to this worthless, inert state, free from the restless neurotic longing that he had been attempting to extinguish throughout the novel. Madness proved to be an impossible resting place for Murphy, but its importance for Beckett would continue. In *Watt*, he would push the novelization of thought disorder even further in preparation for what I will call the novel's psychotic break.

Hearing Things, Namable and Unnamable

Like the schizophrenic that Beckett encountered in Bethlem Royal Hospital, Watt is presented as a virtually empty body. Descriptions of the character reduce him to the most basic bodily functions; he seems incapable of making decisions; his thought processes are often either disordered or mathematical; and he often appears indifferent to his surroundings.

Other characters regard him as an empty conduit of consumption and waste. "Like a sewer pipe, said Mrs. Nixon."[62] While such accounts of the character construct a cypher not unlike the figure of Endon, the novel moves beyond these external descriptions and becomes focalized through Watt in order to disclose his nonnormative patterns of thought. His difficulty in grasping the meaning of language and of simple objects suggests a lack of symbolic orientation and an inability to grasp of the protocols of social behavior that organize a normative phenomenological world. In Watt's earliest encounters with other characters, he exhibits only a hollow mimicry of sociality that recalls Wyndham Lewis's sneering Snooty Baronet. "Watt had watched people smile and thought he understood how it was done ... But there was something wanting to Watt's smile, some little thing was lacking."[63] Though he robotically repeats the external signs and gestures of social interaction, he remains unable to grasp their meaning.

He is mystified by a banal conversation between a piano tuner and his son that they carry on as they attempt to fix Mr. Knott's piano. Watt's disturbance may be provoked by a scene that stages both an inscrutable, paternal relationship as well as the act of correcting an instrument that has gone out of tune. He launches into a frantic effort to interpret behavior and speech that he finds obscure. Watt's capacity for interpretation proves to be as out of tune as the piano; he is unable to determine the difference between meaningful and meaningless data.

> This fragility of outer meaning had a bad effect on Watt, for it caused him to seek for another, for some meaning of what had passed, in the image of how it had passed.
>
> The most meagre, the least plausible, would have satisfied Watt, who had not seen a symbol, nor executed an interpretation, since the age of fourteen, or fifteen and who had lived, miserably it is true, among face values all his adult life, face values at least for him. Some see the flesh before the bones, some see the bones before the flesh, and some never see the bones at all, and some never see the flesh at all, never never see the flesh at all.[64]

It would appear that Watt has carefully eschewed deeper structures or patterns of meaning that might persist beyond immediate sense data – the "bones" beneath the uncanny, shifting flesh of his environment – but a desire for such meaning begins to stir. Whatever significance he is able to ascribe to the scene is quickly replaced with other possibilities, rendering a polymorphous structure of experience.

He "was obliged, because of his peculiar character, to enquire into what they meant, oh not into what they really meant, his character was not so peculiar as all that, but into what they might be induced to mean, with the help of a little patience, a little ingenuity."[65] The text underscores a gap between the everyday, quotidian meaning that might be assigned to his experience and the meaning that he might impose – between normative symbolic organization of experience and the idiosyncratic, delusional meaning that might be created. The narrator indicates that Watt's idiosyncratic relation to signification is a limit to the coherence of both the narrative that is told as well as Watt's world.

> *But what was this pursuit of meaning, in this indifference to meaning? And to what did it tend? These are delicate questions.* [...] *Add to this the obscurity of Watt's communications, the rapidity of his utterance and the eccentricities of his syntax, as elsewhere recorded* ... And some idea will perhaps be obtained of the difficulties experienced in formulating, not only such matters as those here in question, but the entire body of Watt's experience ...[66]

Watt's eccentric speech patterns suggest a fundamental failure of language that is consistent with his difficulty in grasping the meaning of his experiences. These failures suggest that the story comes to us via a series of broken communications systems. Like the piano that the tuner and his son are unable to repair, these language machines are hopelessly dysfunctional.

Watt persists in such attempts to reorient himself through the application of language to his experience, but his attempts continue to falter. The relation between word and thing remains tenuous, and he is plagued by an irreducible sense of unreality.

> Looking at a pot, for example, or thinking of a pot, at one of Mr. Knott's pots, it was in vain that Watt said, Pot, pot. Well, perhaps not quite in vain, but very nearly. For it was not a pot, the more he looked, the more he reflected, the more he felt sure of that, that it was not a pot at all. It resembled a pot, it was almost a pot, but it was not a pot of which one could say, Pot, pot, and be comforted.[67]

His uncanny impression that things are not quite what they should be, his ontological confusion, is a common symptom of psychosis that we have seen described in similar ways in *An Autobiography of a Schizophrenic Girl*.

> When, for example, I looked at a chair or a jug, I thought not of their use or function – a jug not as something to hold water and milk, a chair not as something to sit in – but as having lost their names, their functions and meanings; they became "things" and began to take on life, to exist.[68]

In both accounts, the singularity of the thing refuses to submit to its normative linguistic or ontological category. Both Watt and the schizophrenic girl attempt to achieve some relief, to "be comforted," through the application of the object's given name, but these efforts fail. For Watt, these linguistic and ontological failures redound reflexively upon himself.

> Then when he turned for reassurance to himself, who was not Mr. Knott's, in the sense that the pot was, who had come from without and whom the without would take again, he made the distressing discovery that of himself too he could no longer affirm anything that did not seem as false as if he had affirmed it of a stone.[69]

As in the nightmarish experience of the schizophrenic girl, distinctions between the animate and inanimate or the human and the nonhuman cannot be maintained. Watt feels himself to be *unheimlich*, not at home, in the house of Knott. He is a foreigner to this space that is both divided and sutured through the "Knott" or negation by which fundamental distinctions are made. He cannot claim for himself the status of a subject and is therefore reduced to an inanimate object, a stone. "As for himself, though he could no longer call it a man, as he had used to do, with the intuition that he was perhaps not talking nonsense, yet he could not imagine what else to call it, if not a man … But for all the relief that this afforded him, he might just as well have thought himself as a box, or an urn."[70] Watt feels himself to be indistinguishable from the objects around him, an empty body. This dehumanization has become a familiar experience for him: "he had grown used to his loss of species."[71]

Just as *Murphy* described a failed approach toward madness as an idealized space in which one's full being might be renewed and restored, *Watt* describes an attempt to restore meaning from nothing as a way out of delirium. These novels therefore turn on the same axis of psychosis around which Beckett's career would continue to revolve for several decades. In his subsequent treatments of madness, the form of the novel itself would be subjected to the same radical breakdown that his earlier characters suffer. In the wake of this formal and psychic breakdown, all that remains is a cacophony of indefatigable, autonomous, and often malevolent voices.

Beckett described *Watt* as a writing exercise that he imposed upon himself in order to keep busy during the years of the German occupation of France. It is clear that the novel was more than a mere exercise, as it constituted a significant advance over *Murphy* in his literary simulation of madness. In the late 1940s, he would continue this project with the rapid composition of *Molloy, Malone Dies,* and *The Unnamable* – three texts that would push the form of the novel to a breaking point, leaving him at an aesthetic impasse. I will argue that, with the final installment of this trilogy, Beckett exhausts the novel's formal capacity to replicate the hallucinatory experiences of madness; this state of generic exhaustion prepares the ground for experimentation with other forms and media in order to continue his project.

Like Watt, Molloy's capacity for language is constantly failing and returning. He has trouble maintaining a functional, stable relation between words and things, and language seems to inhabit him like a foreign body.

> Yes, even then, when already all was fading, waves and particles, there could be no things but nameless things, no names but thingless names. I say that now, but after all what do I know now about then, now when the icy words hail down upon me, the icy meanings, and the world dies too, foully named. All I know is what the words know, and the dead things, and that makes a handsome little sum . . .[72]

The wave/particle parallax captures the orthogonal fields of words and things that cannot be sutured. Signification itself seems foreign, life-less, and even painful as it robs things of their being. At other moments, Molloy's being appears to be fleeting and to persist by sheer force of will, "Yes, there were times when I forgot not only who I was, but that I was, forgot to be."[73] The psychotic Judge Schreber famously feared that God may not recognize his existence if he should stop thinking. In a similar delusion, Molloy feels that he must keep his mind occupied with endless, pointless questions in order to persist. "I called that thinking. I thought almost without stopping, I did not dare stop."[74]

Molloy recalls a brief time spent with a woman named Lousse (initially, he thinks her name was "Mrs. Loy"), and this relationship appears to have given him some psychic stability. "During my stay with Lousse no more new symptoms appeared of a pathological nature."[75] However, this reprieve is quickly interrupted when he begins to suspect that she is poisoning him. Even his bicycle, once a beloved source of enjoyment, becomes a source of anxiety. "I left her [Lousse] my bicycle which I had taken a dislike to, suspecting it to be the vehicle of some malignant agency and perhaps the cause of my recent misfortunes."[76] Molloy shares with Flann O'Brien's police officers an obscure fear of the bicycle as an agent of potential dehu-manization. He submits to the voice that tells him to leave the domestic scene, and soon the voice becomes his only guide.

Molloy therefore vacillates erratically through periods of stability, para-noia, and schizophrenic delirium. In his most extreme moments of confu-sion, he becomes unable to recognize his own body, and he believes that his limbs have a life of their own. "And when I see my hands, on the sheet, which they love to floccillate already, they are not mine, less than ever mine, I have no arms, they are a couple, they play with the sheet."[77] The body is reduced to the incoherent and independent part objects. Just as Molloy suspected that his auditory hallucination had its own agenda, the dissociated hands seem to have an uncanny life of their own. Soon all distinctions break down for Molloy, and he is unable to demarcate his own limits. "For all things run together, in the body's long madness, I feel it."[78] This running together recalls the confusion of interiority and exteriority that Murphy experiences when he collapses on the lawn of the Magdalen Mental Mercyseat.

In *Malone Dies,* the title character can only tell his own story through characters that he invents. One such avatar, Macmann, awakes to find himself "in a kind of asylum," surrounded by a group of men and women dressed in white.[79] Malone then interrupts this sequence to describe his own unstable psychic state. "I pause to record what I feel in extraordinary form. Delirium perhaps."[80] The narrator and his character become nearly indiscernible. As with Molloy, this recurrent delirium manifests as auditory hallucination and confusion. Malone writes:

> For a long time now I have been hearing things confusedly. There I go again. What I mean is possibly this, that the noises of the world, so various in themselves and which I used to be so clever at distinguishing from one another, had been dinning at me for so long, always the same old noises, as gradually to have merged into a single noise, so that all I heard was one vast continuous buzzing.[81]

This is the "big blooming buzzing confusion" that Murphy pursued in which figure cannot be distinguished from ground. The moment may also be understood as another instance of the confusions that arise from the ontological monism that appears in the work of Wyndham Lewis and Flann O'Brien. In *The Logic of Sense,* Gilles Deleuze writes, "The univocity of Being signifies that Being is Voice, that it is said, and that it is said in one and the same 'sense' of everything about which it is said. That of which it is said is not at all the same, but Being is the same for everything about which it is said."[82] With this assertion, Deleuze rejects the notion of a transcendental subject, and he would find in schizophrenia an experience of this overwhelming "clamor of being" – an association that had already been implied by Beckett. However, Deleuze arguably repeats Murphy's error by projecting onto psychosis his own fantasy of a direct and euphoric experience of this univocal sense of being. Beckett is far less sanguine, indicating through characters such as Malone that an experience of "one vast continuous buzzing" is hardly euphoric.

While Beckett may not have shared Murphy's idealization of the psychotic patients that he encountered in the asylum, there is ample evidence that extreme mental illness persisted as a source of fascination for him, and psychic self-enclosure and auditory hallucination recur as organizing topoi in his work long after *Murphy*. Beckett's friend Patrick Bowles recalls a conversation about his fascination with such experiences of radical psychic withdrawal and inner voices that, while evident in extreme pathological cases, are perhaps not strictly unique to such conditions:

> Beckett mentioned that self-immersion going by the name of schizophrenia. When that little far-away inner self and voice that *alone* is the real, for him, when it is abandoned, forgotten, when the catatonic leaves his stupor and redirects his attention to the outer world of frills and customs and the conventions of verbal clarity, then he has left what is for him the most profound fact of his existence.
>   I understand that very well. I said to him it was a kind of eternal malady. The one that counts, one of us said, or I thought.[83]

The exchange demonstrates a respect for the hallucinated voices of schizophrenics and perhaps even a form of kinship. We might contrast this attitude with the now dominant psychiatric view that auditory hallucinations are meaningless epiphenomena and are therefore to be ignored. Regarding the dominant tendencies in twentieth-century psychiatry, psychologists Ivan Leudar and Philip Thomas observe, "The pharmacological management of schizophrenia then becomes the priority, and the subject's preoccupation with and self-report of voices becomes little more than an index of the extent to which the underlying illness is controlled by medication."[84] Leudar and Thomas join a growing chorus of recent psychologists and disability scholars who suggest that hallucinations often – though not always – perform pragmatic functions in regulating schizophrenics' behavior and attitudes, and cannot be so easily dismissed. Whether these voices should be ignored or attended to becomes a central problem in *The Unnamable*.

Some, such as Katz, have favored readings of these voices in *The Unnamable* as merely the effects of "language."

> [T]he word "voice" becomes in the trilogy the central term for the phenomenon of interest here – that of the appearance of "language" in the apparent absence of any unequivocal productive source, secure intentional motor, or unquestionable, ideal meaning.[85]

While these ambiguities clearly disturb what remains of a narrator, the attribution of these effects to a generalized theory of "language" is far too abstract, and it ignores the manifest, delusional qualities that distinguish the particular forms of language that are heard and/or spoken within *The Unnamable*.

Through the reduction of the novel to hallucinated voices, Beckett would precipitate not simply the psychic disintegration of a particular character; rather, the form of the novel itself would undergo something like psychotic fragmentation. Describing feelings of thought insertion and persecution, the narrator protests, "these voices are not mine, nor these thoughts, but the voices and thoughts of the devils who beset me."[86] The multiplying voices take on their own shifting, provisional identities, and seem to serve crucial narrative functions: "Decidedly Basil is becoming important, I'll call him Mahood instead. I prefer that, I'm queer. It was he told me stories about me, lived in my stead, issued forth from me, came back to me, entered back into me, heaped stories on my head. I don't know how it was done."[87] If this narrator is delusional, he also demonstrates hyperreflexive insight into his impulses to construct narratives that might render some ad hoc phenomenological world that would give his experiences structure and coherence.

> I invented it all, in the hope it would console me, help me to go on, allow me to think of myself as somewhere on a road, moving between a beginning and an end, gaining ground, losing ground, getting lost, but somehow in the long run making headway. All lies.[88]

Such reflexive moments suggest that the ordering operations of narrative may constitute a form of self-recovery as Dan Zahavi suggests: "Elaborate storytelling might serve a compensatory function; it might be an attempt to make up for the lack of a fragile self-identity."[89]

Yet, if the narrator's voices sometimes generate narratives that would render such minimal identity across time, he just as often interrupts those stories in order to resist any sense of self-identity, or what Paul Ricoeur calls the "humanization of time," that narrative renders. Reflecting upon one of personae that occupy his mental space, the narrator warns:

> The rascal, he's getting humanized, he's going to lose if he doesn't watch out, if he doesn't take care, and with what could he take care, with what could he form the faintest conception of the condition they are decoying him into, with their ears, their eyes, their tears and a brainpan where anything may happen.[90]

Here, "they," may refer to a group of doctors or psychiatrists whom he describes as "a whole college of tyrants, differing in their views as to what should be done with me, in conclave since time began or a little later, listening to me from time to time, then breaking up for a meal or a game of cards."[91] Elsewhere he wonders, "Why don't they wash their hands of me and set me free? That might do me good. I don't know. Perhaps then I could go silent, for good and all."[92] This "college of tyrants" along with references to a "troop of lunatics" and the prevailing feeling of involuntary incarceration suggest that the narrator occupies a psychiatric institution similar to the asylum in *Murphy*.[93] He feels that the malevolent figures of authority make coercive attempts "To make me believe I have an ego all my own, and can speak of it, as they of theirs. Another trap to snap me up among the living."[94] This residual sense of self is linked by the narrator to the conventional, narrative organization of time: "yes, they've inflicted the notion of time on me too."[95] However, against this humanistic experience of temporality, the narrator – and consequently the larger text – often reverts to series of unstructured experiences in the present: "when you have nothing left to say you talk of time, seconds of time, there are some people add them together to make a life, I can't, each one is the first, no, the second, or the third, I'm three seconds old."[96] If madness becomes a recurring problematic that is central to *The Unnamable,* the text explicitly links this problem to its own departures from conventional narrative structures in ways that anticipate recent phenomenological approaches to mental illness.

Shaun Gallagher identifies four features of narrative self-coordination and world building that are often altered or deficient in cases of schizophrenia. These include "the capacity for temporal ordering, the capacity for minimal self-reference, episodic and autobiographical memory, and the capacity for metacognition."[97] As a result, "schizophrenic narratives are characterized by a derailing of thought; by constant tangents, the loss of goal, the loosening of associations, or the compression of a temporally extended story to a single gesture."[98] Gallagher and others demonstrate how narratological analysis can contribute to an understanding of distinctly schizophrenic worlds. *The Unnamable* clearly exhibits many of the formal characteristics that Gallagher and others identify with the altered phenomenology and narrative structures common to schizophrenia: it is marked by an unstable ordering of events, the absence of metacognitive markers that would distinguish memories, fantasies, hallucinations, and sensory experiences, and a narrator whose identity is fractured by the intrusion of voices. These qualities make *The Unnamable* not only another installment in the literary representation of madness but a metatextual reflection upon the formal convergence of experimental fiction and psychotic delusion.

In the absence of plot, character, or temporal structure, *The Unnamable* becomes a report and a reflection upon the strange phenomenology of voice hearing. "The fact is all this business about voices requires to be revised, corrected and then abandoned. Hearing nothing I am none the less a prey to communications. And I speak of voices!"[99] These voices are often described as thought transmissions, though his orientation toward them vacillates dramatically. While at times they clearly persecute him, at other moments he senses that they will lead him to some crucial insight. "This transmission is really excellent. I wonder if it's going to get us somewhere."[100] This somewhere is the final statement, his password or transcendent intonation that will finally silence the cacophony and give him some reprieve. No such primary signifier arrives to suture his thought disorder, and he can only contemplate the source of these transmissions and their meaning. "I have naturally remarked, in a moment of exceptional receptivity, that these exhortations are conveyed to me by the same channel as that used by Malone and Co for their transports. That's suspicious."[101] The text is presented as simply a transcript of these receptions. In place of a mind, the narrator's head is described as "a transformer in which sound is turned, without the help of reason, to rage and terror, that's all that is required, for the moment."[102] He is reduced to a passive machine that receives thought transmissions and produces only dysphoria.

This technological thought transmission recurs in *How It Is,* arguably Beckett's most extreme antinovel. The narrator's rambling monologue strains grammar and is generally lacking punctuation. Instead, a voice frantically broadcasts verbiage without break: "black air nothing left but short waves three hundred four hundred yards per second"; "so many words so many lost one every three two every five first the sound then the sense same ratio or else not one not one lost I hear all understand all and live again have lived again."[103] Our narrator vacillates between the suspicion that he is simply a relay between two audio technologies, offering no contribution of his own and the megalomaniacal claim to omniscient understanding of some divine knowledge. He appears to recognize that his own sanity is questionable – "Krim says I'm mad" – but he rejects this diagnosis: "there's reason in me yet."[104]

Unlike Beckett's earlier narrators, he identifies with the voice that he hears and relies upon it as the source or ground of his being. "I alone my voice no other it leaves me I leave me it comes back to me I come back to me."[105] He worries that should the voice stop, he might vanish: "must sometimes wonder if to these perpetual revictuallings narrations and auditions he might not put an end without ceasing to maintain us in some kind of being."[106] When the rambling voice stops or pauses, he feels himself fading. His being is sustained through a circuit of self-relation that he achieves by hearing his own voice. If he is a puppet, he is his own puppet.

As in Mina Loy's *Insel* and Evelyn Waugh's *The Ordeal of Gilbert Pinfold*, the description of the psychotic mind as a nightmarish machine becomes a recurrent trope in *The Unnamable* and *How It Is*. However, Beckett will find a way to make this mechanized experience more than just metaphor for his audience by turning away from the novel. Having pressed the exhaustion and failure of narrativity to its conclusion, he temporarily abandons the novel in favor of a medium in which the transmission of voice is not only metaphorical but real.

Transmitting Madness

After a two-year period of immense activity that yielded the trilogy (1947–1949), Beckett reached a creative impasse. Knowlson notes that Beckett had become mired creatively and psychologically in the mid-1950s:

> Beckett's depression was very slow to lift, as he began to experience renewed doubt about whether there was any way out of the impasse into which *The Unnamable* and *Fin de partie* had led him. The medium of radio, with the challenge of its technical constraints, offered one possible escape route.[107]

With *The Unnamable* Beckett's novelistic simulations of madness seem to have yielded an endless reverberation of voices, undead in their uncanny persistence. Given the great success he had achieved with *Waiting for Godot* and *Endgame*, it is often suggested that Beckett found on the stage a way out of this aesthetic impasse. While these works marked a clear point of emergence for Beckett's public stature, his radio dramas were crucial, logical developments within the arc of his career and project, though they have received comparatively little critical attention. Ulrika Maude has attributed this relative neglect of Beckett's experimentation with audio technology to the influence of deconstruction within Beckett studies, arguing that its "rejection of 'phonocentrism' has led to a form of phonophobia or aversion to all things heard."[108]

While marking a turn toward technological experimentation that closely followed the technological delusions of *The Unnamable*, these works also advanced the form of the radio drama and demanded methodological innovations for their production. Everett Frost notes that the technical requirements of *All That Fall* (1957) and *Embers* (1959) "led directly to the creation of the BBC's innovative radiophonic workshop at Maida

Vale, with Desmond Briscoe, the sound designer for *All That Fall*, as its first director."[109] Radio offered a medium in which "thought broadcasting," a common symptom of schizophrenia, was not only metaphorical but actual – not simply reported to the audience but produced as lived experienced. Radio became a means by which schizophrenic experiences of auditory hallucination, depersonalization, and a loss of ego boundaries could be narrated and rationalized. Such technical delusions of "thought transmission" continue to be studied as first-rank symptoms of schizophrenia. Psychiatrist Alfred Kraus writes,

> We think it is not by chance that people with schizophrenia so often use technical metaphors to explain their schizophrenic experiences. There must be some analogy between the characteristics of technical processes of the above mentioned kind and the way patients experience their altered psychotic self and world.[110]

Kraus implies that the analogy between the technology and paranoid delusion moves in both directions, and, in its early years, radio was felt by many nonschizophrenic subjects to be a fundamentally depersonalizing experience that rendered what Sconce calls a "leaky ego."[111]

In Samuel Beckett's radio dramas, we find a series of such "leaky egos" that occupy points of convergence between radio technology and the phenomenological conditions of mental illness. Clas Zilliacus writes that, "One reason why Beckett goes to these psychological extremes [. . .] is that radio provides a suitable medium for blurring the distinction between internal and external reality."[112] Similarly, Maude observes, "Because we are more certain of a sound than we are of where it comes from, sound, at times, renders problematic the distinction between the endogenous and the exogenous."[113] Steven Connor similarly notes that Beckett's radio dramas occupy an ambiguous location that is at once no place and a mindspace, and Yoshiki Tajiri finds a similar logic playing out in *Krapp's Last Tape*, where sound technology externalizes "phenomena in the skull."[114] This ambiguity between endogenous, psychic space and exogenous reality is one of the difficulties that often plague schizophrenics, and it is radio's capacity to provoke such confusion that would make it a suitable medium for explorations and simulations of madness. One of the unique challenges of interpreting the radio plays is the difficulty of determining the ontological status of anything that is heard. Beckett refused to adapt his radio dramas for the stage, insisting upon the unique epistemic and ontological uncertainties that are induced by radio, and he explicitly linked these ambiguities to the conditions of madness. Of his 1959 radio drama *Embers*,

Beckett wrote that it "is based on an ambiguity: is the character having a hallucination or is he in the presence of reality? Staging the scene would destroy its ambiguity."[115]

In *Embers*, we hear only what the principal and arguably sole character Henry Bolton hears, and it is doubtful that Henry's experiences are reliable. Henry's hallucinatory psychic world – such as it is – becomes the audience's world through a transmission of voices whose provenance and ontological status remain undefined. *Embers* opens on Henry as he mourns his father's suicide by drowning and contemplates a similar end for himself. While apparently seated near the place of the drowning, Henry recognizes the silent image of his father. This visual knowledge is reported to us by Henry, reminding us of the blindness that radio enforces in its audience. Like many of Beckett's characters, we find our way through this fictional world in the dark with our sensorium disabled and our epistemic limitations made manifest from the beginning of the play. To listen to these plays is to be confronted with a virtually intractable problem of reality testing under compromised circumstances – a problem that is a key nosological condition of psychosis.

The ambient sounds of the sea that rise and fall seem to be empirical evidence confirming Henry's reports about the setting. However, later in the play, Henry's wife Ada also appears to him and casts doubt on his mental stability and epistemic reliability. She worries that his compulsive speech frightens their daughter and urges him to see a doctor.

ADA: Henry
HENRY: Yes.
ADA: You should see a doctor about your talking, it's worse, what must it be like for Addie? [*Pause.*] Do you know what she said to me once, when she was still quite small, she said, Mummy, why does Daddy keep on talking all the time? She heard you in the lavatory. I didn't know what to answer.
HENRY: Daddy! Addie! [*Pause.*] I told you to tell her I was praying. [*Pause.*] Roaring prayers at God and his saints.
ADA: It is very bad for the child. [*Pause.*] It's silly to say it keeps you from hearing it, it doesn't keep you from hearing it, and even if it does you shouldn't be hearing it, there must be something wrong with your brain. [*Pause.*]
HENRY: That! I shouldn't be hearing that!
ADA: I don't think you are hearing it.[116]

Stage directions indicate that Ada speaks in a "low remote voice throughout."[117] This thin, spectral quality distinguishes her voice from Henry's, which moves erratically from frail whispers to tormented screams. That Ada is Henry's hallucination is also suggested by the script's indication that she makes "[No sound as she sits]" – a curious direction that calls for silent action within a medium where only audible action can be detected by the audience.[118] Perhaps even more disorienting is Ada's suggestion that the sound of the sea that torments Henry and that ebbs and flows for us is not real; it is a suggestion from a possibly hallucinated voice that nothing we've heard has any epistemic reliability or ontological stability.

To the extent that Henry's experiences conform to a particular logic, *Embers* remains closer to psychoanalytic topos than to the psychiatric view that "Hallucinations, being psychotic symptoms, have no inherent value or meaning."[119] A series of hallucinated scenes form a pattern of monstrous father figures that cannot be satisfied. These moments consistently begin with a banal exchange between a male authority figure and a child in which mounting anxiety is indexed by audio levels that build to ear piercing shrieks and disturbing sound effects. In the first of these scenes, Henry not only recalls but fully reverts to the child that he once was – a frightened son unwilling to follow his father into the ocean for a swim.

HENRY: Father! [*Pause.*] You wouldn't know me now, you'd be sorry you ever had me, but you were that already, a washout, that's the last I heard from you, a washout. [*Pause. Imitating father's voice.*] "Are you coming for a dip?" "No." "Come on, come on." "No." Glare, stump to the door, turn, glare. "A washout, that's all you are, a washout!" [*Violent slam of door. Pause.*] Again! [*Slam. Pause.*] Slam life shut like that![120]

Henry's hallucinations are far from nonsensical or "ununderstandable" – rather, he struggles with not only his relationship with his father – dead by apparent suicide – but with the abstract role of paternity itself.[121] More than just the epiphenomena of random neural dysfunctions, the hallucinated scene becomes an occasion for compulsive role-playing, as if Henry is trying and failing to master a particular part that has always eluded him. Importantly, the modal status of the scene transforms in ways that are indicated by the production's audio effects: Henry initially describes the sequence as simply another of his stories; he then begins to restage the scene, playing the part of his father and of himself as a child; finally the moment gains nightmarish reality for both Henry and the audience with the violent sounds of shouting and a door being slammed. As is common in experiences of psychosis, the modal categories of memory, narration, and hallucination combine in an unstable auditory environment that collapses for both Henry and the audience the phenomenological coordinates of space, time, self, and other.

In further evidence that Henry's symptoms cluster around the problem of fatherhood, his attention abruptly shifts to his own performance of a similarly monstrous paternal relation to his daughter Addie.

HENRY: I use to walk with her in the fields, Jesus that was awful, she wouldn't let go my hand and I mad to talk. "Run along now Addie, and look at the lambs." [*imitating Addie's voice.*] "No papa." "Go on now, go on." [*Plaintive.*] "No papa." [*Violent.*] "Go on with you when you're told and look at the lambs!" [*Addie's loud wail.*][122]

Again, the scene moves from memory to performed exchange in which Henry plays both roles until Addie's voice is fully hallucinated. Henry's excessive reaction to Addie's demand for intimacy constitutes another instance in which the paternal role is distorted into sadistic persecution – a pattern that conforms to psychoanalytic accounts of psychosis.[123]

These recurrent scenes of failed paternity suggest that Henry's delusional stories are attempts to master through narrative what he has been unable to master in life. However, Henry is hardly the master of his narratives but is instead subject to them. Rather than telling his stories, Henry passively receives them – an experience that is replicated for the audience by the form of radio. Henry's passive relation to the stories that he tells and their escalation from narrative to sensory experience is both a signal feature of psychosis and an effect that the medium of radio affords. It marks an inability to recognize distinctions among one's own thoughts, memories, desires, and sensory experiences, such as the voices of others. The play's erosion of these modal distinctions is one of its most distinctive formal features, and it is made possible through radio drama's strict reduction of all information to audio.

Elsewhere, Henry implies that the voices he hears and perhaps delusional narratives that he passively experiences may serve a compensatory function. He recalls that he began by telling stories and eventually progressed to suffering the voices of strangers until he heard the voices of his family – none of whom may be present.

HENRY: Stories, stories, years and years of stories, til the need came on me, for someone, to be with me, anyone, a stranger, to talk to, imagine he hears me, years of that, and then, now, for someone who ... knew me, in the old days, anyone, to be with me, imagine he hears me, what I am, now.[124]

Henry resorts to narrative for its compensatory, organizing functions, but these functions fail to maintain sufficient phenomenological order. In addition, Henry requires an other to confirm and maintain his existence. Everett Frost suggests that Beckett's radio dramas revise Bishop

Berkeley's famous dictum so that "To be is to be heard."[125] Henry therefore requires a listener who may hear him into some minimal existence, and we as audience are enlisted in this function. Henry's unstable storyworlds are therefore both insufficient and excessive. Rather than autobiographical and temporal orientation, he generates only a few disorganized and fragmentary scenes that elude his narrative control, manifesting as lived experiences and heard voices. The interlocutors that Henry conjures for company ultimately become tormenting voices that he cannot switch off.

Delusions often encode the mediation of social contact through obscure systems of mechanization and thought transmission – a pattern that manifests not only in Beckett's *Embers* but also in his later piece, *Rough for Radio I* (composed in 1961, published in 1973):

SHE: Is it true the music goes on all the time?
HE: Yes.
SHE: Without cease?
HE: Without cease.
SHE: It's unthinkable! [*Pause.*] And the words too? All the time too?
HE: All the time.[126]

Perhaps even more than *Embers, Rough for Radio* integrates experiences of radio and thought insertion: SHE, a novice in the operation of "the apparatus" and its tuning knobs, is instructed by HE, who describes the system as "a need." It is a need for presence and social contact, but that presence quickly becomes excessive and threatening, requiring interruption.[127] HE urgently calls a doctor for assistance, and, referring to the apparatus, complains, "It's crazy! Like one!"[128] The play concludes abruptly with a discussion of "confinement" – a separation and switching off that Joey perfected with his mechanical delusion but that eludes many who suffer similar symptoms.[129] A similar effort to externalize and master emotionally disturbing material through audio technology is staged in *Krapp's Last Tape,* in which thought is switched on, received, and switched off when no longer tolerable. Yet, even here, the subject is placed in a state of increasing passivity toward the speaking machine. Michael Davidson argues that the play presents "the tape recorder as an ultimate agent of mind control, a machine capable of replacing human communication with a prerecorded script."[130]

Returning to *Embers,* we find precisely a convergence between the maddening passivities of auditory hallucination and audio technology. Henry is subject to the insertion of thoughts and perceptions that cannot simply be interrupted. Like Joey in Bettelheim's case study (see Chapter 3), he has developed a technological solution to the voices that will not give him reprieve. However, rather than switching them off, he attempts to drown them out with additional sense data – a strategy that is not uncommon among schizophrenics, as observed by Leudar and Thomas, who write, "The most widely used intervention based on information processing is Walkman therapy. Many people who hear voices find that wearing a Walkman, or portable audiotape, on which they can listen to music helps to damp down voices."[131] When his storytelling fails to establish a stabilized and ordered world and instead only exacerbates his confusion, Henry relies upon a device to overwhelm the voices and the sounds of the sea – a moment that may force a comparison of the audience's reliance upon audio technology for distraction to the state of pathological, technological "distraction" that Henry suffers.

HENRY: Now I walk about with the gramophone. But I forgot it today.
ADA: There is no sense in that. There is no sense in trying to drown it.
        See Holloway.[132]

The moment confirms the recognition that we have been cast in a position similar to that of Henry. If he passively receives voices to varying states of epistemic and even ontological confusion, so do we. The unexpected kinship that the audience may experience with Henry that is achieved through the techniques deployed by the radio drama has far reaching implications for the ways that mental illness has been understood or willfully not understood.

    From *Murphy* to the radio dramas, Beckett moves beyond the misrepresentation of mental illness from the outside – as in Murphy's projections of Endon – toward simulations that take the audience within the lived experiences of the condition. In doing so, Beckett broaches the limitations on empathy that Jaspers draws when he famously defines the symptoms of schizophrenia as fundamentally "un-understandable." In his *General Psychopathology* (1913), Jaspers asserts, "The most profound distinction in psychic life seems to be that between what is meaningful and *allows empathy* and what in its particular way is *ununderstandable*, 'mad' in the literal sense, schizophrenic psychic life."[133] Psychologist Richard Bentall extrapolates the ethical implications of this attitude that has largely dominated the biologically oriented psychiatric conceptions of psychopathology:

> For Jaspers, the empathetic attitude of the psychiatrist towards the patient functions as a kind of diagnostic test. If the empathy scanner returns the reading "ununderstandable" the patient is psychotic and suffering from a biological disease [...] By not empathizing hard enough, we may fail to

recognize the intelligible aspects of the other person's experiences. Moreover, once we have decided that the patient's experiences are unintelligible, we are given an apparent license to treat the patient as a disordered organism, a malfunctioning body that we do not have to relate to in a human way.[134]

To be regarded as merely a "malfunctioning body" or brain whose experiences are not meaningful and are therefore beyond the reach of empathy is, in the view of Bentall and others, to be excluded from the categories of "human" and "person."

It is within this context that the larger consequences of Beckett's simulations of psychosis come into focus. To the extent that the audience experiences the modal ambiguities and metacognitive uncertainties that figures such as Henry Bolton suffer, the radio dramas raise the prospect of an empathic understanding of these conditions. The possibility and imperative of such understanding has been asserted by recent phenomenological psychiatrists such as Josef Parnas, who argues:

> We thus disagree with Jaspers on the issue of incomprehensibility of schizophrenia. We may grasp (at least to a certain degree) the nature of the patient's experience upon adopting a phenomenological stance, in which we suspend our common sense assumption of sharing with the patient the same "modal space." Through this kind of radical empathy, we attempt to make manifest what is most frequently overlooked, namely the altered structures of the patient's lived world, with other forms of spatiality, temporality, and selfhood etc.[135]

It is precisely an altered "modal space" akin to that of schizophrenia that *Embers* renders for its audience by distorting the "common sense" categories of experience such as "spatiality, temporality, and selfhood." If the modal status of Henry's experience is distorted or uncertain, so is ours, and this shared ambiguity enables us to empathize with the altered structure of his experience. As is evident in the statements of Bentall, Price, Parnas, and others, the stakes of this understanding are especially high when its absence leads to a diagnosis that effectively disinherits the patient from the category of human personhood.

The recurrent returns to questions of madness in Beckett's work are therefore not simply the results of morbid curiosity but constitute a sustained inquiry into relations between the formal conditions of our storytelling devices and the formal conditions of psychosis and personhood. If those devices – such as the novel and radio – and our relations to them are theorized within Beckett's work, it is in part because they are also recurrent preoccupations of those suffering from mental illness. In this way, Beckett's simulation of psychosis entails the theorizing of technological media and their relation to the human, because such theorizing is already a common element of modern psychosis and its diagnosis. These simulations therefore reconstruct psychiatric disability in ways that are both minoritizing and universalizing: the phenomenological conditions rendered are specific to particular forms of thought disorder such as schizophrenia; yet their reproduction through radio implies that it is not only the mentally ill who may become "prey to communications."[136]

Conclusion
Contemporary Mediations of Modernist Madness

In 1979, Lawrence Shainberg sent Samuel Beckett a copy of his book *The Brain Surgeon*. In response, Beckett wrote:

> Mere decay is a paltry affair beside the calamities you describe. It is all I can speak of. And the ever acute awareness of it. And the preposterous conviction formed long ago, that here in the end is the last & by far best chance for the writer. Gaping into his synaptic chasms.[1]

As if in response to Beckett's suggestion, Ian McEwan observed the work of a neurosurgeon while writing his novel *Saturday* (2005). The novel deploys free indirect discourse to report the thoughts and experiences of a neurosurgeon over the course of a single day, inevitably drawing comparisons to the methods of high modernist precursors such as *Ulysses* and *Mrs. Dalloway. Saturday* and an earlier novel, *Enduring Love* (1997), are focalized through characters who have absorbed contemporary neuroscience's biological accounts of the mind but who nevertheless find themselves ineluctably compelled to produce narrative forms of knowledge that both adapt the discourses of brainhood and signal the limits of those discourses. Patricia Waugh argues that "A need to find his own position in the celestial panoply of high-modernist novelists seems, for McEwan, to run alongside an enthusiastic engagement with evolution and the neurosciences that insinuates their more advanced grasp of mental interiority."[2]

McEwan is hardly unique in adapting narrative techniques long associated with modernism to engage with the discourses of the brain science and the phenomenology of neurological disorders, although not all examples of the subgenre demonstrate as much enthusiasm for the new discourses of the brain as McEwan sometimes shows. As Lustig and Peacock observe, "the frequency with which contemporary writers address themes relating specifically to molecular biology and what Snow called the 'higher nervous system' deserves further exploration."[3] Such "neuronovels" often take as their central project the representation of the experiences of what Catharine Malabou has called "the new wounded" – a category that designates "people who suffer from psychic wounds that traditional psychoanalysis cannot understand."[4] John Wray's *Lowboy* (2010) tells the story of a schizophrenic character living in New York's subway system; Richard Powers's *The Echo Maker* (2007) represents the experiences of a delusional patient suffering from Capgras syndrome and a writerly neurologist who closely resembles Oliver Sacks; Jonathan Lethem's *Motherless Brooklyn* (2000) features a central character who struggles with Tourette's Syndrome; Mark Haddon's *The Curious Incident of the Dog in the Night-Time* (2004) is narrated by a character whose behavior conforms to many accounts of autism. If late-modernist writers critically responded to the nascent mind sciences and their constructions of psychopathology, a wave of contemporary fiction has similarly responded to the growing awareness of nonneurotypical ways of being in the world and to the growing cultural prestige of neuroscience – a discipline that is often represented as having actualized many of the paranoid delusions of materialist reduction and technological observation that recurred in so many memoirs and late-modernist fictions of madness.

While these examples stretch the periodicity of most accounts of modernism, I would argue that many of them share more with the late-modernist writing that I've assembled in the previous chapters than with classic examples of postmodernism. Reactivations of modernist aesthetics in recent fiction have been observed by several critics.[5] While initial articulations of postmodernism emphasized rupture and discontinuity with modernism, recent approaches to contemporary literature have found modernist techniques renewed rather than subjected to parody or pastiche. David James suggests that, "we can legitimately read the modernist period itself via models of continuity and adaptation (rather than demise) after mid century, so as to enrich the way we reconstruct the story of fiction's postwar development," and come to "an understanding not only of what modernism was but also of what it might still become."[6] In many ways, Tyrus Miller's subtle account of late modernism leaves the door open to the persistence of modernist methods in postwar fiction. Against a periodizing logic of simple succession, Miller adopts the view of architecture critic Charles Jencks, who "emphasizes the overlap and coexistence of late modernism and postmodernism. These are not successive stages but rather alternative responses to the legacy of modernism and its possible continuation."[7] Maintaining the possibility that late-modernist and postmodern aesthetics may remain copresent affords an understanding of the uses to which the methods and concerns of modernism continue to be put in confronting cognate problems in the present. Constellations begin to emerge among texts that were separated by decades and that had been divorced by rigid literary histories.

Within this critical context, I will conclude by observing a resurgence in contemporary fiction of the conceptual and formal elements I've identified in a species of late-modernist fiction. As one of the aims of this book has been to reconstruct a literary history of late modernism's entanglement of psychopathology and information technologies, it is worth recognizing the ways that contemporary fiction has also returned to the scenes of modernism. These novels often engage in conspicuous acts of narrative world building, unreality effects, and altered forms of self-report that are manifestly indebted to the historical moment and discursive methods of modernism. The relation of this recent fiction to the late-modernist techniques and problematics that this book has assembled is rarely one of irony; instead, these works exhibit a shared sense of an ongoing project and legacy that has been reactivated by the claims and problems posed in the present.

In some instances, this return becomes quite explicit in the form of historical fiction that explicitly returns to the constellation of symptoms that includes technological thought transmission, paranoid world building, and the reduction of mind to informatic machine. Set in the early decades of the twentieth century, Tom McCarthy's novel *C* (2010) may be read as a technological *bildungsroman*; the maturation of its protagonist, Serge Carrefax, is closely linked to the development of radio technology.[8] In his youth – and in the early, experimental years of amateur radio transmission – he observes, "The static's like the sound of thinking. Not of any single person thinking, nor even of a group thinking collectively. It's bigger than that, wider – and more direct. It's like the sound of thought itself, its hum and rush."[9] Serge is confronted by a technological conception of information that is disarticulated from individual subjectivity, and the form of the novel vacillates between distinctly modernist modes of subjectless, behaviorist descriptions of outward behavior and first-person accounts of depersonalization. One reviewer of the novel complains that "The deliberately flattened, almost mechanical characters [...] make for joyless reading" – a description that might be applied equally to Wyndham Lewis's acerbic satires of behaviorism such as *Snooty Baronet* and *The Childermass*.[10] As in many of its modernist antecedents, *C* couples the prosthesis afforded by radio with forms of disability: Serge's father runs a school for the deaf, Serge is physically and psychologically maimed at several points in the novel, and his sister exhibits forms of paranoid and magical thinking that arise from her experiments with radio.

The novel links the informatic problem of sorting meaningful signal from meaningless noise to the eroding distinction between life and death as when his sister Sophie attempts to reanimate a dead cat through electrification.

> As she animates the leg over and over again, she shakes with a laughter that's sparked up afresh with each new quickening – as though she were also animated by the current, which was somehow running through her body too. Serge, watching the leg move with the angular stiffness of a clockwork mechanism, thinks of semaphore machines, their angles and positions, then of the strange, moving shapes he saw played out across the sheet. After a while, he starts to wonder if perhaps the morbid and hypnotic sequences being executed by the dead cat's limb contain some kind of information – "contain" in the sense of enclosing, locking in, repeating in a code for which no key's available, at least not to him . . ."

Serge suspects that information is detachable from intention or subjectivity and has an uncanny, automatic existence of its own – a conception that anticipates Claude Shannon's theory of information as a measure not of meaning but of entropy. While occupying a position at the limit of sense and non-sense, he nevertheless detects a dimension of signification to which he does not have access and begins to project patterns where none may exist. Sophie goes further to find hidden signals of world-historical events in the behavior of insects, the structure of flowers, and the letters of newspaper headlines. In Serge's view, "She looks as though she were tuning into something – as though she had somehow turned *herself* into a receiver."[12] The private world of associations that Sophie constructs excludes Serge, and yet they share a technological explanation for the obscure transmissions that only she seems to project and receive. Like Wyndham Lewis's self-styled behaviorist, Kell-Imrie, Serge apprehends only outward, mechanical behavior – phenomena without phenomenology.

While access to normative signification appears foreclosed to him, Serge exhibits the technological megalomania that recurs in Schreber's *Memoirs* and Loy's *Insel.* As a Royal Air Force (RAF) navigator and bombardier, he is granted a vision of total mechanization of the war, "as though he himself had become god-like, elevated by machinery and signal code to a higher post within the overall structure of things."[13] Serge's place within his world vacillates between this megalomaniacal, messianic distinction and depersonalization within the machinery that incorporates him. In a clear reference to F. T. Marinetti's Futurist fantasy of convergence with the automobile and of the mechanistic transcription of "what the propeller told me," Serge imagines becoming one with his machine.[14] In a reference to another modernist meditation on technology, Serge reproduces Heidegger's famous interpretation of Hölderlin: "Where danger is, there rescue grows."[15] Serge's psychological disintegration is coupled with a mythic rebirth in and through a technological *Weltanschauung*.

C develops a decidedly grim appraisal of the coercive, imperial uses to which radio is put. Serge is enlisted to work on the Empire Wireless Chain – a worldwide system of broadcast towers designed to connect the colonies of the British Empire to the governing center of control – a system that was constructed during the 1920s and that arguably became the blueprint for the BBC's world service. The global system enabled the broadcasting of propaganda to controlled territories and the return of intelligence to the empire's nerve center. Such a technological collapse of spatial boundaries through a globalized information system could be regarded as confirmation of the most paranoid fears of thought broadcasting and manipulation – anxieties that recur in the experimental fiction and memoirs of psychosis written in the modernist era in which *C* is set.

The novel therefore not only returns to modernism but recasts the convergence of information technology and psychopathology that defined the work of late-modernist writers such as Wyndham Lewis, Mina Loy, Evelyn Waugh, and Samuel Beckett. At the same time, its treatment of information and global communications systems suggests that the retrospective gaze of *C* is mediated by subsequent technological developments such as information theory, cybernetics, and networked computation. In this way, *C* is a historical novel that not only performs an archaeology of a technological form of madness; it also renders a modernism that responds to conditions and problems of its present moment.

A similar return to the moment and methods of modernism occurs in Will Self's *Umbrella* (2012). Self makes his formal and conceptual debts to modernism clear in an essay entitled "Modernism and Me," and the novel makes multiple allusions to its modernist intertexts.[16] *Umbrella* deploys dense, stream-of-consciousness narration and abrupt shifts in temporality in order to represent the lived experiences of patients suffering from *encephalitis lethargica* – a condition that spread throughout Europe in the 1910s and 1920s and left patients suffering from symptoms of extreme fatigue, involuntary movements, catatonia, and altered experiences of time. These subjects were often misdiagnosed with schizophrenia, and, in the absence of any effective treatment, they sometimes remained in mental institutions for decades. While McCarthy's *C* follows the development of radio technology and psychopathology through the modernist period,

Umbrella represents the era's futile approaches to mental illness and the effects of those treatments upon the patients. As one clinician in the novel observes, "the post-encephalitics have borne the brunt of every successive wave of psychiatric opinion."[17]

In the absence of a decisive etiological explanation of their symptoms, many theories are proposed, including speculations that outbreaks of *encephalitis lethargica* may be correlated with historical periods of intense technological acceleration.

> If we look at the factor it has in common with the others – London on the brink of the first Industrial Revolution, Manchester in the throes of the second, Vienna caught up in a frenzy of wartime armaments production – we might hypothesize that it is not the numbers or density of humans that was the decider, but the density of mechanisation, of … technology.[18]

In this account, the etiology of the condition is not to be found in the individual's psychological conflicts nor in her neural structure; instead, the causes are cultural and historical. The involuntary motions of the central encephalitic patient in the novel, Audrey Death, are ambiguously overdetermined by neurological damage and by the repetitive motions that she performed as a lathe operator in a munitions factory during the Great War and as a typist whose automatisms recalls those of a similar typist in T. S. Eliot's *The Waste Land*. When Audrey spasms during the act of sex, the novel suggests that it is not the result of orgasmic climax but rather the involuntary, neural traces of her assembly-line labor: "She lay beneath him jerking not with pleasure provoked by his caresses but the repetitive motions of operating the lathe – twirling, cranking, pulling – that had been dinned into every nerve-fiber throughout the twelve-hour shift."[19] She is one of the "new wounded" whose symptoms are not signifiers for psychoanalytic interpretation but instead reflect a mechanistic reduction to dysfunctional, neurological substrates.

Novels such as *Umbrella* that invoke such a framework for conceptualizing symptoms pose unique interpretive questions, as T. J. Lustig and James Peacock observe: "If neurology takes center stage, must we reject the notion of hidden meanings, indeed of deep meaningfulness as necessary or desirable? What if a novel, like certain neurological disorders, produces symptoms which are simply random accidents, the results of faulty wiring and hence in no way truly meaningful?"[20] If this is a problem for the contemporary novel, it is not entirely new. As I've argued, it is one that recurs in late-modernist fiction that responds to the mechanistic reduction of symptomatic mind to broken brain, and this may be the primary rationale for the setting and narrative technique of *Umbrella*. If *C* reconstructs its modernism as part of a genealogy of information media and its pathologies, *Umbrella* finds in modernism a genealogy of contemporary neuroculture. In its movements between the first decades of the twentieth century and those of the twenty-first century, *Umbrella* suggests that what Karl Jaspers called "brain mythologies" have only gained force.

Indeed, Joseph Dumit observes that belief and desire persist in the face of failures to establish simple neurological correlations for complex conditions such as schizophrenia: "For the positron emission tomography scan (PET) researcher, the scan shows what the researcher cannot yet imagine. The scan holds a key to the mystery of schizophrenia, but the researcher cannot yet grasp it."[21] The persistence of this belief in the absence of empirical evidence signals a phantasmatic dimension that sustains both producers and consumers of "neuroculture," and this fantasmatic dimension is precisely where cultural analysis is required. For some historians and sociologists of the brain sciences, such as Nicholas Rose and Joelle Abi-Rached, the failure to find the causes of conditions such as schizophrenia in brain scans is the result of a category error that has plagued psychiatry ever since it restricted its attention to neuroanatomy: "At root, the neurobiological project in psychiatry finds its limit in the simple and often repeated fact: mental disorders are problems of persons, not of brains. Mental disorders are not problems of brains in labs, but of human beings in time, space, culture, and history."[22] This, in many ways, is the critique that Will Self's *Umbrella* and other contemporary novels have made.

Rose's and Abi-Rached's critique of this reification of the mind as brain has many precursors. Another late-modernist thinker, Ludwig Wittgenstein asserted that "only of a living human being and what resembles (behaves like) a living human being, can one say it has sensations; it sees, is blind; hears, is deaf; is conscious or unconscious."[23] More recently M. R. Bennett and P. M. S. Hacker have critiqued the "mereological fallacy" of neuroscience, which assigns "properties to genes or brains that properly belong only to persons."[24] Patricia Waugh observes that this tendency "not only somatizes but also molecularizes the self. Mental illnesses are diseases of the brain or central nervous system conceived as evolutionarily wired into localized and dedicated functional modules."[25] *Umbrella* represents such a reduction of patients to subhuman modules to which a psychiatrist struggles to relate in a human way: "They are possessed, he thinks, by ancient subpersonalities, the neural building-blocks of the psyche ... She is gone – or, at least, too far down the corridor to be seen any more a human particle [...] All the subhuman parts of her – can they be observed?"[26] Later, he thinks that "these pecking, bobbing and stuffed bodies were barely human."[27]

Despite his efforts to correlate his patients' symptoms with damage to subcortical regions of their brains, Audrey's psychiatrist sometimes breaks with his colleagues and privately attempts to imagine the structures of their lived experiences:

> Busner has become convinced that whatever the damage to their diencephalons, their hypothalamuses and their substantia nigras, these derelict brains are still inhabited. In the upper storeys of these rundown minds true sentience remains – although surely ferociously disturbed by its decades of imprisonment in a jail within a jail.[28]

In a similar fashion, some neuroscientists have acknowledged that strictly neurological and informatic approaches to mental illness have resulted in inattention to the complexity and specificity of patients' lived experiences. Nancy Andreasen, a neuroscientist who has devoted much of her career to the study of schizophrenia, has melancholically remarked upon the "Death of Phenomenology" in psychiatry, and writes that "there has been a steady decline in the teaching of careful clinical evaluation that is targeted to the individual person's problems and social context and that is enriched by a good general knowledge of psychopathology."[29] Such calls for a return to phenomenological approaches have arisen at a time when works of contemporary fiction have attempted to represent the lived experiences of mental illness and cognitive disorders – a genre that Patricia Waugh describes as the "Neo-Phenomenological Novel."[30]

The reduction of mind to brainhood has consequences not only for doctors' understanding of patients but also for patients' self-understanding, and this extends beyond those who are most directly subjected to psychiatric and neurological explanations. Rose and Abi-Rached argue that "scientific truths and cultural truths are not always so distinct. What happens, then, when these two dimensions transect and intertwine? What happens when the quotidian conception that human beings have of themselves is itself shaped in part by the truth claims made in an esoteric language of science?"[31] These are among the core questions that this book has pursued in the previous chapters by showing how experimental fiction and patients' self-reports have transected and intertwined with psychiatric and neurological reconstructions of the mind as brain.

If the "brain mythologies" that once dominated early psychiatry have returned in force within contemporary neuroculture, some have responded to Andreasen's call for a renewed interest in the phenomenology of psychopathology and to Karl Jasperss's provocative assertion, written over a century ago, that "The methods for knowledge in this field are only acquired through a training in the humanities."[32] While many works of contemporary fiction have attempted to represent the lived experiences of the "new wounded," narrative and phenomenological approaches to mental illness have gained momentum in the mind sciences. Shaun Gallagher observes: "There is a growing consensus, across a number of disciplines, including philosophy, psychology, and neuroscience, that narrative competency provides important structure for the development of something more than a minimal (momentary and immediate sense of) self."[33]

It follows that the study of experimental narrative and narrative theory have much to contribute to the ongoing debates over the understandability of nonnormative minds. We may find in the work of writers such as Wyndham Lewis, Mina Loy, Evelyn Waugh, Anna Kavan, Muriel Spark, Flann O'Brien, and Samuel Beckett acts of narrative worlding and unworlding not unlike those of psychiatric patients. Conversely, literary studies have much to learn from the writings and discourse of mental patients who often develop innovative ways to articulate and manage their lived experiences.[34] If experimental fiction trains us to recognized precariously structured meaning in the delusions of subjects that have often been dismissed as "un-understandable," those delusional memoirs and case studies also illuminate formal features and conceptual problems that distinguish experimental fiction. The study of such writing expands our understanding of what may constitute a world, and how such worlds may be constructed, inhabited, and lost. Such understanding begins with a recognition of the reparative resources of the unreal. Lydia Davis writes that "a mad person not helped out of his trouble by anything real begins to trust what is not real because it helps him and he needs it because real things continue not to help him."[35] As readers of fictions and memoirs of mental illness, we may discover unexpected kinship with those who are helped by "what is not real."

Notes

Introduction: Three Black Boxes

1 Victor Tausk, "On the Origin of the 'Influencing Machine' in Schizophrenia." *Psychoanalytic Quarterly* 22 (1933), 519–556. The article first appeared in the German journal *Internationale Zeitschrift für Psychoanalyse* (1919).

2 Willis K. Wing, Charles Cooke, James Thurber, and Harold Ross, "Talk in Dreams," *The New Yorker*, October 7, 1933, 17–18.

3 The Psycho-Phone was invented by A. B. Saliger, who registered the trademark in 1927 and received U.S. Patent No. 1,886,358 in 1932 for an "automatic time controlled suggestion device." *The New Yorker* reports that by 1933 he had sold over 2,500 Psycho-Phones to mostly satisfied customers.

4 Wing et al., "Talk in Dreams," p. 18.

5 Wyndham Lewis, *Time and Western Man*, (Santa Rosa: Black Sparrow Press, 1993), p. xii.

6 Wyndham Lewis, *The Art of Being Ruled*, (Santa Rosa: Black Sparrow Press, 1989), pp. 105, 106.

7 Pamela Thurschwell, *Literature, Technology, and Magical Thinking, 1880–1920* (Cambridge: Cambridge University Press, 2001), p. 8. For more on the erotic fantasies associated with modernism's audio technologies, see Mark Goble, *Beautiful Circuits: Modernism and the Mediated Life* (New York: Columbia University Press, 2010).

8 Theodor Adorno, "The Problem of a New Type of Human Being," in Robert Hullot-Kentor (ed. and trans.), *Current of Music* (Malden, MA: Polity Press, 2006), pp. 461–468.

9 Adorno, "The Problem of a New Type of Human Being," *Current of Music*, p. 463.

10 Adorno, "The Radio Voice," *Current of Music*, p. 373.

11 Hadley Cantril and Gordon W. Allport, *The Psychology of Radio* (New York: Harper & Bros., 1935), p. 3, p. vii.

12 Rudolf Arnheim, *Radio* (London: Faber & Faber, 1936), p. 263.

13 Arnheim, *Radio*, p. 274.

14 Asa Briggs, *The History of Broadcasting in the United Kingdom*, Vol. 1: *The Birth of Broadcasting* (Oxford: Oxford University Press, 1961), p. 14.

15 Debra Rae Cohen, "Intermediality and the Problem of the Listener," *Modernism/Modernity* 19.3 (2012), 579. Cohen quotes *Listener*, September 11, 1929, p. 355; "Discussion Groups," *Listener*, September 23, 1929, p. 60.

16 Harold Nicolson, "Myself and the Microphone," *Listener*, April 29, 1931, p. 722; quoted in Cohen, "Intermediality and the Problem of the Listener," p. 585.

17 Cohen, "Intermediality and the Problem of the Listener," p. 586.

18 On the links among modernist writing, propaganda, and media, see especially Mark Wollaeger, *Modernism, Media, and Propaganda: British Narrative From 1900 to 1945* (Princeton: Princeton University Press, 2008).

19 Lisa Blackman, *Hearing Voices: Embodiment and Experience* (London: Free Association Press, 2001), p. 2.

20 Karl Jaspers, *General Psychopathology*, J. Hoenig and Marian W. Hamilton (trans.) (Johns Hopkins University Press, 1997), p. 459.

21 Wayne Shorter, *A History of Psychiatry: From the Era of the Asylum to the Age of Prozac* (New York: Wiley, 1998), p. 80.

22 Written in the late 1930s, this novel was recovered from Loy's papers and published posthumously in 1991. Mina Loy, *Insel*, Elizabeth Arnold (ed.) (Santa Rosa: Black Sparrow Press, 1991).

23 Shorter, *A History of Psychiatry*, p. 80.

24 Wyndham Lewis, *The Childermass* (New York: Covici & Friede, 1928).

25 Marguerite Sechehaye, *Autobiography of a Schizophrenic Girl: Reality Lost and Regained*, Grace Rubin-Rabson (trans.) (New York: Grune & Stratton, 1951). This "autobiography" was transcribed and published with commentary by Sechehaye, who treated the anonymous patient. Daniel Paul Schreber, *Memoirs of My Nervous Illness*, Ida Macalpine and Richard Hunter (trans.) (New York: New York Review of Books, 2000).

26 Paul Ricoeur, *Time and Narrative*, Vol. 1, Kathleen McLaughlin and David Pellauer (trans.) (Chicago: University of Chicago Press, 1990).

27 Charles Taylor, *The Sources of the Self: The Making of Modern Identity* (Cambridge: Harvard University Press, 1989), p. 52.

28 Antonio Damasio, *The Feeling of What Happens: Body and Emotion in the Making of Consciousness* (New York: Harcourt, 1999), pp. 222–233.

29 Thomas Metzinger, *The Ego Tunnel: The Science of Mind and the Myth of the Self* (New York: Basic Books, 2009).

30 Eve Kosofsky Sedgwick, "Paranoid Reading, Reparative Reading, or, You're So Paranoid, You Probably Think This Essay Is about You," *Touching Feeling: Affect, Pedagogy, Performativity* (Durham: Duke University Press, 2003), p. 131, emphasis original.

31 Eric Santner, *My Own Private Germany: Daniel Paul Schreber's Secret History of Modernity* (Princeton: Princeton University Press, 1996).

32 Santner, *My Own Private Germany*, p. 37.

33 David Trotter, *Paranoid Modernism: Literary Experiment, Psychosis, and the Professionalization of English Society* (Oxford: Oxford University Press, 2001).

34 For a fascinating reading about avant-garde aesthetics in light of neurasthenia, see Amelia Jones, *Irrational Modernism: A Neurasthenic History of New York Dada* (Cambridge: MIT Press, 2004).

35 Emil Kraepelin, *Dementia Praecox and Paraphrenia*, R. M. Barclay (trans.) (Huntington, NY: Robert E. Krieger, 1971); Eugen Bleuler, *The Schizophrenic Disorders*, S. M. Clemens (trans.) (New Haven and London: Yale University Press, 1978).

36 Richard Bentall, *Madness Explained: Psychosis and Human Nature* (New York: Penguin, 2004), p. 50.

37 Michel Foucault, *History of Madness*, Jean Khalfa (ed.), Jonathan Murphy and Jean Khalfa (trans.) (New York: Routledge, 2006), p. 194. Foucault revisited these arguments in his 1973–1974 College de France Lectures. Michel Foucault, *Psychiatric Power*, ed. Jacques Lagrange and Arnold Davidson, trans. Graham Burchell (New York: Picador, 2008).

38 Mary Boyle, *Schizophrenia: A Scientific Delusion* (London: Routledge, 1990).

39 Blackman, *Hearing Voices*, p. 18, p. 38.

40 Angela Woods, *The Sublime Object of Psychiatry: Schizophrenia in Clinical and Cultural Theory* (Oxford: Oxford University Press, 2011), p. 2.

41 Darian Leader, *What Is Madness?* (New York: Penguin Press, 2012), p. 75.

42 Bentall, *Madness Explained*, p. 39, emphasis added.

43 Leslie Barber, "The Age of Schizophrenia," *Harper's Monthly Magazine*, December 1, 1937, p. 70.

44 Morton Prince, *A Dissociation of a Personality: A Biographical Study in Abnormal Personality* (New York: Longmans and Green, 1906).

45 Particularly illuminating studies of modernism's confrontations with technology include Friedrich Kittler, *Discourse Networks 1800/1900*, Michael Metteer (trans.) (Stanford: Stanford University Press, 1990); Mark Seltzer, *Bodies and Machines* (New York: Routledge, 1992); Tim Armstrong, *Modernism, Technology and the Body: A Cultural Study* (Cambridge: Cambridge University Press, 1998); Jeffrey Herf, *Reactionary Modernism: Technology, Culture, and Politics in Weimar and the Third Reich* (Cambridge: Cambridge University Press, 1986).

46 Catherine Prendergast in Lennard J. Davis (ed.), "*The Unexceptional Schizophrenic: A Post-Postmodern Introduction,*" (New York: Routledge, 2013), pp. 236–245.

47 Sechehaye, *Autobiography of a Schizophrenic Girl*, p. 10, p. 12.

48 Rene Descartes, *The Philosophical Works of Descartes*, Vol. 1, Elizabeth Haldane and G. R. T. Ross (ed. and trans.) (Cambridge: Cambridge University Press, 1969), p. 155.

49 For a rich comparison Descartes's treatment of the subject as an object in the world to schizophrenic experiences of depersonalization, see Louis Sass, "Heidegger, Schizophrenia, and the Ontological Difference," *Philosophical Psychology* 5.2 (1992), pp. 109–133.

50 Sechehaye, *Autobiography of a Schizophrenic Girl*, p. 25.

51 Friedrich Kittler, *Discourse Networks 1800/1800;* Laura Otis, *Networking: Communicating with Bodies and Machines in the Nineteenth Century* (Ann Arbor: University of Michigan Press, 2001).

52 Carl Jung, *The Psychology of Dementia Praecox*, A. A. Brill (trans.) (New York: Nervous and Mental Disease Publishing Company, 1936). Avital Ronell gives a deliriously inventive reading of this delusion that connects it to Heidegger's notorious "call of conscience" in *The Telephone Book: Technology, Schizophrenia, Electric Speech* (Lincoln: University of Nebraska Press, 1989).

53 Kittler cites Flechsig's inaugural lecture as professor of psychiatry at the University of Leipzig in which he claims that there are "no independent illnesses of the mind without those of the body." Kittler, *Discourse Networks 1800/1900*, p. 294.

54 Schreber, *Memoirs of My Nervous Illness*, p. 46.

55 Schreber, *Memoirs of My Nervous Illness*, p. 21.

56 Schreber, *Memoirs of My Nervous Illness*, 120.

57 Kittler, *Discourse Networks 1800/1900*, p. 294.

58 For another valuable discussion of early, somatic psychiatry as a framework for early modernism, see Kylie Valentine, *Psychoanalysis, Psychiatry and Modernist Literature* (New York: Palgrave Macmillan, 2003), pp. 63–89.

59 For an account of Helmholtzian materialism's influences on Freud, see Frank Sulloway, *Freud, Biologist of the Mind: Beyond the Psychoanalytic Legend* (New York: Basic Books, 1979); Siefried Bernfeld, "Freud's Earliest Theories and the School of Helmholtz," *Psychoanalytic Quarterly* 13 (1944): 341–62. For challenges to this account, see Richard Boothby, *Freud as Philosopher: Metapsychology After Lacan* (New York: Routledge, 2001), pp. 241–280, and Slavoj Zizek, *Tarrying with the Negative: Kant, Hegel, and the Critique of Ideology* (Durham, Duke University Press, 1993), pp. 178–180.

60 Among papers that follow Tausk's study of machine-identification in schizophrenia are R. Ekstein, "The Space Child's Time Machine: On 'Reconstruction' in the Psychotherapeutic Treatment of a Schizophrenoid Child," *American Journal of Orthopsychiatry* 24 (1954), 492–506; P. Elkisch and M. S. Mahler, "On Infantile Precursors of the 'Influencing Machine' (Tausk)," *Psychoanalytic Study of the Child* 14 (1959), 219–235; E. Furman, "An Ego Disturbance in a Young Child," *Psychoanalytic Study of the Child* 11 (1956), 312–335; E. Jacobson, "Depersonalization," *Journal of the American Psychoanalytic Association* 7 (1959), 581–610; H. Sachs, "The Delay of the Machine Age," *Psychoanalytic Quarterly* 2 (1933), 404–424; L. J. Sachs, "On changes in identification from machine to cripple," *Psychoanalytic Study of the Child* 12 (1957), 356–375.

61 Henry Maudsley, *Responsibility in Mental Disease*, (London: Macmillan, 1874), p. 15.

62 Jaspers, General Psychopathology, p. 18.

63 Eugen Bleuler, *Naturgeschichte der Seele und irhes beisstwerdens, eine Elementarpsychologie*, 1921, quoted in Verena Kuni, " 'Je Suis Radio' – from the 'Influencing Machine' to the 'Radio- Self,' " in Thomas Roske and Bettina Brand-Claussen (eds.), *The Air Loom and Other Dangerous Influencing Machines* (Heidelberg: Wunderhorn, 2006), p. 243.

64 Kuni, " 'Je Suis Radio' – from the 'Influencing Machine' to the 'Radio- Self,' " p. 245.

65 "Human Radio Emanations," *New York Times*, September 28, 1925, p. 27; cited by Jeffrey Sconce, "Wireless Ego: The Pulp Physics of Psychoanalysis," in Debra Rae Cohen, Michael Coyle, and Jane Lewty (eds.), *Broadcasting Modernism* (Gainesville: University Press of Florida, 2009), p. 38. Also see "Radio's Aid is Invoked to Explore Telepathy," *New York Times*, August 30, 1925, p. XX3.

66 L.F. Haas, "Hans Berger (1873–1941), Richard Caton (1842–1926), and Electroencephalography," *Journal of Neurology, Neurosurgery & Psychiatry* 74.1 (2003), n.p.

67 Sconce, "Wireless Ego"; see also Jeffrey Sconce, *Haunted Media: Electronic Presence from Telegraphy to Television* (Durham: Duke University Press, 2000).

68 John B. Watson, *Behaviorism* (Chicago: University of Chicago Press, 1928), p. 11.

69 Edward Boring, "Mind and Mechanism," *American Journal of Psychology* 59.2 (1946), 183, 185, emphasis added.

70 Boring, "Mind and Mechanism," p. 191.

71 Boring, "Mind and Mechanism," p. 177.

72 Rhodri Hayward, "'Our Friends Electric': Mechanical Models of Mind in Postwar Britian," in G. C. Bunn, A. D. Lovie, and G. D. Richards (eds.), *Psychology in Britain: Historical Essays and Personal Reflections* (Leicester, UK: British Psychologist Society, 2001), p. 304.

73 Andrew Pickering, *Cybernetic Brain: Sketches of Another Future* (Chicago: University of Chicago Press), p. 93; Ross Ashby, *Design For a Brain* (London: Chapman & Hall, 1952).

74 Ross Ashby, "Cybernetics," in G. W. T. H. Fleming (ed.), *Recent Progress in Psychiatry*, special issue of *Journal of Mental Science*, 2nd ed. (London: Churchill, 1950), 107. Cited in Pickering, *Cybernetic Brain*, p. 133.

75 Pickering, *Cybernetic Brain*, p. 17.

76 Norbert Wiener, *The Human Use of Human Beings: Cybernetics and Society* (New York: Avon, 1967 [1950]); cited in Pickering, *Cybernetic Brain*, p. 132.

77 The interview was conducted in 1966, but, on his condition, only published after Heidegger's death in 1976. "Only a God Can Save Us," in Richard Wolin (ed.), *The Heidegger Controversy: A Critical Reader* (Cambridge: MIT Press, 1991), pp. 91–118.

78 For an historical survey and philosophical defense of this position, see Thomas Hardy Leahy, "Psychology as Engineering," in Christina E. Erneling and David M. Johnson (eds.), *The Mind as a Scientific Object: Between Brain and Culture* (Oxford: Oxford University Press, 2005), pp. 126–143.

79 Blackman, *Hearing Voices*, pp. 42–43.

80 Barbara O'Brien, *Operators and Things: The Inner Life of a Schizophrenic* (Cambridge: Arlington, 1958), p. 135.

81 Ian Hacking, *Rewriting the Soul: Multiple Personality and the Sciences of Memory* (Princeton: Princeton University Press, 1995), p. 21.

82 Jean-Pierre Dupuy, *On the Origins of Cognitive Science: The Mechanization of the Mind*, trans. M. B. DeBevoise (Cambridge: MIT Press, 2009), p. 49.

83 Jaspers, *General Psychopathology*, pp. 537, 772; Gilbert Ryle, *The Concept of Mind* (Chicago: University of Chicago Press, 2000), especially pp. 19–21, pp. 319–324.

84 Jacques Lacan, *The Seminar of Jacques Lacan, Book II: The Ego in Freud's Theory and in the Technique of Psychoanalysis, 1954–1955*, ed. Jacques-Alain Miller, trans. Sylvana Tomaselli (New York: Norton, 1991), pp. 294–326.

85 Jean-Pierre Dupuy, *On The Origins of Cognitive Science: The Mechanization of the Mind* (Cambridge: MIT Press, 2009), p. 19.

86 Gregory Bateson, *Steps to an Ecology of Mind: Collected Essays in Anthropology, Psychiatry, Evolution, and Epistemology* (Chicago: University of Chicago Press, 2000); Kenneth Colby, *Artificial Paranoia: A Computer Simulation of Paranoid Processes* (New York: Pergamon, 1975).

87 W. R. Ashby, "Passing through Nature" (unpublished notebook), referenced in Pickering, p. 112.

88 For more on the links between psychoanalysis and cybernetics, see Lydia H. Liu, *The Freudian Robot: Digital Media and the Future of the Unconscious* (Chicago: University of Chicago Press, 2010).

89 See Bruce Clarke and Linda Dalrymple Henderson (eds.), *From Energy to Information: Representation in Science and Technology, Art, and Literature* (Palo Alto: Stanford University Press, 2002). David Trotter also discusses this transition in light of modernism in *Literature and the First Media Age* (Cambridge: Harvard University Press, 2013), p. 22.

90 "As I neither fear criticism nor shy away from self-criticism, I have no motive for avoiding mention of a similarity that may damage our libido theory in the judgment of many readers. Schreber's 'rays of God,' composed of a condensation of solar rays, nerve fibers, and spermatozoa, are in fact nothing other than the libidinal investments, concretely represented and projected outwards, and so lend his delusion a striking conformity with our theory." Sigmund Freud, *The Schreber Case*, trans. Andrew Webber (New York: Penguin, 2003), p. 66.

91 R. D. Laing, *The Divided Self: An Existential Study of Sanity and Madness* (New York: Penguin, 1960), p. 22.

92 Jaspers, *General Psychopathology*, p. 462.

93 Daniel Dennett, *The Intentional Stance* (Cambridge: MIT Press, 1987).

94 Richard Bentall, *Madness Explained: Psychosis and Human Nature* (New York: Penguin, 2004), p. 530.

95 Bentall, *Madness Explained*, 29.

96 Heather Love, "Safe," *American Literary History* 25.1 (2013), 170.

97 Samuel Beckett, *The Unnamable* in *Three Novels* (New York: Grove Press, 2009), p. 360.

98 *Diagnostic and Statistical Manual of Mental Disorders, 5th Edition: DSM-5* (New York: American Psychiatric Association, 2013).

99 Leader, *What Is Madness?* p. 31, emphasis added. Elsewhere, Leader notes that "A recent survey of MEDLINE publications on schizophrenia showed that a mere 0.17 per cent of articles were related to the subjective experience of the patient." p. 32.

100 Bentall, *Madness Explained*, p. 498.

101 Blackman, *Hearing Voices*, p. 78. See also Rita Charon, *Narrative Medicine: Honoring the Stories of Illness* (Oxford: Oxford University Press, 2008); Ann Jurecic, *Illness as Narrative* (Pittsburgh: University of Pittsburgh Press, 2012); Arthur W. Frank: *The Wounded Storyteller: Body, Illness, and Ethics* (Chicago: University of Chicago Press, 2013); Ivan Leudar and Philip Thomas, *Voices of Reason, Voices of Insanity: Studies of Verbal Hallucinations* (New York: Routledge, 2000).

102 Martin Heidegger, "The Thing," in *Poetry, Language, Thought*, Albert Hofstadter (trans.) (New York: Harper Collins, 1971), p. 164.

103 Sechehaye, *An Autobiography of a Schizophrenic Girl*, p. 59.

104 Sechehaye, *An Autobiography of a Schizophrenic Girl*, p. 28.

105 K. Tylen, P. Christensen, A. Roepstorff, T. Lund, S. Ostergaard, and M. Donald, "Brains Striving for Coherence: Long-Term Cumulative Plot Formation in the Default Mode Network," *Neuroimage*, (2015), 107.

106 Dan Zahavi, "Self and Other: The Limits of Narrative Understanding," in Daniel Hutto (ed.), *Narrative Understanding and Persons* (Cambridge: Cambridge University Press, 2007), p. 183.

107 Shaun Gallagher, "Pathologies in Narrative Structures," in Hutto (ed.), *Narrative and Understanding Persons*, p. 224.

108 Paul Ricoeur, "Life: A Story in Search of a Narrator," in *On Psychoanalysis: Writings and Lectures*, Vol. 1, David Pellauer (trans.) (New York: Polity Press, 2012), p. 193.

109 Anthony Giddens, *Modernity and Self-Identity: Self and Society in the Late-Modern Age* (Palo Alto: Stanford University Press, 1991), p. 54; cited in Jurecic, *Illness as Narrative*, p. 20.

110 Sigmund Freud, "Neurosis and Psychosis" (1924), in *The Standard Edition of the Complete Psychological Works of Sigmund Freud*, Vol. 19, James Strachey (trans.) (London: Hogarth Press, 2001), p. 151.

111 Schreber, Memoirs of My Nervous Illness, p. 54.

112 Oliver Sacks, "Foreword," in A. R. Luria, *The Man with a Shattered World: The History of a Brain Wound* (Cambridge: Harvard University Press, 1987), p. xvii.

113 Larry Davidson, "Storytelling and Schizophrenia: Using Narrative Structure in Phenomenological Research," *Humanistic Psychologist* 21.2 (1991), 200–220.

114 James Phillips, "Schizophrenia and the Narrative Self," in Tilo Kircher and Anthony David (eds.), *Self in Neuroscience and Psychiatry* (Cambridge: Cambridge University Press, 2003), p. 328.

115 Paul Lysaker and John Lysaker, "Narrative Structure in Psychosis: Schizophrenia and Disruptions in the Dialogical Self," *Theory & Psychology* 12.2 (2002), 207–220; Paul Lysaker, Amanda Wickett, and Louanne Davis, "Narrative Qualities in Schizophrenia: Associations with Impairments in Neurocognition and Negative Symptoms," *Journal of Nervous and Mental Disease* 193.4 (2005), 244–249; Paul Lysaker et al., "Changes in Narrative Structure and Content in Schizophrenia in Long

Term Individual Psychotherapy: A Single Case Study," *Clinical Psychology and Psychotherapy* 12 (2005), 406–416; Paul Lysaker and John Lysaker, "A Typology of Narrative Impoverishment in Schizophrenia: Implications for Understanding the Processes of Establishing and Sustaining Dialogue in Individual Psychotherapy," *Counseling Psychology Quarterly* 19.1 (2006), 57–68; Paul Lysaker, Jack Tsai, Alyssa Maulucci, and Giovanni Stanghellini, "Narrative Accounts of Illness in Schizophrenia: Association of Different Forms of Awareness with Neurocognition and Social Function over Time," *Consciousness and Cognition* 17 (2008), 1143–1151; Paul Lysaker, Jamie Ringer, Alan McGuire, and Tania Lecomte, "Personal Narratives and Recovery from Schizophrenia," *Schizophrenia Research* 121 (2010), 271–276.

116 Sedgwick, "Paranoid Reading, Reparative Reading, or, You're So Paranoid You Probably Think This Essay Is about You."

117 Jurecic, *Illness as Narrative*, p. 4.

118 Bruno Latour, "Why Has Critique Run Out of Steam? From Matters of Fact to Matters of Concern," *Critical Inquiry* 30 (Winter 2004), 246; cited in Jurecic, *Illness as Narrative*, p. 16.

119 Leader, *What is Madness?* p. 77.

120 Leader, *What is Madness?* p. 73, emphasis added.

121 Ricoeur, "Life: A Story in Search of a Narrator," pp. 195–196.

122 Ricoeur, "Life: A Story in Search of a Narrator," p. 196.

123 Friedrich Kittler, *Discourse Networks 1800/1900*, trans. Michael Metteer (Stanford: Stanford University Press, 1990), pp. 265–346.

124 Steven Connor offers a similar critique of Kittler's analysis when he writes, "Machinery cannot be said to have replaced dreamwork, since machines are in large part formed of dreamwork. The mechanical magic of the phono-graph does not so much capture and denature the voice as release a kind of magical mechanism. We have not passed out of imaginary relations into the real, as Kittler maintains, since that real is now more than ever itself a phan-tasmal precipitate." Steven Connor, "*Scilicet:* Kittler, Media and Madness," in *Kittler Now*, ed. Stephen Sale and Laura Salisbury (Malden, MA: Polity Press, 2015), p. 127.

125 John Sadler, "The Instrument Metaphor, Hyponarrativity, and the Generic Clinician," in James Phillips (ed.), *Philosophical Perspectives on Technology and Psychiatry* (Oxford: Oxford University Press, 2010), p. 30.

126 Sadler, "The Instrument Metaphor, Hyponarrativity, and the Generic Clinician," p. 26. Unfortunately, Sadler seems to deploy a somewhat narrow model for narrative that is predicated upon a strictly linear trajectory of per-sonal history organized by desires for future outcomes, and less conventional narrative structures may be found in the discourse of such patients.

127 Sadler, "The Instrument Metaphor, Hyponarrativity, and the Generic Clinician," p. 31.

128 Giovanni Stanghellini, *Disembodied Spirits and Deanimated Bodies: The Psychopathology of Common Sense* (Oxford: Oxford University Press, 2004), p. 3.

129 Stanghellini, *Disembodied Spirits and Deanimated Bodies*, p. 4.

130 Louis Sass, *The Paradoxes of Delusion: Wittgenstein, Schreber, and the Schizophrenic Mind* (Ithaca: Cornell University Press, 1995), p. 95.

131 Steven Connor, "Scilicet: Kittler, Media and Madness," pp. 129–130.

132 Patricia Waugh, "Thinking in Literature: Modernism and Contemporary Neuroscience," in David James (ed.), *The Legacies of Modernism: Historicising Postwar and Contemporary Fiction* (Cambridge University Press, 2012), pp. 92–93.

133 Muriel Spark, *The Comforters* (New York: New Directions, 2014), p. 189.

134 Evelyn Waugh, "Review of *The Comforters*," *Spectator*, February 22, 1957; reprinted in Donat Gallagher (ed.), *The Essays and Articles of Evelyn Waugh* (London: Methuen, 1983), p. 519.

135 Fredric Jameson, *Postmodernism, or the Cultural Logic of Late Capitalism* (Durham: Duke University Press, 1992), p. 17.

136 Tyrus Miller, *Late Modernism: Politics, Fiction, and the Arts between the Wars* (Berkeley: University of California Press, 1999), p. 10.

137 Here I follow Miller's suggestion that the beginnings of late-modernism may be observed in the "stock-taking" works of the late 1920s that included many of Lewis's attempts to "rethink past experiences and hunker down to the much bleaker future that had come to pass despite all avant-garde 'renewals.'" Miller, *Late Modernism*, p. 3.

138 Paul Saint-Amour, *Tense Future: Modernism, Total War, Encyclopedic Form* (New York: Oxford University Press, 2015).

139 Lubomír Doležel, *Heterocosmica: Fiction and Possible Worlds* (Baltimore: Johns Hopkins University Press, 2000); Marie-Laure Ryan, *Possible Worlds, Artificial Intelligence, and Narrative Theory* (Bloomington: Indiana University Press, 1992); Ruth Ronen, *Possible Worlds in Literary Theory* (Cambridge: Cambridge University Press, 1994).

140 Ryan, *Possible Worlds, Artificial Intelligence, and Narrative Theory*, p. 3.

141 Ryan, *Possible Worlds, Artificial Intelligence, and Narrative Theory*, p. 26.

142 Schreber, *Memoirs of My Nervous Illness*, p. 70.

143 Sechehaye, *An Autobiography of a Schizophrenic Girl*, p. 54.

144 Eric Hayot, *On Literary Worlds* (Oxford: Oxford University Press, 2012), p. 25.

145 Martin Heidegger, *Being and Time*, trans. Joan Stambaugh (Albany: State University of New York, 2010), p. 74.

146 Jean-Luc Nancy, *The Creation of the World or Globalization*, trans. Francois Raffoul and David Pettigrew (Albany: State University of New York Press, 2007), pp. 42–43; cited in Hayot, *On Literary Worlds*, p. 23.

147 Lewis, *The Art of Being Ruled*, pp. 162, 148.

148 Flann O'Brien, *Flann O'Brien: The Complete Novels*, ed. Keith Donohue (New York: Alfred Knopf, 2008), p. 296.

149 While radio stations sporadically appeared in the first decades of the twentieth century, the British Broadcasting Corporation primarily emerged as a national and international institution in the late 1920s and the 1930s. See Todd Avery, *Radio Modernism: Literature, Ethics, and the BBC, 1922–1938* (Burlington: Ashgate, 2006); Asa Briggs, *The History of Broadcasting in the*

United Kingdom, Vol I: The Birth of Broadcasting (Oxford: Oxford University Press, 1961).

150 Lewis, *Time and Western Man*, p. xii.

1 Fables of Regression: Wyndham Lewis and Machine Psychology

1 Wyndham Lewis, *Rude Assignment: An Intellectual Autobiography* (Santa Barbara: Black Sparrow Press, 1984), p. 219.

2 Lewis, *The Childermass*, p. 147.

3 Lewis, *The Childermass*, p. 156.

4 Lewis, *The Childermass*, p. 154.

5 Lewis, *The Childermass*, p. 185.

6 Ed Commentale similarly reads Pullman and Satters as "schizoid," although his analysis advances a Deleuzian, anti-oedipal analysis. See Ed Commentale, "The Shropshire Schizoid and the Machines of Modernism," *Modernist Cultures* 1.1 (2005), 22–46.

7 Lewis, *The Childermass*, p. 3. Trotter compares some of the linguistic effects in *The Childermass* to schizophrenics' tendency to produce neologisms. Trotter, *Paranoid Modernism*, p. 348.

8 Lewis, *The Childermass*, p. 3.

9 Lewis, *The Childermass*, p. 6.

10 Lewis, *The Childermass*, p. 85.

11 Lewis, *The Childermass*, p. 15.

12 Lewis, *The Childermass*, p. 115.

13 Andy Clark, *Supersizing the Mind: Embodiment, Action, and Cognitive Extension* (Oxford: Oxford University Press, 2010); Andy Clark and David Chalmers, "The Extended Mind," in Richard Menary (ed.), *The Extended Mind* (Cambridge: MIT Press, 2012), pp. 27–42; Edwin Hutchins, *Cognition in the Wild* (Cambridge: MIT Press, 1996).

14 Lewis, *The Childermass*, p. 64.

15 Trotter also observes the hallucinatory experiences represented in *The Childermass* and emphasizes their possible connections to the unstable "time philosophies" of Bergson and Whitehead that Lewis rejects. Trotter, *Paranoid Modernism*, p. 346.

16 Marguerite Sechehaye, *An Autobiography of a Schizophrenic Girl* (London: Grune & Stratton, 1951), pp. 10–11.

17 Sechehaey, *Autobiography of a Schizophrenic Girl*, pp. 28–29.

18 Lewis, *The Childermass*, p. 97.

19 Lewis, *The Art of Being Ruled*, p. 35.

20 Lewis, *The Art of Being Ruled*, pp. 346–347.

21 Alice Reeve-Tucker and Nathan Waddell, "Wyndham Lewis, Evelyn Waugh and Inter-war British Youth: Conflict and Infantilism," in Andrzej Gasiorek and Alice Glen-Reeve (eds.), *Wyndham Lewis and the Cultures of Modernity* (London: Ashgate, 2011), p. 175.

22 Lewis, *The Art of Being Ruled*, p. 346.

23 Lewis, *The Art of Being Ruled*, p. 344.

24 Sedgwick, "Paranoid Reading," p. 134.

25 Silvan Tomkins, *Affect, Imagery, Consciousness*, Vol. II (New York: Springer, 1963), pp. 433–434.

26 Lewis, *The Art of Being Ruled*, p. 362.

27 Hal Foster, *Prosthetic Gods* (Cambridge, MA: MIT Press, 2004), pp. 109–151. Foster especially emphasizes shock and trauma as constituting the pathological dimensions of Lewis's visual and literary art.

28 Trotter, *Paranoid Modernism*, pp. 284–325.

29 Lewis, *Rude Assignment*, p. 54.

30 Foster, *Prosthetic Gods*, p. 380, ft. 5.

31 Marshall McLuhan, *Understanding Media: The Extensions of Man* (New York: McGraw-Hill, 1964).

32 Lewis, *The Art of Being Ruled*, p. 105.

33 On the logic of prosthesis in Lewis's work, also see Jessica Burstein, "Waspish Segments: Lewis, Prosthesis, Fascism," *Modernism/Modernity* 4.2 (1997), 139–164.

34 Adorno, "Radio Voice," p. 372.

35 Adorno, "Radio Voice," p. 368.

36 Andrzej Gasiorek, "Wyndham Lewis on Art, Culture and Politics in the 1930s," in Andrzej Gasiorek and Alice Glen-Reeve (eds.), *Wyndham Lewis and the Cultures of Modernity* (London: Ashgate, 2011), p. 213.

37 Lewis, *The Art of Being Ruled*, p. 148.

38 Lewis, *The Art of Being Ruled*, p. 166.

39 Adorno, "Theses about the Idea and Form of Collaboration of the Princeton Radio Research Project," *Current of Music* (Malden MA: Polity Press, 2009), p. 479.

40 Adorno, "Theses about the Idea and Form of Collaboration of the Princeton Radio Research Project," p. 480.

41 Adorno, "Theses about the Idea and Form of Collaboration of the Princeton Radio Research Project," p. 480.

42 Lewis, *The Art of Being Ruled*, p. 162.

43 Lewis, *The Art of Being Ruled*, p. 167.

44 Bruce Fink elaborates, "The paternal function is not the function played by the individual's father, regardless of his particular style and personality, the role he plays in the family circle, and so on. A flesh-and-blood father does not immediately and automatically fulfill the paternal function, nor does the absence of a real, live father in any way automatically ensure the nonexistence of the paternal function. This function may be fulfilled despite the early death or disappearance of the father due to war or divorce; it may be fulfilled by another man who becomes a 'father figure,' and it may be fulfilled in other ways as well." Bruce Fink, *A Clinical Introduction to Lacanian Psychoanalysis* (Cambridge, MA: Harvard University Press, 1997), p. 79.

45 Jacques Lacan, Jacques-Alain Miller (ed.), Russell Grigg (trans.), *The Seminar of Jacques Lacan, Book III, 1955–1956* (New York: W. W. Norton, 1991), pp. 196–205; Freud, *The Schreber Case*, pp. 52, 58, 64.

46 Adorno, "The Problem of a New Type of Human Being," p. 462.

47 Adorno, *Current of Music*, p. 371, emphasis added.

48 Lewis, *The Childermass*, p. 147.

49 Lewis, *The Childermass*, p. 146.

50 Wyndham Lewis, *Men without Art* (London: Cassell, 1934), p. 131.

51 In another discussion of Lewis's views on monism versus pluralism, Daniel Schenker writes, "He says that even though Oneness may have it all over plurality in the contest for the real, this hardly matters for us as human beings, because *as* human beings, we live only amidst plurality and are not, in that sense, real." Daniel Schnenker, *Wyndham Lewis, Religion and Modernism* (Tuscaloosa: Alabama Press, 1992), p. 124.

52 Lewis, *The Childermass*, p. 134.

53 Lewis, *The Childermass*, p. 135, emphasis added.

54 For a discussion of the modern reduction of the body to a monist ontology of "energy," see Anson Rabinbach, *The Human Motor: Energy, Fatigue, and the Origins of Modernity* (Berkeley: University of California Press, 1990). A monist ontology of information is evident in Norbert Wiener, *Cybernetics, or, Control and Communication in the Animal and the Machine* (Cambridge, MA: Technology Press, 1948).

55 F. T. Marinetti, R. W. Flint (ed. and trans.), *Selected Writings* (New York: Farrar Straus and Giroux), p. 98.

56 Marinetti, *Selected Writings*, p. 136.

57 Lewis, *The Childermass*, p. 152.

58 Lewis, *The Art of Being Ruled*, p. 27.

59 Jacques Lacan, Jacques-Alain Miller (ed.), *Le séminaire: Livre XIX … ou pire, 1971–1972* (Paris: Seuil, 2011).

60 Fink, A Clinical Introduction to Lacanian Psychoanalysis, p. 111.

61 John Watson, *Behavior: An Introduction to Comparative Psychology* (New York: Henry Holt, 1914); John Watson, *Behaviorism* (Chicago: University of Chicago Press, 1930).

62 John B. Watson, "Psychology as the Behaviorist Views It," *Psychological Review* 20 (1913), 163.

63 Watson, "Psychology as the Behaviorist Views It," p. 174.

64 Watson, "Psychology as the Behaviorist Views It," p. 174, ft. 2.

65 Paul Scott Stanfield, " 'This Implacable Doctrine': Behaviorism in Wyndham Lewis's *Snooty Baronet*," *Twentieth-Century Literature* 47.2 (2001), 242, 246.

66 Lewis, *The Childermass*, p. 4.

67 Trotter, *Paranoid Modernism*, p. 351.

68 Lewis, *Times and Western Man*, p. 320.

69 Watson, *Behaviorism*, p. 11.

70 Lewis, *Time and Western Man*, p. 321, emphasis added.

71 Lewis, *Time and Western Man*, p. 322.

72 Robert M. Yerkes, "Report of the Psychological Committee of the National Research Council," *Psychological Review* XXVI (1919), 83. Cited in Kerry W. Buckley, *Mechanical Man: John Broadus Watson and the Beginnings of Behaviorism* (New York: Guilford Press, 1989), p. 99.

73 Buckley, *Mechanical Man*, p. 80; E. B. Titchener, "On 'Psychology as the Behaviorist Views It,'" *Proceedings of the American Philosophical Society* 53 (1914), 1–17. For another critical reposte to Watson's paper, see Mary Whiton Calkins, "Psychology and the Behaviorist," *Psychological Bulletin* 10 (1913), 288–291.

74 Buckley, *Mechanical Man*, p. 119.

75 Lewis, *Time and Western Man*, p. 328.

76 Lewis, *Time and Western Man*, pp. 320–321.

77 Paul Edwards, "Wyndham Lewis and the Uses of Shellshock: Meat and Postmodernism," in Andrzej Gasiorek and Alice Glen-Reeve (eds.), *Wyndham Lewis and the Cultures of Modernity* (London: Ashgate, 2011), p. 236.

78 Wyndham Lewis, *Wyndham Lewis: An Anthology of His Prose*, ed. E. W. F. Tomlin (London: Methuen, 1969), pp. 315–316.

79 Lewis, *The Childermass*, p. 16.

80 Lewis, *The Childermass*, p. 30.

81 Lewis, *The Childermass*, p. 33.

82 Lewis, *The Childermass*, p. 31.

83 Fredric Jameson, *Fables of Aggression: Wyndham Lewis, the Modernist as Fascist* (Berkeley: University of California Press 1979), pp. 35–61.

84 Hugh Kenner, *Wyndham Lewis* (Norfolk, CT: New Directions, 1954), p. 107.

85 Erik M. Bachman, "How to Misbehave as a Behaviourist (If You're Wyndham Lewis)," *Textual Practice* 9 (2013), 10.

86 Stanfield, "'This Implacable Doctrine': Behaviorism in Wyndham Lewis's *Snooty Baronet*," p. 250.

87 Lewis, *The Art of Being Ruled*, p. 125.

88 Lewis, *Snooty Baronet*, p. 80.

89 Stanfield, "'This Implacable Doctrine': Behaviorism in Wyndham Lewis's *Snooty Baronet*," p. 254.

90 Lewis, *Snooty Baronet*, p. 138.

91 Lewis, *Snooty Baronet*, p. 63.

92 Lewis, *Snooty Baronet*, p. 131, emphasis original.

93 Lewis, *Snooty Baronet*, p. 131.

94 Lewis, *Snooty Baronet*, p. 135.

95 Lewis, *Snooty Baronet*, p. 135, emphasis original.

96 Lewis, *Snooty Baronet*, p. 136, emphasis original.

97 R. D. Laing, *The Divided Self: An Existential Study in Sanity and Madness* (New York: Penguin, 1965), p. 22.

98 Laing, *The Divided Self*, p. 46.

99 Sechehaye, *An Autobiography of a Schizophrenic Girl*, p. 18.

100 Lewis, *Snooty Baronet*, p. 136, emphasis original.

101 Sechehaye, *Autobiography of a Schizophrenic Girl*, pp. 40–41, emphasis added.

102 Sechehaye, *Autobiography of a Schizophrenic Girl*, p. 10, emphasis added.

103 Lewis, *Snooty Baronet*, p. 136.

104 Lewis, *Snooty Baronet*, p. 138.

105 Schreber, *Memoirs of My Nervous Illness*, p. 70.
106 Laing, *The Divided Self*, p. 48.

2 Modernist Influencing Machines: From Mina Loy to Evelyn Waugh

1 For discussions of the novel, see Miller, *Late Modernism*, pp. 207–221; Christina Walter, *Optical Impersonality: Science, Images, and Literary Modernism* (Baltimore: Johns Hopkins University Press, 2014), pp. 151–169.
2 Loy, *Insel* (1991), p. 31.
3 Loy, *Insel*, p. 115.
4 Loy, *Insel*, p. 32.
5 Loy, *Insel* (1991), p. 96.
6 Loy, *Insel* (1991), p. 167.
7 Loy, *Insel* (1991), p. 139.
8 Loy, *Insel* (1991), p. 102.
9 Loy, *Insel* (1991), p. 144.
10 Letter to Istvan Hollos in 1928, quoted in Woods, *The Sublime Object of Psychiatry*, p. 158, ft. 11.
11 For a fine account of the difficulties facing the psychoanalytic treatment of psychotics, see Fink, *A Clinical Introduction to Lacanian Psychoanalysis*, pp. 79–112.
12 Carolyn Burke describes this meeting with Freud in *Becoming Modern: A Life of Mina Loy* (New York: Farrar, Straus Giroux, 1996), p. 313. For an examination of Loy's psychoanalytic interest and research, also see Keith Tuma, "Mina Loy's 'Anglo-Mongrels and the Rose,'" in Maeera Schreiber and Keith Tuma (eds.), *Mina Loy: Woman and Poet* (Orono: National Poetry Foundation, 1998), pp. 181–204.
13 For histories of psychoanalysis and its continuities with earlier forms of psychological treatment, see Henri Ellenburger, *The Discovery of the Unconscious* (New York: Basic Books, 1979), pp. 53–109; W. F Bynum, Roy Porter, and Michael Shepherd (eds.), *The Anatomy of Madness: Essays in the History of Psychiatry* (London: Tavistock, 1985); Mark Micale (ed.), *The Mind of Modernism: Medicine, Psychology, and the Cultural Arts in Europe and America, 1880–1940* (Stanford: Stanford University Press, 2004).
14 For a study of mesmerism's historical and cultural influence and its relation to Freudian psychoanalysis, see Adam Crabtree, *From Mesmer to Freud: Magnetic Sleep and the Roots of Psychological Healing* (New Haven: Yale University Press, 1993).
15 John Durham Peters, "Broadcasting and Schizophrenia," *Media, Culture, and Society* 32.1 (2010), 128–129.
16 Loy, *Insel* (1991), p. 96.
17 Pamela Thurschwell, *Literature, Psychology, and Magical Thinking, 1820–1920* (Cambridge: Cambridge University Press, 2005).
18 See Anne Harrington, "Hysteria, Hypnosis, and the Lure of the Invisible: The Rise of Neo-Mesmerism in Fin-de-siecle French Psychiatry," in W. F. Bynum,

Roy Porter, and Michael Shepherd (eds.), *The Anatomy of Madness*, Vol. 3 (London: Routledge, 1988), 226–245.

19 For a evidence of the ways that transference emerged as an early subject of scrutiny, see August Forel, *Hypnotism; or Suggestion and Psychotherapy* (1889), trans. H. Armit (London: Rebman, 1906).

20 Victor Tausk, "On the Origins of the Influencing Machine Delusion in Schizophrenia," *Psychoanalytic Quarterly* 2 (1933), pp. 519–556, p. 544.

21 Tausk, "On the Origins of the Influencing Machine Delusion in Schizophrenia," p. 544.

22 Mina Loy, *Insel*, ed. Sarah Hayden (New York: Neversink Press, 2014), p. 161.

23 Loy, Insel (2014), p. 161.

24 Peters, "Broadcasting and Schizophrenia," 124.

25 Tausk, "On the Origins of the Influencing Machine Delusion in Schizophrenia," p. 533.

26 Tausk, "On the Origins of the Influencing Machine Delusion in Schizophrenia," p. 556.

27 Tausk, "On the Origins of the Influencing Machine Delusion in Schizophrenia," p. 549.

28 Tausk, "On the Origins of the Influencing Machine Delusion in Schizophrenia," p. 544.

29 Loy, *Insel* (1991), p. 166.

30 Loy, *Insel* (1991), p. 157.

31 Loy, *Insel* (1991), p. 170.

32 Loy, *Insel* (1991), p. 166. Tyrus Miller argues that Insel, rather than Mrs. Jones, assumes the role of lay or "wild" analyst; Miller, *Late Modernism*, p. 215. In my reading, Jones's primary role in rehabilitating Insel is dominant, although the instability of roles is also evident.

33 Loy, *Insel* (1991), p. 149.

34 Loy, *Insel* (1991), p. 151.

35 Loy, *Insel* (1991), pp. 154–155.

36 Loy, *Insel* (1991), p. 151.

37 Thurschwell, *Literature, Technology, and Magical Thinking*, p. 150.

38 Thurschwell, *Literature, Technology, and Magical Thinking*, p. 117; Thurschwell quotes Ernest Jones, *The Life and Work of S. Freud*, vol. III (New York: Basic Books, 1955), p. 407. Also see Gyorgy Hidas, "Flowing Over – Transference, Countertransference, Telepathy: Subjective Dimensions of the Psychoanalytic Relationship in Ferenczi's Thinking," in Lewis Aron and Adrienne Harris (eds.), *The Legacy of Sandor Ferenczi* (New York: Routledge, 1993), pp. 207–215.

39 Loy, *Insel* (1991), p. 174.

40 In a eulogistic article, William James pronounced that Myers's work would have the greatest influence on future psychological research. William James, "Frederic Myers's Service to Psychology" (1901), in Robert A. McDermott (ed), *Essays in Psychical Research* (Cambridge: Harvard University Press, 1986).

41 Loy, *Insel* (2014), p. 163.

42 Loy, *Insel* (2014), p. 163.

43 Loy, *Insel* (2014), p. 163.

44 The abiding interest in the case study as an ethically fraught genre in not only psychoanalysis and psychiatry but also legal studies, sociology, and literary studies is taken up in a special issue of *Critical Inquiry*, "On the Case," edited by Lauren Berlant, 33.4 (Summer 2007). For other valuable meditations on the problem of the case study as genre, see Charles Bernheimer and Claire Kahane (eds.), *In Dora's Case: Freud – Hysteria – Feminism* (New York: Columbia University Press, 1985); Charles Ragin and Howard S. Becker (eds.), *What Is a Case? Exploring the Foundations of Social Inquiry* (New York: Cambridge University Press, 1992).

45 Loy, *Insel* (1991), p. 148.

46 Kittler, *Discourse Networks 1800/1900*, pp. 265–346.

47 Loy, *Insel* (1991), p. 178.

48 Evelyn Waugh, *The Ordeal of Gilbert Pinfold: A Conversation Piece* (New York: Back Bay Books, 1957), p. 8.

49 Stephen L. Post suggests that the Box is also "reminiscent of Wilhelm Reich's orgone box, well known in the 1950s." See Stephen Post, "His and Hers: Breakdown as Depicted by Evelyn Waugh and Charlotte Perkins Gilman," *Literature and Medicine*, 9 (1990), 172–180, p. 174.

50 Waugh, *The Ordeal of Gilbert Pinfold*, p. 8.

51 Waugh, *The Ordeal of Gilbert Pinfold*, p. 11.

52 Waugh, *The Ordeal of Gilbert Pinfold*, p. 18.

53 Waugh, *The Ordeal of Gilbert Pinfold*, p. 20.

54 Waugh, *The Ordeal of Gilbert Pinfold*, p. 20.

55 Waugh, *The Ordeal of Gilbert Pinfold*, p. 22.

56 Waugh, *The Ordeal of Gilbert Pinfold*, pp. 34–35.

57 Waugh, *The Ordeal of Gilbert Pinfold*, p. 65.

58 Waugh, *The Ordeal of Gilbert Pinfold*, p. 71.

59 Waugh, *The Ordeal of Gilbert Pinfold*, p. 82.

60 Slavoj Zizek, *The Plague of Fantasies* (New York: Verso, 1997), p. 114.

61 Franz Kafka, *The Trial*, trans. Breon Mitchell (New York: Schocken, 1998), pp. 80–87.

62 Waugh, *The Ordeal of Gilbert Pinfold*, pp. 88–89.

63 Waugh, *The Ordeal of Gilbert Pinfold*, p. 89.

64 Waugh, *The Ordeal of Gilbert Pinfold*, p. 96.

65 Waugh, *The Ordeal of Gilbert Pinfold*, p. 102.

66 Waugh, *The Ordeal of Gilbert Pinfold*, p. 103.

67 Waugh, *The Ordeal of Gilbert Pinfold*, p. 105.

68 Waugh, *The Ordeal of Gilbert Pinfold*, p. 186, emphasis original.

69 Waugh, *The Ordeal of Gilbert Pinfold*, pp. 186–187.

70 Waugh, *The Ordeal of Gilbert Pinfold*, p. 188.

71 Waugh, *The Ordeal of Gilbert Pinfold*, p. 190.

72 Waugh, *The Ordeal of Gilbert Pinfold*, p. 195.

73 Waugh, *The Ordeal of Gilbert Pinfold*, p. 62.

74 Waugh, *The Ordeal of Gilbert Pinfold*, p. 196, emphasis original.

75 Waugh, *The Ordeal of Gilbert Pinfold*, pp. 199–200.
76 Waugh, *The Ordeal of Gilbert Pinfold*, p. 183.
77 Waugh, *The Ordeal of Gilbert Pinfold*, p. 203.
78 Waugh, *The Ordeal of Gilbert Pinfold*, p. 203.
79 Waugh, *The Ordeal of Gilbert Pinfold*, p. 209, emphasis added.
80 Waugh, *The Ordeal of Gilbert Pinfold*, p. 215.
81 Waugh, *The Ordeal of Gilbert Pinfold*, p. 221.
82 Waugh, *The Ordeal of Gilbert Pinfold*, p. 231.
83 R. Neill Johnson, "Shadowed by the Gaze: Evelyn Waugh's 'Vile Bodies' and 'The Ordeal of Gilbert Pinfold,'" *The Modern Language Review* 91.1 (1996), 15.
84 Waugh, *The Ordeal of Gilbert Pinfold*, p. 221.
85 Waugh, *The Ordeal of Gilbert Pinfold*, p. 32.
86 Ivan Leudar and Philip Thomas, *Voices of Reason, Voices of Insanity: Studies of Verbal Hallucinations* (New York: Routledge, 2000), p. 53.
87 Waugh, *The Ordeal of Gilbert Pinfold*, p. 11.
88 Evelyn Waugh, *The Essays, Articles and Reviews of Evelyn Waugh*, ed. Donat Gallagher, (London: Methuen, 1983), p. 442. Also quoted in James J. Lynch, "Evelyn Waugh during the *Pinfold* Years," *mfs: Modern Fiction Studies* 32.4 (1986), 549.
89 Lynch, "Evelyn Waugh During the Pinfold Years," p. 550.
90 Lynch, "Evelyn Waugh During the Pinfold Years," p. 554, ft. 12.
91 Margaret Price, *Mad At School: Rhetorics of Mental Disability and Academic Life* (Ann Arbor: University of Michican Press, 2011), p. 27.
92 Waugh, *The Ordeal of Gilbert Pinfold*, p. 200.
93 Waugh, *The Ordeal of Gilbert Pinfold*, p. i.
94 Waugh, *The Ordeal of Gilbert Pinfold*, p. i.
95 Pamela White Hadas, "Madness and Medicine: The Graphomaniac's Cure," *Literature and Medicine* 9 (1990), 182.
96 Robert J. Kloss, "Evelyn Waugh: His Ordeal," *American Imago* 42:1 (1985), 100.
97 J. B. Priestley, "What Was Wrong with Pinfold," *New Statesman* (1957), quoted in David Pryce-Jones (ed.), *Evelyn Waugh and His World* (Boston: Little, Brown & Co., 1973), p. 3.
98 Waugh, *The Ordeal of Gilbert Pinfold*, p. 96.
99 Waugh, *The Ordeal of Gilbert Pinfold*, p. 103.
100 Post, "His and Hers," p. 173.
101 Post, "His and Hers," p. 173.
102 Examples of critics who are compelled to psychoanalyze Waugh in ways that are similar to Priestley's review include Johnson, Post, and Kloss, among others. The latter speculates extensively about Waugh's childhood relationship with his mother, and writes, "It is as if he is impelled to re-enact in his fiction the significant ordeals of his childhood in an attempt to undo their traumata." Kloss, "Evelyn Waugh: His Ordeal," 104.
103 Evelyn Waugh, "Anything Wrong with Priestley?" *Spectator*, September 13, 1957.

3 On Worlding and Unworlding in Fiction and Delusion:
Muriel Spark and Anna Kavan

1 Evelyn Waugh, "Something Fresh: Review of *The Comforters* by Muriel Spark," *The Essays, Articles and Reviews of Evelyn Waugh*, p. 519. The review originally appeared in *Spectator*, February 22, 1957.
2 Waugh, "Something Fresh," p. 518.
3 Muriel Spark, *The Comforters* (New York: New Directions, 2014), p. 45 emphasis added.
4 Spark, *The Comforters*, p. 64.
5 Spark, *The Comforters*, p. 64.
6 Spark, *The Comforters*, p. 65.
7 Spark, *The Comforters*, p. 108.
8 Spark, *The Comforters*, pp. 106–107.
9 Spark, *The Comforters*, p. 189.
10 Spark, *The Comforters*, pp. 108–109.
11 John Lanchester, "In Sparkworld," in Robert E. Hosmer, Jr. (ed.), *Hidden Possibilities: Essays in Honor of Muriel Spark* (South Bend, IN: Notre Dame University Press, 2014), p. 188.
12 Spark, *The Comforters*, p. 154.
13 Spark, *The Comforters*, p. 148.
14 Spark, *The Comforters*, p. 105.
15 Spark, *The Comforters*, p. 191.
16 Spark, *The Comforters*, p. 164.
17 Spark, *The Comforters*, p. 195.
18 Spark, *The Comforters*, p. 70, emphasis original.
19 Kittler, *Discourse Networks 1800/1900*, pp. 265–346.
20 Spark, *The Comforters*, p. 81, emphasis added.
21 Spark, *The Comforters*, p. 82.
22 Spark, *The Comforters*, p. 99.
23 David Lewis, *Counterfactuals*, (Cambridge: Harvard University Press, 1978); David Lewis, "Truth in Fiction," *American Philosophical Quarterly* 15 (1983), 37–46; Saul Kripke, "Semantic Considerations on Modal Logic," *Acta Philosophica Fennica* 16 (1963), 83–94; Jaakko Hintikka, "Individuals, Possible Worlds, and Epistemic Logic," *Nous* 1 (1967), 33–62; Michael Loux (ed.), *The Possible and the Actual: Readings in the Metaphysics of Modality* (Ithaca: Cornell University Press, 1979).
24 Thomas Pavel, *Fictional Worlds* (Cambridge: Harvard University Press, 1986); Lubomír Doležel, *Heterocosmica: Fiction and Possible Worlds* (Baltimore: Johns Hopkins University, 2000); Marie-Laure Ryan, *Possible Worlds, Artificial Intelligence, and Narrative Theory* (Bloomington: Indiana University Press, 1992); Ruth Ronen, *Possible Worlds in Literary Theory* (New York: Cambridge University Press, 1994).
25 Ryan, *Possible Worlds, Artificial Intelligence, and Narrative Theory*, p. 3.
26 Ronen, *Possible Worlds in Literary Theory*, p. 5.

27 Ronen, *Possible Worlds in Literary Theory*, p. 6, emphasis original.
28 Ronen, *Possible Worlds in Literary Theory*, p. 93.
29 David Herman, *The Basic Elements of Narrative* (New York: Wiley-Blackwell, 2009), p. 107.
30 Ryan, *Possible Worlds, Artificial Intelligence, and Narrative Theory*, p. 26.
31 Ryan, *Possible Worlds, Artificial Intelligence, and Narrative Theory*, p. 4.
32 Ronen, *Possible Worlds in Literary Theory*, p. 94.
33 Lyndsey Stonebridge, "Hearing Them Speak: Voices in Wilfred Bion, Muriel Spark and Penelope Fitzgerald," *Textual Practice* 19.4 (2005), 453.
34 Spark, *The Comforters*, pp. 189–190.
35 Waugh, "Something Fresh," p. 519.
36 Lanchester, "In Sparkworld," p. 189.
37 Patricia Waugh, "Muriel Spark and the Metaphysics of Modernity: Art, Secularization, and Psychosis," in David Herman (ed.), *Muriel Spark: Twenty-First-Century Perspectives* (Baltimore: Johns Hopkins University Press), p. 64.
38 Waugh, "Muriel Spark and the Metaphysics of Modernity: Art, Secularization, and Psychosis," p. 72.
39 Spark, *The Comforters*, p. 57.
40 Spark, *The Comforters*, p. 109.
41 Quoted in Martin Stannard, *Muriel Spark: The Biography* (New York: W. W. Norton, 2009), p. 152.
42 Stannard, *Muriel Spark*, p. 151.
43 Stannard, *Muriel Spark*, p. 154. Interview with Jerzy Peterkiewicz, May 9, 1994.
44 Stannard, *Muriel Spark*, p. 157. Letter, March 26, 1954, Spark to Stanford.
45 Muriel Spark, *Loitering with Intent* (New York: New Directions, 2014), p. 83.
46 Spark, *Loitering With Intent*, p. 70.
47 Spark, *Loitering With Intent*, p. 71.
48 Frank Kermode, "Unrivalled Deftness: The Novels of Muriel Spark," in Hosmer (ed.), *Hidden Possibilities*, pp. 107–108.
49 Spark, *Loitering with Intent*, p. 91.
50 Spark, *Loitering with Intent*, p. 85.
51 Spark, *The Comforters*, p. 45.
52 Muriel Spark, *Memento Mori* (New York: New Directions, 2000), p. 168.
53 Stonebridge, "Hearing Them Speak: Voices in Wilfred Bion, Muriel Spark and Penelope Fitzgerald," p. 447.
54 Muriel Spark, *Voices at Play*, (London: Macmillan, 1961).
55 Eugen Bleuler, *Dementia Praecox, or the Group of Schizophrenias*, p. 440.
56 Spark, *Voices at Play*, pp. 229–248.
57 Spark, "Author's Note," *Voices at Play*, p. v.
58 D. A. Callard, *The Case of Anna Kavan: A Biography* (London: Peter Owen, 1992), p. 64.
59 Callard, *The Case of Anna Kavan*, p. 112.
60 Callard, *The Case of Anna Kavan*, p. 123.
61 Callard, *The Case of Anna Kavan*, pp. 151–152.

62 Callard, *The Case of Anna Kavan*, p. 40; Kavan's diary entry, December 10, 1926.

63 Callard, *The Case of Anna Kavan*, p. 34.

64 Quoted in Callard, *The Case of Anna Kavan*, p. 83.

65 Jane Garrity, "Nocturnal Transgressions in *The House of Sleep:* Anna Kavan's Maternal Registers," *Modern Fiction Studies* 40.2 (1994), p. 253.

66 Garrity, "Nocturnal Transgressions in *The House of Sleep:* Anna Kavan's Maternal Registers," p. 254.

67 *The Listener*, April 5, 1945. Cited by Victoria Walker in her "Foreword" to Anna Kavan, *I Am Lazarus* (1945), (London: Peter Owen, 2013), p. 6.

68 Anna Kavan, *Asylum Piece* (1940), (London: Peter Owen, 2002), p. 31.

69 Kavan, *Asylum Piece*, p. 71.

70 Kavan, *Asylum Piece*, pp. 43–44.

71 Kavan, *Asylum Piece*, p. 92.

72 Kavan, *Asylum Piece*, pp. 79–80.

73 Kavan, *Asylum Piece*, pp. 32–33.

74 Kavan, *Asylum Piece*, p. 115.

75 Kavan, *Asylum Piece*, p. 116.

76 Kavan, *Asylum Piece*, p. 75.

77 Kavan, *Asylum Piece*, p. 139.

78 Kavan, *Asylum Piece*, p. 118.

79 Karl Jaspers, *General Psychopathology* (Baltimore: Johns Hopkins University Press, 1997), p. 313.

80 Kenneth Kendler, "Introduction: Why Does Psychiatry Need Philosophy?" in Kenneth S. Kendler and Josef Parnas (eds.), *Philosophical Issues in Psychiatry: Explanation, Phenomenology, and Nosology* (Baltimore: Johns Hopkins University Press, 2008), p. 6.

81 Jaspers, *General Psychopathology*, p. 576. Quoted in Christoph Hoerl, "Jaspers on Explaining and Understanding in Psychiatry," in Giovanni Stanghellini and Thomas Fuchs (eds.), *One Century of Karl Jaspers's General Psychopathology*, (Oxford: Oxford University Press, 2013), p. 118.

82 Hoerl, "Jaspers on Explaining and Understanding in Psychiatry," p. 119, emphasis added.

83 Nancy Andreasen, *The Broken Brain: The Biological Revolution in Psychiatry* (New York: Harper & Row, 1984).

84 Jaspers, *General Psychopathology*, p. 459.

85 Jaspers, *General Psychopathology*, p. 459.

86 Jaspers, *General Psychopathology*, p. 302.

87 Jaspers, *General Psychopathology*, p. 459.

88 Jaspers, *General Psychopathology*, p. 293, emphasis added.

89 Looking back on the response to the first edition of his *General Psychopathology*, Jaspers would write, "this present book (1913) [was] greeted as something radically new, although all I had done was to link psychiatric reality with the traditional humanities." Jaspers, *General Psychopathology*, pp. 301–302, ft. 1.

90 Bruno Bettelheim, *The Empty Fortress: Infantile Autism and the Birth of the Self* (New York: Free Press, 1967), p. 234.

91 Bettelheim, *The Empty Fortress*, p. 252.

92 Bettelheim, *The Empty Fortress*, p. 239.

93 Bettelheim, *The Empty Fortress*, p. 234.

94 Bettelheim, *The Empty Fortress*, p. 259.

95 Bettelheim, *The Empty Fortress*, p. 252.

96 Bettelheim, *The Empty Fortress*, p. 256.

97 Bettelheim, *The Empty Fortress*, p. 281.

98 Bettelheim, *The Empty Fortress*, p. 268.

99 Anna Kavan, *Who Are You?* (Lowestoft, Suffolk: Scorpion Press, 1963); Quoted in Callard, p. 26 emphasis added.

100 Bettelheim, *The Empty Fortress*, p. 234.

101 Bettelheim, *The Empty Fortress*, p. 235.

102 Bettelheim, *The Empty Fortress*, p. 238.

103 Jaspers, *General Psychopathology*, p. 447.

104 Thomas Fuchs, "Being a Psycho-Machine: on the Phenomenology of the Influencing-Machine," in Bettina Brand-Clausen and Thomas Roeske (eds.), *Air Loom* (Heidelberg: Wunderhorn, 2006), p. 41, emphasis added.

105 Kavan, *I Am Lazarus*, p. 7.

106 Kavan, *I Am Lazarus*, pp. 9–10.

107 Kavan, *I Am Lazarus*, p. 10.

108 Kavan, *I Am Lazarus*, p. 11.

109 Kavan, *I Am Lazarus*, p. 13.

110 Kavan, *I Am Lazarus*, p. 11.

111 Kavan, *I Am Lazarus*, p. 23.

112 Kavan, *I Am Lazarus*, p. 24.

113 Kavan, *I Am Lazarus*, p. 25.

114 Kavan, *I Am Lazarus*, p. 27, emphasis added.

115 Kavan, *I Am Lazarus*, p. 42.

116 Kavan, *I Am Lazarus*, p. 42.

117 Kavan, *I Am Lazarus*, p. 22.

118 Kavan, *I Am Lazarus*, p. 55.

119 Kavan, *I Am Lazarus*, p. 60.

120 Herman, *The Basic Elements of Narrative*, p. 133.

121 Kavan, *I Am Lazarus*, p. 67.

122 Barbara O'Brien, *Operators and Things: The Inner Life of a Schizophrenic* (Cambridge: Arlington, 1958), xi.

123 Bettelheim, *The Empty Fortress*, p. 281.

4 Flann O'Brien and Authorship as a Practice of "Sane Madness"

1 J. C. C. Mays, "Brian O'Nolan: Literalist of the Imagination," in Timothy O'Keefe (ed.), *Myles: Portraits of Brian O'Nolan* (London: Martin Brian & O'Keeffe, 1973), pp. 77–119.

2 Flann O'Brien in *The Complete Novels*, ed. Keith Donohue (New York: Alfred Knopf, 2008), p. 296.

3 Bruno Latour, *We Have Never Been Modern* (Cambridge: Harvard University Press, 1993). Against the notion that modernity achieves this "work of purification," he argues that there is instead a historical proliferation of "hybrid objects" that ontologically occupy a middle ground between the human and the inhuman, the social and the natural, the rational and the irrational.

4 Anne Clissman, *Flann O'Brien: A Critical Introduction to His Writings* (New York: Barnes and Noble, 1975), p. 37. Clissman cites "Cruiskeen Lawn," July 3, 1953.

5 Clissmann, *Flann O'Brien*, p. 1.

6 O'Brien, The Complete Novels, p. 269.

7 See Ondrej Pilny, "'Did You Put Charcoal Adroitly in the Vent?' Brian O'Nolan and Pataphysics," in Ruben Borg, Paul Fagan, and Werner Huber (eds.), *Flann O'Brien: Contesting Legacies*, (Cork: Cork UP, 2014), pp. 156–180. Also see Anthony Adams, "Butter-Spades, Footnotes, and Omnium: *The Third Policeman* as Pataphysical Fiction," in Neil Murphy and Keith Hopper (eds.), *Review of Contemporary Fiction: Flann O'Brien Centenary Essays* 31.3 (2011), 106–119.

8 O'Brien, *The Complete Novels*, p. 238.

9 Louis Sass, *Madness and Modernism* (New York: Basic Books, 1992), p. 44. Sass translates, "die Wahrnehmungstarre," from German psychiatric discourse.

10 Sass, *Madness and Modernism*, p. 44.

11 Tvetan Todorov, *The Fantastic: A Structural Approach to a Literary Genre* (Ithaca: Cornell University Press, 1975).

12 O'Brien, *The Complete Novels*, p. 220.

13 Myles na gCopaleen, "Cruiskeen Lawn," *Irish Times*, October 5, 1945, p. 2. Also cited by Sean Pryor, "Making Evil, with Flann O'Brien," in Julian Murphet, Ronan McDonald, and Sascha Morrell (eds.), *Flann O'Brien and Modernism* (New York: Bloomsbury Academic, 2014), p. 20.

14 Erwin Schrödinger, *What Is Life?* (Cambridge: Cambridge University Press, 2012), p. 84.

15 Schrödinger, *What Is Life?* p. 88.

16 "Cruiskeen Lawn," *Irish Times*, March 10, 1947, p. 4. See also Alana Gillespie, "'Banjaxed and Bewildered' *Cruiskeen Lawn* and the Role of Science in Independent Ireland," in Ruben Borg, Paul Fagan, and Werner Huber (eds.), *Flann O'Brien: Contesting Legacies* (Cork: Cork UP, 2014), p. 178.

17 O'Brien, *The Complete Novels*, p. 296.

18 Jacques Lacan, in *Seminar VII: The Ethics of Psychoanalysis*, ed. Jacques-Alain Miller, trans. Dennis Porter (New York: Norton, 1992), pp. 101–114.

19 O'Brien, *The Complete Novels*, p. 237.

20 O'Brien, *The Complete Novels*, p. 239.

21 O'Brien, *The Complete Novels*, p. 239.

22 Daniel Dennett, *Consciousness Explained* (New York: Penguin, 1991), p. 107. Dirk van Hulle makes a similar comparison in "Flann O'Brien's *Ulysses*: Marginalia

and the Modernist Mind," in Julian Murphet, Ronan McDonald, and Sascha Morrell (eds.), *Flann O'Brien and Modernism* (London: Bloomsbury, 2014), p. 116.

23 Julian Murphet, "Flann O'Brien and Modern Character," Julian Murphet, Ronan McDonald, and Sascha Morrell *Flann O'Brien and Modernism* (New York: Bloomsbury Academic, 2014), p. 152.

24 O'Brien, *The Complete Novels*, p. 252.

25 O'Brien, *The Complete Novels*, p. 240.

26 O'Brien, *The Complete Novels*, p. 240.

27 O'Brien, *The Complete Novels*, p. 240.

28 O'Brien, *The Complete Novels*, p. 241.

29 O'Brien, *The Complete Novels*, p. 242.

30 O'Brien, *The Complete Novels*, p. 245.

31 O'Brien, *The Complete Novels*, p. 250.

32 O'Brien, *The Complete Novels*, p. 273.

33 O'Brien, *The Complete Novels*, p. 273.

34 O'Brien, *The Complete Novels*, p. 293.

35 O'Brien, *The Complete Novels*, p. 294.

36 O'Brien, *The Complete Novels*, p. 295.

37 O'Brien, *The Complete Novels*, p. 296.

38 O'Brien, *The Complete Novels*, pp. 296, 300.

39 O'Brien, *The Complete Novels*, pp. 318–319.

40 Julian Murphet, "Flann O'Brien and Modern Character," p. 161.

41 Lewis, *The Art of Being Ruled*, p. 131.

42 O'Brien, *The Complete Novels*, p. 324.

43 O'Brien, *The Complete Novels*, p. 327.

44 O'Brien, *The Complete Novels*, p. 329, emphasis original.

45 Leo Bersani, "Pynchon, Paranoia, and Literature," *Representations*, 25 (Winter 1989), 109. Lacan first makes this claim in "Aggressiveness in Psychoanalysis," Bruce Fink (trans.), *Ecrits* (New York: Norton, 2006), pp. 82–101.

46 O'Brien, *The Complete Novels*, p. 300.

47 Patricia Marks, *Bicycles, Bangs, and Bloomers: The New Woman in the Popular Press* (Lexington: University Press of Kentucky, 1990). Also see Ann Ardis, *New Women, New Novels: Feminism and Early Modernism* (New Brunswick: Rutgers University Press, 1990).

48 O'Brien, *The Complete Novels*, p. 299, emphasis original.

49 For a discussion of queerness in *The Third Policeman*, see Andrea Bobotis, "Queering Knowledge in Flann O'Brien's *The Third Policeman*," *Irish University Review: A Journal of Irish Studies*, Autumn–Winter, 32.2 (2002), 242–58.

50 O'Brien, *The Complete Novels*, p. 327.

51 Slavoj Zizek, *Enjoy Your Symptom* (New York: Routledge, 2001), p. 137, emphasis original.

52 O'Brien, *The Complete Novels*, p. 624.

53 For details of O'Brien's medical conditions, see Anthony Cronin, *No Laughing Matter: The Life and Times of Flann O'Brien* (London: Paladin, 1990), pp. 253–255.

54 O'Brien, *The Complete Novels*, p. 730.
55 Pryor, "Making Evil, with Flann O'Brien," pp. 14, 21.
56 O'Brien, *The Complete Novels*, p. 21.
57 Schrödinger, *What Is Life? p.* 85.
58 For a critical discussion of Lucia Joyce's diagnosis and treatment, see Carol Loeb Schloss, *Lucia Joyce: To Dance in the Wake* (New York: Farrar Straus Giroux, 2003).
59 For an exegesis of Lacan's seminar on Joyce, see Roberto Harari, *How Joyce Made His Name: A Reading of the Final Lacan* (New York: Other Press, 2002).
60 Rabaté argues that Joyce's formal innovations in *Finnegans Wake* were motivated in part by a desire to help Lucia resolve her schizophrenic thought disorder. See Jean-Michel Rabaté, *James Joyce and the Politics of Egoism* (Cambridge: Cambridge University Press, 2001), pp. 7–10.
61 O'Brien, *The Complete Novels*, p. 772.
62 O'Brien, *The Complete Novels*, p. 772.
63 O'Brien, *The Complete Novels*, p. 772.
64 Pryor, "Making Evil, with Flann O'Brien," p. 20.
65 Freud, *The Schreber Case*, p. 61.
66 O'Brien, *The Complete Novels*, p. 672.
67 O'Brien *The Complete Novels*, p. 672.
68 O'Brien, *The Complete Novels*, p. 706.
69 O'Brien, *The Complete Novels*, p. 674.
70 O'Brien, *The Complete Novels*, p. 712.
71 Murphet, "Flann O'Brien and Modern Character," p. 152.
72 O'Brien, *The Complete Novels*, p. 712.
73 O'Brien, *The Complete Novels*, p. 714.
74 O'Brien, *The Complete Novels*, p. 714.
75 O'Brien, *The Complete Novels*, p. 712.
76 O'Brien, *The Complete Novels*, p. 758.
77 O'Brien, *The Complete Novels*, p. 748.
78 O'Brien, *The Complete Novels*, p. 768.
79 O'Brien, *The Complete Novels*, p. 769.
80 O'Brien, *The Complete Novels*, p. 766.

5 "Prey to Communications": Voice Hearing, Thought Transmission, and Samuel Beckett

1 For a discussion of Beckett's work in light of Bion, see Steven Connor, "Beckett and Bion," *Journal of Beckett Studies* 17.1 (2008), 9–34.
2 For more on Beckett's encounters with psychiatric patients, see James R. Knowlson, *Damned to Fame: The Life of Samuel Beckett* (New York: Simon & Schuster, 1996), pp. 197–200.
3 For a rich discussion of Beckett's psychology notes and his reading list, see Michael Feldman, *Beckett's Books: A Cultural History of the Interwar Notes* (New York: Continuum, 2006).

4 Discussions of mental illness in Beckett's work include Thomas A. Warger, "Going Mad Systematically in Beckett's *Murphy*," *Modern Language Studies* 16.2 (1986), 13–18; Michael Beausang, "*Watt*: Logic, Insanity, Aphasia," trans. Valerie Galiussi, *Style* 30.3 (1996), 495–513. Benjamin Keating, "Beckett and Language Pathology," *Journal of Modern Literature* 31.4 (2008), 86–101.

5 See especially the special issue of *The Journal of Beckett Studies* devoted to "Beckett, Language, and the Mind" 17.1 (2008), which addresses clinical and neurological questions, including, Laura Salisbury, "'What Is the Word': Beckett's Aphasic Modernism," *Journal of Beckett Studies* 17.1 (2008), 78–126; Ulrika Maude, "'A Stirring beyond Coming and Going': Beckett and Tourette's," *Journal of Beckett Studies* 17.1 (2008), 153–168; Peter Fifield, 'Beckett, Cotard's Syndrome and the Narrative Patient," *Journal of Beckett Studies* 17.1 (2008), 169–186; Lois Oppenheim, "A Twenty-First Century Perspective on a Play by Samuel Beckett," *Journal of Beckett Studies* 17.1 (2008), 187–198.

6 Karl Jaspers, *General Psychopathology*, J. Hoenig and Marian W. Hamilton (trans.). Baltimore: Johns Hopkins University Press, 1997, pp. 704–705.

7 Margaret Price, *Mad at School* (Ann Arbor: University of Michicagn Press, 2011), p. 9, emphasis added.

8 Beckett's translations appeared in a special edition of *This Quarter* (September 1932), which was one of the earliest and most important surveys of French Surrealism for anglophone audiences.

9 Knowlson, *Damned to Fame*, p. 113.

10 Daniel Albright, *Beckett and Aesthetics* (Cambridge: Cambridge University Press, 2003), p. 10.

11 Samuel Beckett, *Murphy* (New York: Grove Press, 2011), p. 49.

12 Tajiri organizes the motifs of mechanized bodies through Beckett's career under the category of the "prosthetic body" and begins to link these motifs to psychic regression and psychosis but stops short of fully developing this connection to psychopathology in preference for a more broad approach: "an in-depth pathological analysis of Beckett's work is beyond the scope of this book and it is more important to concentrate on distinct features of the instability of boundaries revealed in his texts." Yoshiki Tajiri, *Samuel Beckett and the Prosthetic Body: The Senses and Organs of Modernism* (New York: Palgrave, 2007), p. 61.

13 J. D. O'Hara, *Samuel Beckett's Hidden Drives: Structural Uses of Depth Psychology* (Gainesville: University of Florida Press, 1997), p. 43.

14 Phil Baker, *Beckett and the Mythology of Psychoanalysis* (New York: St. Martin's Press, 1997).

15 Beckett, *Murphy*, pp. 7, 57.

16 Robert Woodworth, *Contemporary Schools of Psychology* (New York: Ronald Press, 1931).

17 Kurt Koffka, *Principles of Gestalt Psychology* (New York: Harcourt Brace & Co., 1935).

18 Beckett, *Murphy*, p. 4. In Rabaté's view, Neary's eastern origin and frequent Hegelian references constitute further evidence that Beckett's therapist

Wilfred Bion was a likely source for the character. Jean-Michel Rabaté *Ghosts of Modernity* (Gainesville: University Press of Florida, 1996), pp. 148–170.

19 Carl Jung, *The Symbolic Life: Miscellaneous Writings* (London: Routledge and Kegan Paul, 1977), p. 209.

20 Beckett, *Murphy*, p. 49.

21 Harry Guntrip, *Schizoid Phenomena, Object-Relations, and the Self* (London: International Universities Press, 1992).

22 Beckett, *Murphy*, p. 6.

23 Hugh Kenner, *Samuel Beckett: A Critical Study* (Berkeley: University of California Press, 1973), p. 117.

24 C. J. Ackerley, *Demented Particulars: The Annotated Murphy* (Gainesville: Journal of Beckett Studies Books, 1998), p. 29.

25 Beckett, *Murphy*, p. 30.

26 Beckett, *Murphy*, p. 29.

27 Beckett, *Murphy*, p. 49.

28 Beckett, *Murphy*, p. 11.

29 Beckett, *Murphy*, p. 12.

30 Beckett, *Murphy*, p. 18.

31 Ulrika Maude, "Beckett, Body and Mind," in Dirk Van Hulle (ed.), *The New Cambridge Companion to Samuel Beckett* (Cambridge: Cambridge University Press, 2015); for a discussion of the parodic treatments of behaviorism in *Murphy*, see John Bolin, *Beckett and the Modern Novel* (Cambridge: Cambridge University Press, 2013), p. 43–61.

32 Maude, "Beckett, Body and Mind," p. 183. Maude writes that Beckett's reading included "a number of turn-of-the-century medical books, including Sir William Osler's *The Principles and Practice of Medicine*, Pierre Gernier's *Onanisme Seul et a Deux*, Max Nordau's *Degeneration*, as well as works of psychology and psychoanalysis, among them Robert Woodworth's *Contemporary Schools of Psychology* and Karin Stephen's *Psychoanalysis and Medicine: A Study of the Wish to Fall Ill.*" Maude, "Beckett, Body and Mind," p. 174.

33 Beckett, *Murphy*, p. 111.

34 Beckett, *Murphy*, p. 111.

35 Beckett, *Murphy*, p. 111.

36 Beckett, *Murphy*, p. 112.

37 Quoted in Slavoj Zizek, *Enjoy Your Symptom!* (New York: Verso, 2001), p. 50.

38 Beckett, *Murphy*, p. 113.

39 Beckett, *Murphy*, p. 113.

40 Beckett, *Murphy*, p. 112.

41 Ackerley, *Demented Particulars*, p. 129.

42 Beckett, *Murphy*, p. 65.

43 Beckett, *Murphy*, p. 87.

44 Beckett, *Murphy*, p. 89.

45 Beckett, *Murphy*, p. 94.

46 Beckett, *Murphy*, p. 168.

47 Samuel Beckett, *Collected Letters*, Vol. 1., Martha Dow Fehsenfeld, Lois Overbeck, Dan Gunn, and George Craig, eds. (Cambridge: Cambridge University Press, 2009), p. 277 emphasis added.
48 Beckett, *Murphy*, p. 178.
49 Knowlson, *Damned to Fame*, p. 198.
50 Beckett, *Murphy*, pp. 179–180.
51 Beckett, *Murphy*, p. 183.
52 Beckett, *Murphy*, p. 183, emphasis original.
53 Beckett, *Murphy*, p. 241.
54 Beckett, *Murphy*, p. 242.
55 Beckett, *Murphy*, p. 245.
56 Beckett, *Murphy*, p. 246.
57 George Berkeley, *Principles of Human Knowledge and Three Dialogues*, ed. Howard Robinson (Oxford: Oxford University Press, 2009), p. 24.
58 Beckett, *Murphy*, p. 250.
59 Beckett, *Murphy*, p. 251.
60 Beckett, *Murphy*, p. 252.
61 Arnold Geulincx, Han Van Ruler and Anthony Uhlmann (eds.), Martin Wilson (trans.), *Ethics, with Samuel Beckett's Notes* (London: Brill, 2006), p. 178.
62 Samuel Beckett, *Watt* (New York: Grove Press, 1994), p. 18.
63 Beckett, *Watt*, p. 25.
64 Beckett, *Watt*, p. 73.
65 Beckett, *Watt*, p. 75.
66 Beckett, *Watt*, p. 75, emphasis added.
67 Beckett, *Watt*, p. 81.
68 Sechehaye, *An Autobiography of a Schizophrenic Girl*, pp. 40–41.
69 Beckett, *Watt*, p. 82.
70 Beckett, *Watt*, p. 83.
71 Beckett, *Watt*, p. 85.
72 Beckett, *Three Novels*, p. 31.
73 Beckett, *Three Novels*, p. 49.
74 Beckett, *Three Novels*, p. 49.
75 Beckett, *Three Novels*, p. 55.
76 Beckett, *Three Novels*, p. 59.
77 Beckett, *Three Novels*, p. 66.
78 Beckett, *Three Novels*, p. 56.
79 Beckett, *Three Novels*, p. 255.
80 Beckett, *Three Novels*, p. 257.
81 Beckett, *Three Novels*, p. 207.
82 Gilles Deleuze, Mark Lester (trans.), *The Logic of Sense*, (New York: Columbia University Press, 1990). For more on Deleuze's ontology of "univocal being," see Alain Badiou, Louise Burchill (trans.), *Deleuze: The Clamor of Being*, (Minneapolis: University of Minnesota Press, 1999), pp. 19–30.

83 James Knowlson and Elizabeth Knowlson (eds.), *Beckett Remembering/ Remembering Beckett: A Centenniary Celebration* (London: Bloomsbury, 2006), p. 113.

84 Ivan Leuder and Phillip Thomas, *Voice of Reason, Voices of Insanity: Studies of Verbal Hallucination* (New York: Routledge, 2000), p. 114.

85 Daniel Katz, *Saying I No More: Subjectivity and Consciousness in the Prose of Samuel Beckett* (Evanston: Northwestern University Press, 1999), p. 83.

86 Beckett, *Three Novels*, p. 347.

87 Beckett, *Three Novels*, p. 309.

88 Beckett, *Three Novels*, p. 314.

89 Dan Zahavi, "Self and Other: The Limits of Narrative Understanding," in Daniel Hutto (ed.), *Narrative and Understanding Persons*, (Cambridge: Cambridge University Press, 2012), p. 183.

90 Beckett, *Three Novels*, p. 360.

91 Beckett, *Three Novels*, p. 310.

92 Beckett, *Three Novels*, p. 314.

93 Beckett, *Three Novels*, p. 308.

94 Beckett, *Three Novels*, p. 345.

95 Beckett, *Three Novels*, p. 325.

96 Beckett, *Three Novels*, p. 395.

97 Gallagher, "Self-Narrative in Schizophrenia," p. 205.

98 Gallagher, "Self-Narrative in Schizophrenia," pp. 217–218.

99 Beckett, *Three Novels*, p. 336.

100 Beckett, *Three Novels*, p. 351.

101 Beckett, *Three Novels*, p. 336.

102 Beckett, *Three Novels*, p. 356.

103 Samuel Beckett, *How It Is* (New York: Grove Press, 1994), pp. 94–95.

104 Beckett, *How It Is*, pp. 82, 94.

105 Beckett, *How It Is*, p. 95.

106 Beckett, *How It Is*, p. 139.

107 Knowlson, *Damned to Fame*, pp. 387–388.

108 Ulrika Maude, *Beckett, Technology, and the Body* (Cambridge: Cambridge University Press, 2009), p. 47.

109 Everett Frost, "Mediatating On: Beckett, Embers, and Radio Theory," in Lois Oppenheim (ed.), *Samuel Beckett and the Arts: Music, Visual Arts, and Non-Print Media* (New York: Garland, 1999), p. 314.

110 Alfred Kraus, "Schizophrenic Delusion and Hallucination as the Expression and Consequence of an Alteration of the Existential a Prioris," in Man Chung, Bill Fulford, and George Graham (eds.), *Reconceiving Schizophrenia* (Oxford: Oxford University Press, 2007), p. 103.

111 Sconce, "Wireless Ego: The Pulp Physics of Psychoanalysis," p. 40.

112 Clas Zilliacus, *Beckett and Broadcasting: A Study of the Works of Samuel Beckett for and in Radio and Television* (Åbo: Abo Akademi, 1976), p. 81.

113 Maude, *Beckett, Technology, and the Body*, p. 57.

114 Steven Connor, "I Switch Off: Beckett and the Ordeals of Radio," in Debra Rae Cohen, Michael Coyle, and Jane Lewty (eds.), *Broadcasting Modernism* (Gainesville: University Press of Florida, 2009), p. 274; Tajiri, *Samuel Beckett and the Prosthetic Body*, p. 161.

115 Samuel Beckett, *The Letters of Samuel Beckett, Vol. 1: 1929–1940*, eds. Martha Dow Fehsenfeld, Lois More Overbeck, Dan Gunn, and George Craig (Cambridge: Cambridge University Press, 2009), p. 278.

116 Samuel Beckett, *Collected Shorter Plays* (New York, Grove Press, 1984), p. 100.

117 Beckett, *Collected Shorter Plays*, p. 97.

118 Beckett, *Collected Shorter Plays*, p. 97.

119 Leudar and Thomas, *Voices of Reason, Voices of Insanity*, p. 114.

120 Beckett, *Collected Shorter Plays*, p. 96.

121 For a reading of *Embers* as a scene of psychoanalytic working through, see David Alpaugh, "*Embers* and the Sea: Beckettian Intimations of Mortality," *Modern Drama* 16 (1973), pp. 317–28.

122 Beckett, *Collected Shorter Plays*, p. 96.

123 Jacques Lacan, *The Seminar of Jacques Lacan, Book III: The Psychoses, 1955–1956*, ed. Jacques-Alain Miller, trans. Russell Grigg (New York: Norton & Company, 1993), p. 285. See also Eric L. Santner, *My Own Private Germany: Daniel Paul Schreber's Secret History of Modernity* (Princeton: Princeton University Press, 1996).

124 Beckett, *Collected Shorter Plays*, p. 95.

125 Frost, "Mediatating On: Beckett, *Embers*, and Radio Theory," p. 316.

126 Beckett, *Collected Shorter Plays*, p. 107.

127 For a rich discussion of the thematics of "switching" on and off in Beckett's work for radio and stage, see Connor, "I Switch Off: Beckett and the Ordeals of Radio," pp. 284–287.

128 Beckett, *Collected Shorter Plays*, p. 110.

129 Beckett, *Collected Shorter Plays*, p. 111.

130 Michael Davidson, "Technologies of Presence: Orality and the Tapevoice of Contemporary Poetics," in Adalaide Morris (ed.), *Sound States: Innovative Poetics and Acoustical Technologies* (Chapel Hill: University of North Carolina Press, 1997), p. 99.

131 Leudar and Thomas, *Voices of Reason, Voices of Insanity*, p. 122.

132 Beckett, *Collected Shorter Plays*, p. 101.

133 Jaspers, *General Psychopathology*, p. 577, emphasis original.

134 Bentall, *Madness Explained*, 29.

135 Josef Parnas, "On Psychosis: Karl Jaspers and Beyond," in Giovanni Stanghellini and Thomas Fuchs (eds.), *One Century of Karl Jaspers's General Psychopathology* (Oxford: Oxford Unviersity Press, 2013), p. 220.

136 Beckett, *Three Novels*, p. 336.

Conclusion: Contemporary Mediations of Modernist Madness

1 I am indebted to Ulrika Maude, who provides this valuable archival reference in Dirk Van Hulle (ed.), "Beckett, Body and Mind," *The New Cambridge*

Companion to Samuel Beckett (Cambridge: Cambridge University Press, 2015), pp. 182–183. Beckett to Lawrence Shainberg, Paris, July 15, 1979, University of Reading MS JEK A/2/268.

2 Waugh, "Thinking in Literature: Modernism and Contemporary Neuroscience," p. 79.

3 T. J. Lustig and James Peacock (ed.), *Diseases and Disorders in Contemporary Fiction: The Syndrome Syndrome* (New York: Routledge, 2013), p. 3.

4 Catherine Malabou, *The New Wounded: From Neurosis to Brain Damage* (New York: Fordham University Press, 2012), p. 9.

5 See David James (ed.), *The Legacies of Modernism: Historicizing Postwar and Contemporary Fiction* (Cambridge: Cambridge University Press, 2012); David James, *Modernist Futures: Innovation and Inheritance in the Contemporary Novel* (Cambridge: Cambridge University Press, 2012); Michael D'Arcy and Mathias Nilges (eds.), *The Contemporaneity of Modernism: Literature, Media, Culture* (New York: Routledge Press, 2015).

6 David James, "Introduction: Mapping Modernist Continuities," in David James (ed.), *The Legacies of Modernism: Historicizing Postwar and Contemporary Fiction* (Cambridge: Cambridge University Press, 2012), pp. 2–3.

7 Miller, *Late Modernism*, p. 9.

8 Tom McCarthy, *C* (New York, Knopf, 2010). McCarthy's interest in the relation between radio technology and literature extends well beyond his novel. He has produced radio art installations and pirate radio projects, and, to promote the publication of *C*, he published a rich essay on the history of literature and information technology. Tom McCarthy, "Technology and the Novel, From Blake to Ballard," *Guardian Review*, July 24, 2010, p. 2.

9 McCarthy, *C*, p. 79.

10 Quoted in Jenny Turner, "Seeing Things Flat," *London Review of Books* 32.17, September 9, 2010, pp. 7–8. Turner refers to a review of *C* on BBC Radio 4's *Saturday Review* program.

11 McCarthy, *C*, p. 77.

12 McCarthy, *C*, p. 93, emphasis original.

13 McCarthy, *C*, p 177.

14 F. T. Marinetti, "The Founding Manifesto of Futurism" (1909), and "The Technical Manifesto of Futurist Literature" (1912), in Lawrence Rainey, Christine Poggi, and Laura Wittman (eds.), *Futurism: An Anthology* (New Haven: Yale University Press, 2009), pp. 49–53; pp. 119–125.

15 McCarthy, *C*, p. 189. Heidegger quotes these lines from Holderlin's poem "Patmos" in his essay "The Turning," in *The Question Concerning Technology and Other Essays*, ed. and trans. William Levitt (New York: Harper Books, 1977), p. 42.

16 Will Self, "Modernism and Me," *Guardian*, August 3, 2012. Web. https://www.theguardian.com/books/2012/aug/03/will-self-modernism-and-me

17 Will Self, *Umbrella* (London: Bloomsbury, 2012), p. 120.

18 Self, *Umbrella*, p. 380.

19 Self, *Umbrella*, p. 216.

20 T. J. Lustig and James Peacock (eds.), *Diseases and Disorders in Contemporary Fiction: The Syndrome Syndrome* (New York: Routledge, 2013), p. 10.

21 Joseph Dumit, *Picturing Personhood: Brain Scans and Biomedical Identity* (Princeton: Princeton University Press, 2004), p. 104.

22 Nikolas Rose and Joelle Abi-Rached, *Neuro: The New Brain Sciences and the Management of the Brain* (Princeton: Princeton University Press, 2013), p. 140.

23 Ludwig Wittgenstein, *Philosophical Investigations* (Oxford: Basil Blackwell, 1958), section 281.

24 M. R. Bennett and P. M. S. Hacker "The Mereological Fallacy in Neuroscience," in *Philosophical Foundations of Neuroscience* (New York: Wiley-Blackwell, 2003), p. 68; quoted in Rose and Abi-Rached, *Neuro*, p. 84.

25 Patricia Waugh, "The Naturalistic Turn, the Syndrome, and the Rise of the Neo-Phenomenological Novel," in James Peacock and Tim Lustig (eds.), *Diseases and Disorders in Contemporary Fiction: The Syndrome Syndrome* (New York: Routledge, 2013), pp. 17–34 at 18.

26 Self, *Umbrella*, p. 13.

27 Self, *Umbrella*, p. 188.

28 Self, *Umbrella*, p. 136.

29 Nancy Andreasen, "DSM and the Death of Phenomenology in America: An Example of Unintended Consequences," *Schizophrenia Bulletin* 33.1 (2006), 108.

30 Waugh, "The Naturalistic Turn, the Syndrome, and the Rise of the Neo-Phenomenological Novel,"p. 24.

31 Rose and Abi-Rached, *Neuro*, p. 219.

32 Jaspers, *General Psychopathology*, p. 293, emphasis added.

33 Gallagher, "Pathologies in Narrative Structure," p. 211.

34 For accounts of transdisciplinary exchanges between the mind sciences and the humanities, see Melissa Littlefield and Jenell Johnson (eds.), *The Neuroscientific Turn: Transdisciplinarity in the Age of the Brain* (Ann Arbor: University of Michigan Press, 2012); David Herman (ed.), *Narrative Theory and the Cognitive Sciences* (Palo Alto: Stanford University Press, 2003); David Herman, *Storytelling and the Sciences of the Mind* (Cambridge: MIT Press, 2013).

35 Lydia Davis, "Liminal: The Little Man," in *The Collected Stories of Lydia Davis* (New York: Picador, 2010), p. 13.

Bibliography

Ackerley, C. J. *Demented Particulars: The Annotated Murphy*. Gainesville, FL: Journal of Beckett Studies Books, 1998.

Adams, Anthony. "Butter-Spades, Footnotes, and Omnium: *The Third Policeman* as Pataphysical Fiction," *The Review of Contemporary Fiction: Flann O'Brien Centenary Essays*. Edited by Neil Murphy and Keith Hopper 31.3 (2011), 106–119.

Adorno, Theodor. "The Problem of a New Type of Human Being." *Current of Music*. Edited and translated by Robert Hullot-Kentor. Malden, MA: Polity Press, 2006. pp. 461–468.

"The Radio Voice." *Current of Music*. Edited and translated by Robert Hullot-Kentor. Malden, MA: Polity Press, 2009. pp. 345–391.

"Theses about the Idea and Form of Collaboration of the Princeton Radio Research Project." *Current of Music*. Edited and translated by Robert Hullot-Kentor. Malden, MA: Polity Press, 2009. pp. 477–480.

Albright, Daniel. *Beckett and Aesthetics*. New York: Cambridge University Press, 2003.

Alpaugh, David. "*Embers* and the Sea: Beckettian Intimations of Mortality," *Modern Drama* 16 (1973), 317–328.

Andreasen, Nancy. *The Broken Brain: The Biological Revolution in Psychiatry*. New York: Harper & Row, 1984.

"DSM and the Death of Phenomenology in America: An Example of Unintended Consequences," *Schizophrenia Bulletin* 33.1 (2006), 108–112.

Ardis, Ann. *New Women, New Novels: Feminism and Early Modernism*. New Brunswick, NJ: Rutgers University Press, 1990.

Armstrong, Tim. *Modernism, Technology and the Body: A Cultural Study*. Cambridge: Cambridge University Press, 1998.

Arnheim, Rudolf. *Radio*. London: Faber & Faber, 1936.

Ashby, Ross. "Cybernetics." *Recent Progress in Psychiatry*, Vol. 2. Edited by G. W. T. H. Fleming. London: Churchill, 1950, 93–110.

Design For a Brain. London: Chapman & Hall, 1952.

Avery, Todd. *Radio Modernism: Literature, Ethics, and the BBC, 1922–1938*. Burlington, VT: Ashgate, 2006.

Bachman, Erik M. "How to Misbehave as a Behaviourist (If You're Wyndham Lewis)," *Textual Practice* 28:3 (2014), 427–451.

Badiou, Alain. *Deleuze: The Clamor of Being*. Translated by Louise Burchill. Minneapolis: University of Minnesota Press, 1999.

Baker, Phil. *Beckett and the Mythology of Psychoanalysis*. New York: St. Martin's Press, 1997.

Barber, Leslie. "The Age of Schizophrenia," *Harper's Monthly Magazine* December 1, 1937, 70–78.

Bateson, Gregory. *Steps to an Ecology of Mind: Collected Essays in Anthropology, Psychiatry, Evolution, and Epistemology*. Chicago: University of Chicago Press, 2000.

Beausang, Michael. "*Watt*: Logic, Insanity, Aphasia." Translated by Valerie Galiussi. *Style* 30.3 (1996), 495–513.

Beckett, Samuel. *Collected Shorter Plays*. New York, Grove Press, 1984.

How It Is. New York: Grove Press, 1994.

Watt. New York: Grove Press, 1994.

Collected Letters, Vol. 1. Edited by Martha Dow Fehsenfeld, Lois Overbeck, Dan Gunn, and George Craig. Cambridge: Cambridge University Press, 2009.

Three Novels: Molloy, Malone Dies, The Unnamable. New York: Grove Press, 2009.

Murphy. New York: Grove Press, 2011.

Bennett, M. R. and P. M. S. Hacker. *Philosophical Foundations of Neuroscience*. New York: Wiley-Blackwell, 2003.

Bentall, Richard. *Madness Explained: Psychosis and Human Nature*. New York: Penguin, 2004.

Berkeley, George. *Principles of Human Knowledge and Three Dialogues*. Edited by Howard Robinson. Oxford: Oxford University Press, 2009.

Berlant, Lauren. "On the Case: A Special Issue," *Critical Inquiry* 33.4 (2007), 663–672.

Bernfeld, Siefried. "Freud's Earliest Theories and the School of Helmholtz," *Psychoanalytic Quarterly* 13 (1944), 341–362.

Bernheimer, Charles and Claire Kahane (eds.). *In Dora's Case: Freud – Hysteria – Feminism*. New York: Columbia University Press, 1985.

Bersani, Leo. "Pynchon, Paranoia, and Literature," *Representations* 25 (Winter 1989), 99–118.

Bettelheim, Bruno. *The Empty Fortress; Infantile Autism and the Birth of the Self*. New York: Free Press, 1967.

Blackman, Lisa. *Hearing Voices: Embodiment and Experience*. London: Free Association Press, 2001.

Bleuler, Eugen. *Dementia Praecox, or the Group of Schizophrenias*. Translated by Joseph Zinkin. New York: International Universities Press, 1950.

Naturgeschichte der Seele und irhes beisstwerdens, eine Elementarpsychologie. Berlin: Springer-Verlag, 1921.

The Schizophrenic Disorders. Translated by S. M. Clemens. New Haven, CT: Yale University Press, 1978.

Bobotis, Andrea. "Queering Knowledge in Flann O'Brien's *The Third Policeman*," *Irish University Review: A Journal of Irish Studies* Autumn–Winter, 32.2 (2002), 242–258.

Bolin, John. *Beckett and the Modern Novel.* Cambridge: Cambridge University Press, 2013.

Boothby, Richard. *Freud as Philosopher: Metapsychology after Lacan.* New York: Routledge, 2001.

Boring, Edwin G. "Mind and Mechanism," *The American Journal of Psychology* 59.2 (1946), 173–192.

Boyle, Mary. *Schizophrenia: A Scientific Delusion.* London: Routledge, 1990.

Breton, Andre. *The Immaculate Conception.* Translated by David Gascoyne, Antony Melville, and Jon Graham. London: Atlas Press, 1997.

Briggs, Asa. *The History of Broadcasting in the United Kingdom, Vol. 1: The Birth of Broadcasting.* Oxford: Oxford University Press, 1961.

Buckley, Kerry W. *Mechanical Man: John Broadus Watson and the Beginnings of Behaviorism.* New York: Guilford Press, 1989.

Burke, Carolyn. *Becoming Modern: A Life of Mina Loy.* New York: Farrar, Straus Giroux, 1996.

Burn, Stephen (ed.). "Neuroscience and Modern Fiction," Special Issue of *Modern Fiction Studies* 61.2 (2015).

Burstein, Jessica. "Waspish Segments: Lewis, Prosthesis, Fascism," *Modernism/ Modernity* 4.2 (1997), 139–164.

Bynum, W. F, Roy Porter, and Michael Shepherd (eds.). *The Anatomy of Madness: Essays in the History of Psychiatry.* London: Tavistock, 1985.

Calkins, Mary Whiton. "Psychology and the Behaviorist," *Psychological Bulletin* 10 (1913), 288–291.

Callard, D. A. *The Case of Anna Kavan: A Biography.* London: Peter Owen, 1992.

Cantril, Hadley and Gordon W. Allport. *The Psychology of Radio.* New York: Harper & Bros., 1935.

Charon, Rita. *Narrative Medicine: Honoring the Stories of Illness.* Oxford: Oxford University Press, 2008.

Clark, Andy. *Supersizing the Mind: Embodiment, Action, and Cognitive Extension.* Oxford: Oxford University Press, 2010.

Clark, Andy and David Chalmers. "The Extended Mind." *The Extended Mind.* Edited by Richard Menary. Cambridge: MIT Press, 2012. pp. 27–42.

Clarke, Bruce and Linda Dalrymple (eds.). *From Energy to Information: Representation in Science and Technology, Art, and Literature.* Palo Alto: Stanford University Press, 2002.

Clissman, Anne. *Flann O'Brien: A Critical Introduction to His Writings.* New York: Barnes and Noble, 1975.

Cohen, Debra Rae. "Intermediality and the Problem of the Listener." *Modernism/ Modernity* (2012) 19.3, 569–592.

Colby, Kenneth. *Artificial Paranoia: A Computer Simulation of Paranoid Processes.* New York: Pergamon, 1975.

Comentale, Edward. *Modernism, Cultural Production, and the British Avant-Garde.* New York: Cambridge University Press, 2004.

"The Shropshire Schizoid and the Machines of Modernism," *Modernist Cultures* 1.1 (2005), 22–46.

Connor, Steven. "Beckett and Bion." *Journal of Beckett Studies* 17.1 (2008), 9–34.

"I Switch Off: Beckett and the Ordeals of Radio." *Broadcasting Modernism.* Edited by Debra Rae Cohen, Michael Coyle, and Jane Lewty. Gainesville: University Press of Florida, 2009. pp. 274–293.

"*Scilicet:* Kittler, Media and Madness." *Kittler Now.* Edited by Stephen Sale and Laura Salisbury. Malden, MA: Polity Press, 2015. pp. 115–130.

Cooper, J. E., R. E. Kendell, B. J. Gurland, L. Sharpe, J. R. M. Copeland and R. Simon. *Psychiatric Diagnosis in New York and London: Maudsley Monograph No. 2.* Oxford: Oxford University Press, 1972.

Crabtree, Adam. *From Mesmer to Freud: Magnetic Sleep and the Roots of Psychological Healing.* New Haven: Yale University Press, 1993.

Cronin, Anthony. *No Laughing Matter: The Life and Times of Flann O'Brien.* London: Grafton, 1990.

Dalí, Salvador. *Oui: The Paranoid-Critical Revolution, Writings 1927–1933.* Edited by Robert Descharnes. Translated by Yvonne Shafir. Boston: Exact Change, 1998.

Maniacal Eyeball: The Unspeakable Confessions of Salvador Dalí, Translated by André Parinaud. New York: Creation, 2004.

Damasio, Antonio. *The Feeling of What Happens: Body and Emotion in the Making of Consciousness.* New York: Harcourt, 1999.

D'Arcy, Michael and Mathias Nilges (eds.). *The Contemporaneity of Modernism: Literature, Media, Culture.* New York: Routledge Press, 2015.

Davidson, Larry. "Storytelling and Schizophrenia: Using Narrative Structure in Phenomenological Research," *Humanistic Psychologist* 21.2 (1991), 200–220.

Davidson, Michael. "Technologies of Presence: Orality and the Tapevoice of Contemporary Poetics." *Sound States: Innovative Poetics and Acoustical Technologies.* Edited by Adalaide Morris. Chapel Hill: University of North Carolina Press, 1997. pp. 97–125.

Davis, Lydia. "Liminal: The Little Man." *The Collected Stories of Lydia Davis.* New York: Picador, 2010. pp. 12–17.

Deleuze, Gilles. *The Logic of Sense.* Translated by Mark Lester. New York: Columbia University Press, 1990.

Dennett, Daniel. *The Intentional Stance.* Cambridge: MIT Press, 1987.

Consciousness Explained. New York: Penguin, 1991.

Descartes, Rene. *The Philosophical Works of Descartes.* Edited and translated by Elizabeth Haldane and G. R. T. Ross. Cambridge: Cambridge University Press, 1969.

Diagnostic and Statistical Manual of Mental Disorders, 5th Edition: DSM-5. New York: American Psychiatric Association, 2013.

Dolezel, Lubimir. *Heterocosmica: Fiction and Possible Worlds.* Baltimore: Johns Hopkins University Press, 2000.

Dumit, Joseph. *Picturing Personhood: Brain Scans and Biomedical Identity.* Princeton: Princeton University Press, 2004.

Dupuy, Jean-Pierre. *On the Origins of Cognitive Science: The Mechanization of the Mind.* Translated by M. B. DeBevoise. Cambridge: MIT Press, 2009.

Edwards, Paul. "Wyndham Lewis and the Uses of Shellshock: Meat and Post-modernism." *Wyndham Lewis and the Cultures of Modernity.* Edited by Andrzej Gasiorek and Alice Glen-Reeve. London: Ashgate, 2011. pp. 223–241.

Ekstein, R. "The Space Child's Time Machine: On 'Reconstruction' in the Psychotherapeutic Treatment of a Schizophrenoid Child," *American Journal of Orthopsychiatry* 24 (1954), 492–506.

Elkisch, P and Mahler, M. S. "On Infantile Precursors of the 'Influencing Machine' (Tausk)," *Psychoanalytic Study of the Child* 14 (1959), 219–235.

Ellenburger, Henri. *The Discovery of the Unconscious.* New York: Basic Books, 1979.

Feldman, Michael. *Beckett's Books: A Cultural History of the Interwar Notes.* New York: Continuum, 2006.

Fifield, Peter. "Beckett, Cotard's Syndrome and the Narrative Patient." *Journal of Beckett Studies* 17.1 (2008), 169–186.

Fink, Bruce. *A Clinical Introduction to Lacanian Psychoanalysis: Theory and Technique.* Cambridge: Harvard University Press, 1997.

Forel, August. *Hypnotism; or Suggestion and Psychotherapy* (1889). Translated by H. Armit. London: Rebman, 1906.

Foster, Hal. *Prosthetic Gods.* Cambridge: MIT Press, 2004.

Foucault, Michel. *History of Madness.* Edited by Jean Khalfa. Translated by Jonathan Murphy and Jean Khalfa. New York: Routledge, 2006.

Psychiatric Power. Edited by Jacques Lagrange and Arnold Davidson. Translated by Graham Burchell. New York: Picador, 2008.

Frank, Arthur W. *The Wounded Storyteller: Body, Illness, and Ethics.* Chicago: University of Chicago Press, 2013.

Freud, Sigmund. "Neurosis and Psychosis" (1924). *The Standard Edition of the Complete Psychological Works of Sigmund Freud.* Vol. 19. Translated by James Strachey. London: Hogarth Press, 2001. pp. 149–156.

"The Ego and the Id" (1923), *The Standard Edition of the Complete Psychological Works of Sigmund Freud.* Vol. 19. Translated by James Strachey. London: Hogarth Press, 2001. pp. 12–68.

The Schreber Case. Translated by Andrew Webber. New York: Penguin, 2003.

Frost, Everett. "Mediatating on: Beckett, Embers, and Radio Theory." *Samuel Beckett and the Arts: Music, Visual Arts, and Non-Print Media.* Edited by Lois Oppenheim. New York: Garland Publishing, 1999. pp. 311–331.

Fuchs, Thomas. "Being a Psycho-Machine: on the Phenomenology of the Influencing-Machine." *Air Loom.* Edited by Bettina Brand-Clausen and Thomas Roeske. Heidelberg: Wunderhorn, 2006. pp. 25–43.

"Brain Mythologies: Jaspers' Critique of Reductionism from a Current Perspective." *Karl Jaspers' Philosophy and Psychopathology.* Edited by T. Fuchs, Thiemo Breyer, and Christoph Mundt. New York: Springer, 2013. pp. 75–84.

Furman, E. "An Ego Disturbance in a Young Child," *Psychoanalytic Study of the Child* 11 (1956): 312–335.

Gaedtke, Andrew. "Halluci-nation: Mental Illness, Modernity, and Metaphoricity in Salman Rushdie's *Midnight's Children*," *Contemporary Literature* 55.4 (2014), 701–725.

Gallagher, Shaun. "Self-Narrative in Schizophrenia." *The Self in Neuroscience and Psychiatry*. Edited by Tilo Kircher and Anthony David. New York: Cambridge University Press, 2003. pp. 336–357.

"Pathologies in Narrative Structures." *Narrative and Understanding Persons*. Edited by Daniel D. Hutto. Cambridge: Cambridge University Press, 2007. pp. 203–224.

Garrity, Jane. "Nocturnal Transgressions in *The House of Sleep:* Anna Kavan's Maternal Registers," *Modern Fiction Studies* 40.2 (1994), 253–277.

Gasiorek, Andrzej. "Wyndham Lewis on Art, Culture and Politics in the 1930s." *Wyndham Lewis and the Cultures of Modernity*. Edited by Andrzej Gasiorek and Alice Glen-Reeve. London: Ashgate, 2011. pp. 201–221.

Geulincx, Arnold. *Arnold Geulincx Ethics, with Samuel Beckett's Notes*. Edited by Han Van Ruler and Anthony Uhlmann. Translated by Martin Wilson. London: Brill, 2006.

Giddens, Anthony. *Modernity and Self-Identity: Self and Society in the Late-Modern Age*. Palo Alto: Stanford University Press, 1992.

Gillespie, Alana. "'Banjaxed and Bewildered' *Cruiskeen Lawn* and the role of science in independent Ireland." *Flann O'Brien: Contesting Legacies*. Edited by Ruben Borg, Paul Fagan, and Werner Huber. Cork: Cork UP, 2014. pp. 169–180.

Goble, Mark. *Beautiful Circuits: Modernism and the Mediated Life*. New York: Columbia University Press, 2012.

Gordon, Rae Beth. "From Charcot to Charlot: Unconscious Imitations and Spectatorship in French Cabaret and Early Cinema." *The Mind of Modernism: Medicine, Psychology, and the Cultural Arts in Europe and American, 1880–1940*. Edited by Mark Micale. Stanford: Stanford University Press, 2004. pp. 93–124.

Guntrip, Harry. *Schizoid Phenomena, Object-Relations, and the Self*. London: International Universities Press, 1992.

Haas, L. F. "Hans Berger (1873–1941), Richard Caton (1842–1926), and Electroencephalography," *Journal of Neurology, Neurosurgery & Psychiatry* 74.1 (2003): 9.

Hacking, Ian. *Rewriting the Soul: Multiple Personality and the Sciences of Memory*. Princeton: Princeton University Press, 1995.

Hadas, Pamela White. "Madness and Medicine: The Graphomaniac's Cure," *Literature and Medicine* 9 (1990), 181–193.

Harari, Roberto. *How James Joyce Made His Name: A Reading of the Final Lacan*. Translated by Luke Thurston. New York: Other Press, 2002.

Harrington, Anne. "Hysteria, Hypnosis, and the Lure of the Invisible: The Rise of Neo-Mesmerism in Fin-de-siècle French Psychiatry." *The Anatomy of Madness*.

Edited by W. F. Bynum, Roy Porter, and Michael Shepherd. London: Routledge, 1988. Vol. 3. pp. 226–245.

Hayles, N. Katherine. *How We Became Post-Human: Virtual Bodies in Cybernetics, Literature, and Informatics.* Chicago: University of Chicago Press, 1999.

Hayot, Eric. *On Literary Worlds.* Oxford: Oxford University Press, 2012.

Hayward, Rhodri. "'Our Friends Electric': Mechanical Models of Mind in Postwar Britain," *Psychology in Britain: Historical Essays and Personal Reflections,* ed. G. C. Bunn, A. D. Lovie, and G. D. Richards. Leicester: British Psychologist Society, 2001. pp. 290–308.

Heidegger, Martin. "The Thing," in *Poetry, Language, Thought.* Translated by Albert Hofstadter. New York: Harper Collins, 1971. pp. 161–184.

"The Turning," *The Question Concerning Technology and Other Essays.* Translated by William Levitt. New York: Harper Books, 1977. pp. 36–52.

"Only a God Can Save Us." *The Heidegger Controversy: A Critical Reader.* Edited by Richard Wolin. Cambridge: MIT Press, 1991. pp. 91–118.

Being and Time. Translated by Joan Stambaugh. Albany: State University of New York, 2010.

Herf, Jeffrey. *Reactionary Modernism: Technology, Culture, and Politics in Weimar and the Third Reich.* Cambridge: Cambridge University Press, 1986.

Herman, David. *The Basic Elements of Narrative.* New York: Wiley-Blackwell, 2009.

Storytelling and the Sciences of the Mind. Cambridge: MIT Press, 2013.

Herman, David (ed.). *Narrative Theory and the Cognitive Sciences.* Palo Alto: Stanford University Press, 2003.

Hidas, Gyorgy. "Flowing Over – Transference, Countertransference, Telepathy: Subjective Dimensions of the Psychoanalytic Relationship in Ferenczi's Thinking." *The Legacy of Sandor Ferenczi.* Edited by Lewis Aron and Adrienne Harris, New York: Routledge, 1993. pp. 207–215.

Hintikka, Jaakko. "Individuals, Possible Worlds, and Epistemic Logic." *Nous* 1 (1967), 33–62.

Hoerl, Christopher. "Jaspers on Explaining and Understanding in Psychiatry." *One Century of Karl Jaspers's General Psychopathology.* Edited by Giovanni Stanghellini and Thomas Fuchs. Oxford: Oxford University Press, 2013. pp. 107–120.

"Human Radio Emanations," *New York Times,* September 28, 1925, 27.

Hutchins, Edwin. *Cognition in the Wild.* Cambridge: MIT Press, 1996.

Jacobson, E. "Depersonalization." *Journal of the American Psychoanalytic Association* 7 (1959): 581–610.

James, David. "Introduction." *The Legacies of Modernism: Historicizing Postward and Contemporary Fiction.* Edited by David James. Cambridge: Cambridge University Press, 2012. pp. 1–19.

The Legacies of Modernism: Historicizing Postward and Contemporary Fiction. Edited by David James. Cambridge: Cambridge University Press, 2012.

Modernist Futures: Innovation and Inheritance in the Contemporary Novel. Cambridge: Cambridge University Press, 2012.

(ed.), *The Legacies of Modernism: Historicizing Postward and Contemporary Fiction.* Cambridge: Cambridge University Press, 2012.

James, William. "Frederic Myers's Service to Psychology." *Popular Science Monthly* (August 1901), 380–389.

Jameson, Fredric. *Fables of Aggression: Wyndham Lewis, the Modernist as Fascist.* Berkeley: University of California Press, 1979.

Postmodernism, or the Cultural Logic of Late Capitalism. Durham: Duke University Press, 1992.

Jaspers, Karl. *General Psychopathology.* Translated by J. Hoenig and Marian W. Hamilton. Baltimore: Johns Hopkins University Press, 1997.

Johnson, R. Neill. "Shadowed by the Gaze: Evelyn Waugh's 'Vile Bodies' and 'The Ordeal of Gilbert Pinfold,'" *Modern Language Review* 91.1 (1996), 9–19.

Jones, Amelia. *Irrational Modernism: A Neurasthenic History of New York Dada.* Cambridge: MIT Press, 2004.

Jung, Carl. *The Psychology of Dementia Praecox.* Translated by A. A. Brill. New York: Nervous and Mental Disease Publishing Company, 1936.

The Symbolic Life: Miscellaneous Writings. London: Routledge and Kegan Paul, 1977.

Jurecic, Ann. *Illness as Narrative.* Pittsburgh: University of Pittsburgh Press, 2012.

Kafka, Franz. *The Trial.* Translated by Breon Mitchell. New York: Schocken, 1998.

Katz, Daniel. *Saying I No More: Subjectivity and Consciousness in the Prose of Samuel Beckett.* Evanston: Northwestern University Press, 1999.

Kavan, Anna. *Asylum Piece* (1940). London: Peter Owen, 2002.

I Am Lazarus (1945). London: Peter Owen, 2013.

Who Are You? Lowestoft, Suffolk: Scorpion Press, 1963.

Keating, Benjamin. "Beckett and Language Pathology," *Journal of Modern Literature* 31.4 (2008), 86–101.

Kendler, Kenneth. "Introduction: Why Does Psychiatry Need Philosophy?" *Philosophical Issues in Psychiatry: Explanation, Phenomenology, and Nosology.* Edited by Kenneth S. Kendler and Josef Parnas. Baltimore: Johns Hopkins University Press, 2008. pp. 1–18.

Kenner, Hugh. *Wyndham Lewis.* Norfolk, CT: New Directions, 1954.

Samuel Beckett: A Critical Study. Berkeley: University of California Press, 1973.

Kermode, Frank. "Unrivalled Deftness: The Novels of Muriel Spark." *Hidden Possibilities: Essays in Honor of Muriel Spark.* Edited by Robert E. Hosmer, Jr. South Bend, IN: Notre Dame University Press, 2014. pp. 107–118.

Kittler, Friedrich. *Discourse Networks 1800/1900.* Translated by Michael Metteer. Stanford: Stanford University Press, 1990.

Kloss, Robert J. "Evelyn Waugh: His Ordeal," *American Imago* 42:1 (1985), 99–110.

Knowlson, James. *Damned to Fame: The Life of Samuel Beckett.* New York: Simon & Schuster, 1996.

Knowlson, James and Elizabeth Knowlson (eds.). *Beckett Remembering/ Remembering Beckett: A Centenniary Celebration.* London: Bloomsbury, 2006.

Koffka, Kurt. *Principles of Gestalt Psychology.* New York: Harcourt Brace & Co., 1935.

Kraepelin, Emil. *Dementia Praecox and Paraphrenia.* Translated by R. M. Barclay. Huntington, NY: Robert E. Krieger, 1971.

Kraus, Alfred. "Schizophrenic Delusion and Hallucination as the Expression and Consequence of an Alteration of the Existential a Prioris." *Reconceiving Schizophrenia*. Edited by Man Chung, Bill Fulford, and Graham George. Oxford: Oxford University Press, 2007. pp. 97–112.

Kripke, Saul. "Semantical Considerations on Modal Logic," *Acta Philosophica Fennica* 16 (1963), 83–94.

Kuni, Verena. " 'Je Suis Radio' – from the 'Influencing Machine' to the 'Radio-Self.' " *The Air Loom and Other Dangerous Influencing Machines*. Edited by Thomas Roske and Bettina Brand-Claussen. Heidelberg: Wunderhorn, 2006. pp. 239–253.

Lacan, Jacques. *The Seminar of Jacques Lacan, Book II: The Ego in Freud's Theory and in the Technique of Psychoanalysis, 1954–1955*. Edited by Jacques-Alain Miller. Translated by Sylvana Tomaselli. New York: W. W. Norton, 1991.

The Seminar of Jacques Lacan, Book III, 1955–1956. Edited by Jacques-Alain Miller. Translated by Russell Grigg. New York: W. W. Norton, 1991.

The Seminar of Jacques Lacan, Book VII: The Ethics of Psychoanalysis. Edited by Jacques-Alain Miller. Translated by Dennis Porter. New York: W. W. Norton, 1992.

"Aggressiveness in Psychoanalysis." *Ecrits*. Translated by Bruce Fink. New York: W. W. Norton, 2006. 82–101.

Le séminaire: Livre XIX ... ou pire, 1971–1972. Edited by Jacques-Alain Miller. Paris: Seuil, 2011.

Laing, R.D. *The Divided Self: An Existential Study of Sanity and Madness*. New York: Penguin, 1960.

Lanchester, John. "In Sparkworld." *Hidden Possibilities: Essays in Honor of Muriel Spark*. Edited by Robert E. Hosmer, Jr. South Bend, IN: Notre Dame University Press, 2014. pp. 187–196.

Latour, Bruno. *We Have Never Been Modern*. Cambridge: Harvard University Press, 1993.

"Why Has Critique Run Out of Steam? From Matters of Fact to Matters of Concern." *Critical Inquiry* 30 (2004), 225–248.

Leader, Darian *What Is Madness?* New York: Penguin Press, 2012.

Leahy, Thomas Hardy. "Psychology as Engineering." *The Mind as a Scientific Object: Between Brain and Culture*. Oxford: Oxford University Press, 2005. pp. 126–143.

Leudar, Ivan and Philip Thomas. *Voices of Reason, Voices of Insanity: Studies of Verbal Hallucinations*. New York: Routledge, 2000.

Lewis, David. *Counterfactuals*. Cambridge: Harvard University Press, 1978.

"Truth in Fiction," *American Philosophical Quarterly* 15 (1983), 37–46.

Lewis, Wyndham. *The Childermass*. New York: Covici & Friede, 1928.

Men without Art. London: Cassell, 1934.

Wyndham Lewis: An Anthology of His Prose. Edited by E. W. F. Tomlin. London: Methuen, 1969.

Rude Assignment: An Intellectual Autobiography. Santa Barbara: Black Sparrow Press, 1984.

The Art of Being Ruled (1926). Edited by Reid Way Dasenbrock. Santa Rosa: Black Sparrow Press, 1989.

Time and Western Man. (1927) Santa Rosa: Black Sparrow Press, 1993.

Littlefield, Melissa and Jenell Johnson (eds.). *The Neuroscientific Turn: Transdisciplinarity in the Age of the Brain.* Ann Arbor: University of Michigan Press, 2012.

Liu, Lydia H. *The Freudian Robot: Digital Media and the Future of the Unconscious.* Chicago: University of Chicago Press, 2010.

Loux, Michael (ed.). *The Possible and the Actual: Readings in the Metaphysics of Modality.* Ithaca: Cornell University Press, 1979.

Love, Heather. "Safe," *American Literary History* 25.1(2013), 164–175.

Loy, Mina. *Insel.* Edited by Elizabeth Arnold. Santa Rosa: Black Sparrow Press, 1991.

Insel. Edited by Sarah Hayden. New York: Neversink Press, 2014.

Luria, A.R. *The Man with a Shattered World: The History of a Brain Wound.* Cambridge: Harvard University Press, 1987.

Lustig, T. J. and James Peacock (ed.). *Diseases and Disorders in Contemporary Fiction: The Syndrome Syndrome.* New York: Routledge, 2013.

Lynch, James J. "Evelyn Waugh during the *Pinfold* Years." *mfs: Modern Fiction Studies* 32.4 (1986), 543–559.

Lysaker, Paul et al., "Changes in Narrative Structure and Content in Schizophrenia in Long Term Individual Psychotherapy: A Single Case Study," *Clinical Psychology and Psychotherapy* 12 (2005), 406–416.

Lysaker, Paul and John Lysaker. "Narrative Structure in Psychosis: Schizophrenia and Disruptions in the Dialogical Self," *Theory & Psychology* 12.2 (2002), 207–220.

"A Typology of Narrative Impoverishment in Schizophrenia: Implications for Understanding the Processes of Establishing and Sustaining Dialogue in Individual Psychotherapy," *Counseling Psychology Quarterly* 19.1 (2006), 57–68.

Lysaker, Paul, Jamie Ringer, Alan McGuire, and Tania Lecomte, "Personal Narratives and Recovery from Schizophrenia," *Schizophrenia Research* 121 (2010), 271–276.

Lysaker, Paul, Jack Tsai, Alyssa Maulucci, and Giovanni Stanghellini, "Narrative Accounts of Illness in Schizophrenia: Association of Different Forms of Awareness with Neurocognition and Social Function over Time," *Consciousness and Cognition* 17 (2008), 1143–1151.

Lysaker, Paul, Amanda Wickett, Louanne Davis. "Narrative Qualities in Schizophrenia: Associations with Impairments in Neurocognition and Negative Symptoms." *The Journal of Nervous and Mental Disease* 193.4 (2005), 244–249.

Malabou, Catherine. *The New Wounded: From Neurosis to Brain Damage.* New York: Fordham University Press, 2012.

Marinetti, F. T. "The Founding Manifesto of Futurism" (1909). *Futurism: An Anthology,* Ed. Lawrence Rainey, Christine Poggi, and Laura Wittman. New Haven: Yale University Press, 2009. pp. 49–53.

"The Technical Manifesto of Futurist Literature" (1912). *Futurism: An Anthology*, Edited by Lawrence Rainey, Christine Poggi, and Laura Wittman (New Haven: Yale University Press, 2009), 119–125.

Selected Writings. Edited and translated by R. W. Flint. New York: Farrar Straus and Giroux, 1972.

Marks, Patricia. *Bicycles, Bangs, and Bloomers: The New Woman in the Popular Press*. Lexington: University Press of Kentucky, 1990.

Maude, Ulrika. "'A Stirring beyond Coming and Going': Beckett and Tourette's." *Journal of Beckett Studies* 17.1 (2008), 153–168.

Beckett, Technology, and the Body. Cambridge: Cambridge University Press, 2009.

"Beckett, Body and Mind." *The New Cambridge Companion to Samuel Beckett.* Ed. Dirk Van Hulle. Cambridge: Cambridge University Press, 2015. 170–184.

Maudsley, Henry. *Responsibility in Mental Disease*. London: Macmillan and Co, 1874.

Mays, J. C. C. "Brian O'Nolan: Literalist of the Imagination," *Myles: Portraits of Brian O'Nolan*. London: Martin Brian & O'Keeffe, 1973. pp. 77–119.

McCarthy, Tom. *C*. New York: Knopf, 2010.

"Technology and the Novel, From Blake to Ballard." *Guardian Review*, July, 24, 2010, p. 2.

McLuhan, Marshall. *Understanding Media: The Extensions of Man*. New York: McGraw-Hill, 1964.

Mettrie, Julien Offray de la. *Man a Machine* (1748). Edited and translated by Ann Thomson. Cambridge: Cambridge University Press, 1996.

Metzinger, Thomas. *Being No One: The Self-Model Theory of Subjectsivity*. Cambridge: MIT Press, 2004.

The Ego Tunnel: The Science of Mind and the Myth of the Self. New York: Basic Books, 2009.

Micale, Mark (ed.). *The Mind of Modernism: Medicine, Psychology, and the Cultural Arts in Europe and America, 1880–1940*. Stanford: Stanford University Press, 2004.

Approaching Hysteria: Disease and Its Interpretations. Princeton: Princeton University Press, 1994.

Miller, Tyrus. *Late Modernism: Politics, Fiction, and the Arts between the World Wars*. Berkeley: University of California Press, 1999.

Murphet, Julian. "Flann O'Brien and Modern Character." *Flann O'Brien and Modernism*. Edited by Julian Murphet, Ronan McDonald, and Sascha Morrell. New York: Bloomsbury Academic, 2014. pp. 149–161.

na gCopaleen, Myles. "Cruiskeen Lawn." *Irish Times*, October 2, 1945.

Nancy, Jean-Luc. *Creation of the World, or Globalization*. Translated by Francois Raffoul and David Pettigrew. Albany: State University of New York Press, 2007.

Nicolson, Harold. "Myself and the Microphone," *Listener* 29 (April 1931), 722–723.

O'Brien, Barbara. *Operators and Things: The Inner Life of a Schizophrenic*. Cambridge: Arlington, 1958.

O'Brien, Flann. *Flann O'Brien: The Complete Novels*. Edited by Keith Donohue. New York: Alfred Knopf, 2008.

O'Hara, J. D. *Samuel Beckett's Hidden Drives: Structural Uses of Depth Psychology*. Gainesville: University of Florida Press, 1997.

Oppenheim, Lois. "A Twenty-First Century Perspective on a Play by Samuel Beckett." *Journal of Beckett Studies* 17.1 (2008), 187–198.

Otis, Laura. *Networking: Communicating with Bodies and Machines in the Nineteenth Century*. Ann Arbor: University of Michigan Press, 2001.

Parnas, Josef. "On Psychosis: Karl Jaspers and Beyond." *One Century of Karl Jaspers's General Psychopathology*. Edited by Giovanni Stanghellini and Thomas Fuchs. Oxford: Oxford Unviersity Press, 2013. pp. 208–228.

Pavel, Thomas. *Fictional Worlds*. Cambridge: Harvard University Press, 1986.

Phillips, James. "Schizophrenia and the Narrative Self." *Self in Neuroscience and Psychiatry*. Edited by Tilo Kircher and Anthony David. Cambridge: Cambridge University Press, 2003. pp. 319–335.

Pickering, Andrew. *Cybernetic Brain: Sketches of Another Future*. Chicago: University of Chicago Press, 2011.

Pilny, Ondrej. "'Did You Put Charcoal Adroitly in the Vent?' Brian O'Nolan and Pataphysics." *Flann O'Brien: Contesting Legacies*. Edited by Ruben Borg, Paul Fagan, and Werner Huber. Cork: Cork UP, 2014. pp. 156–180.

Porter, Roy. *The Greatest Benefit to Mankind: A Brief History of Medicine*. New York: Norton, 1997.

Post, Stephen L. "His and Hers: Breakdown as Depicted by Evelyn Waugh and Charlotte Perkins Gilman." *Literature and Medicine* 9 (1990), 172–180.

Prendergast, Catherine. "The Unexceptional Schizophrenic: A Post-Postmodern Introduction." *The Disability Studies Reader*. Edited by Lennard J. Davis. New York: Routledge, 2013. pp. 236–245.

Price, Margaret. *Mad at School: Rhetorics of Mental Disability and Academic Life*. Ann Arbor: University of Michican Press, 2011.

Prince, Morton. *A Dissociation of a Personality: A Biographical Study in Abnormal Personality*. New York: Longmans and Green, 1906.

Pryce-Jones, David (ed.). *Evelyn Waugh and His World*. Boston: Little, Brown & Co., 1973.

Pryor, Sean. "Making Evil, with Flann O'Brien." *Flann O'Brien and Modernism*. Edited by Julian Murphet, Ronan McDonald, and Sascha Morrell. New York: Bloomsbury Academic, 2014. pp. 11–26.

Rabaté, Jean-Michel. *Ghosts of Modernity*. Gainesville: University Press of Florida, 1996.

  James Joyce and the Politics of Egoism. Cambridge: Cambridge University Press, 2001.

  "Loving Freud Madly: Surrealism between Hysterical and Paranoid Modernism," *Journal of Modern Literature* 25.3 (2002), 58–74.

Rabinbach, Anson. *The Human Motor: Energy, Fatigue, and the Origins of Modernity*. Berkeley: University of California Press, 1990.

"Radio's Aid is Invoked to Explore Telepathy" *New York Times*, August 30, 1925.

Ragin, Charles and Howard S. Becker (ed.). *What Is a Case?: Exploring the Foundations of Social Inquiry*. New York: Cambridge University Press, 1992.

Reeve-Tucker, Alice and Nathan Waddell. "Wyndham Lewis, Evelyn Waugh and Inter-war British Youth: Conflict and Infantilism." *Wyndham Lewis and the Cultures of Modernity*. Edited by Andrzej Gasiorek and Alice Glen-Reeve. London: Ashgate, 2011. pp. 162–184.

Ricoeur, Paul. *Time and Narrative*, Vol. 1. Translated by Kathleen McLaughlin and David Pellauer. Chicago: University of Chicago Press, 1990.

"Life: A Story in Search of a Narrator." *On Psychoanalysis: Writings and Lectures*. Translated by David Pellauer. New York: Polity Press, 2012. pp. 187–200.

Ronell, Avital. *The Telephone Book: Technology, Schizophrenia, Electric Speech*. Lincoln: University of Nebraska Press, 1989.

Ronen, Ruth. *Possible Worlds in Literary Theory*. Cambridge: Cambridge University Press, 1994.

Rose, Nikolas and Joelle Abi-Rached. *Neuro: The New Brain Sciences and the Management of the Brain*. Princeton: Princeton University Press, 2013.

Roudinesco, Elizabeth. *Jacques Lacan*. Translated by Barbara Bray. New York: Columbia University Press, 1997.

Rushdie, Salman. *Midnight's Children*. New York: Random House, 1981.

East, West. New York: Vintage, 1994.

Ryan, Marie-Laure. *Possible Worlds, Artificial Intelligence, and Narrative Theory*. Bloomington: Indiana University Press, 1992.

Ryle, Gilbert. *The Concept of Mind*. Chicago: University of Chicago Press, 2000.

Sachs, H. "The Delay of the Machine Age," *Psychoanalytic Quarterly* 2 (1933): 404–424.

Sachs, L. J. "On Changes in Identification from Machine to Cripple," *Psychoanalytic Study of the Child* 12 (1957): 356–375.

Sacks, Oliver. "Foreword." In A.R. Luria, *The Man with a Shattered World: The History of a Brain Wound*. Cambridge: Harvard University Press, 1987. pp. vii–xviii.

Sadler, John. "The Instrument Metaphor, Hyponarrativity, and the Generic Clinician." *Philosophical Perspectives on Technology and Psychiatry*. Edited by James Phillips. Oxford: Oxford University Press, 2010. pp. 23–34.

Saint-Amour, Paul. *Tense Future: Modernism, Total War, Encyclopedic Form*. New York: Oxford University Press, 2015.

Salisbury, Laura. " 'What Is the Word': Beckett's Aphasic Modernism," *Journal of Beckett Studies* 17.1 (2008), 78–126.

Santner, Eric *My Own Private Germany: Daniel Paul Schreber's Secret History of Modernity*. Princeton: Princeton University Press, 1996.

Sass, Louis. "Heidegger, Schizophrenia, and the Ontological Difference," *Philosophical Psychology* 5.2 (1992), 109–133.

Madness and Modernism: Insanity in Light of Modern Art, Literature, and Thought. New York: Basic Books, 1992.

The Paradoxes of Delusion: Wittgenstein, Schreber, and the Schizophrenic Mind. Ithaca: Cornell University Press, 1995.

Schenker, Daniel. *Wyndham Lewis, Religion and Modernism*. Tuscaloosa: University of Alabama Press, 1992.

Schloss, Carol Loeb. *Lucia Joyce: To Dance in the Wake*. New York: Farrar Straus Giroux, 2003.

Schreber, Daniel Paul. *Memoirs of My Nervous Illness*. Translated by Ida Macalpine and Richard A. Hunter. New York: New York Review of Books Classics, 2000.

Schrödinger, Erwin. *What Is Life?* Cambridge: Cambridge University Press, 2012.

Sconce, Jeffrey. *Haunted Media: Electronic Presence from Telegraphy to Television*. Durham: Duke University Press, 2000.

'Wireless Ego: The Pulp Physics of Psychoanalysis.' *Broadcasting Modernism*. Edited by Debra Rae Cohen, Michael Coyle, and Jane Lewty. Gainesville: University Press of Florida, 2009. pp. 31–50.

Searles, Ralph. *The Nonhuman Environment in Normal Development and in Schizophrenia*. New York: International Universities Press, 1960.

Sechehaye, Marguerite. *Autobiography of a Schizophrenic Girl: Reality Lost and Regained*. Translated by Grace Rubin-Rabson. New York: Grune & Stratton, 1951.

Sedgwick, Eve Kosofsky. "Paranoid Reading, Reparative Reading, or, You're So Paranoid, You Probably Think This Essay Is about You." *Touching Feeling: Affect, Pedagogy, Performativity*. Durham: Duke University Press, 2003, pp. 123–152.

Self, Will. "Modernism and Me." *Guardian*, August 3, 2012. Web.

Umbrella. London: Bloomsbury, 2012.

Seltzer, Mark. *Bodies and Machines*. New York: Routledge, 1992.

Shorter, Wayne. *A History of Psychiatry: From the Era of the Asylum to the Age of Prozac*. New York: Wiley, 1998.

Spark, Muriel. *Voices at Play*. London: Macmillan, 1961.

Memento Mori. New York: New Directions, 2000.

The Comforters. New York: New Directions, 2014.

Loitering with Intent. New York: New Directions, 2014.

Stanfield, Paul Scott. "'This Implacable Doctrine': Behaviorism in Wyndham Lewis's *Snooty Baronet*." *Twentieth-Century Literature* 47.2 (2001), 241–267.

Stanghellini, Giovanni. *Disembodied Spirits and Deanimated Bodies: The Psychopathology of Common Sense*. Oxford: Oxford University Press, 2004.

Stannard, Martin. *Muriel Spark: The Biography*. New York: W.W. Norton, 2009.

Stonebridge, Lyndsey. "Hearing Them Speak: Voices in Wilfred Bion, Muriel Spark and Penelope Fitzgerald," *Textual Practice* 19.4 (2005), 445–465.

Sulloway, Frank. *Freud, Biologist of the Mind: Beyond the Psychoanalytic Legend*. New York: Basic Books, 1979.

Tajiri, Yoshiki. *Samuel Beckett and the Prosthetic Body: The Senses and Organs of Modernism*. New York: Palgrave, 2007.

Tausk, Victor. "On the Origin of the 'Influencing Machine' in Schizophrenia," *Psychoanalytic Quarterly* 2 (1933), 519–556.

Taylor, Charles. *The Sources of the Self: The Making of Modern Identity*. Cambridge: Harvard University Press, 1989.

Thurschwell, Pamela. *Literature, Technology, and Magical Thinking, 1820–1920.* Cambridge: Cambridge University Press, 2001.

Titchener, E. B. "On 'Psychology as the Behaviorist Views It,'" *Proceedings of the American Philosophical Society* 53 (1914), 1–17.

Todorov, Tvetan. *The Fantastic: A Structural Approach to a Literary Genre.* Ithaca: Cornell University Press, 1975.

Tomkins, Silvan. *Affect, Imagery, Consciousness,* Vol. II. New York: Springer, 1963.

Trotter, David. *Paranoid Modernism: Literary Experiment, Psychosis, and the Professionalization of English Society.* Oxford: Oxford University Press, 2001.

Literature in the First Media Age. Cambridge: Harvard University Press, 2013.

Tuma, Keith. "Mina Loy's 'Anglo-Mongrels and the Rose.'" *Mina Loy: Woman and Poet.* Edited by Maeera Schreiber and Keith Tuma. Orono: National Poetry Foundation, 1998. pp. 181–204.

Turner, Jenny. "Seeing Things Flat." *London Review of Books* 32.17 (September 9, 2010), 7–8.

Tylen, K., P. Christensen, A. Roepstorff, T. Lund, S. Ostergaard, and M. Donald. "Brains Striving for Coherence: Long-term cumulative plot formation in the default mode network," *Neuroimage* 121 (2015), 106–114.

Valentine, Kylie. *Psychoanalysis, Psychiatry and Modernist Literature.* New York: Palgrave Macmillan, 2003.

Van Hulle, Dirk. "Flann O'Brien's *Ulysses*: Marginalia and the Modernist Mind." *Flann O'Brien and Modernism.* Edited by Julian Murphet, Ronan McDonald, and Sascha Morrell. London: Bloomsbury, 2014. pp. 107–120.

Walker, Victoria. "Foreword." In Anna Kavan, *I Am Lazarus.* London: Peter Owen, 2013.

Walter, Christina. *Optical Impersonality: Science, Images, and Literary Modernism.* Baltimore: Johns Hopkins University Press, 2014.

Warger, Thomas A. "Going Mad Systematically in Beckett's *Murphy,*" *Modern Language Studies* 16.2 (1986), 13–18.

Watson, John B. "Psychology as the Behaviorist Views It," *Psychological Review* 20, (1913), 158–177.

Behavior: An Introduction to Comparative Psychology. New York: Henry Holt, 1914.

Behaviorism. Chicago: University of Chicago Press, 1928.

Waugh, Evelyn. "Anything Wrong with Priestley?" *Spectator,* September 13, 1957, 8–10.

The Ordeal of Gilbert Pinfold: A Conversation Piece. New York: Back Bay Books, 1957.

"Something Fresh: Review of *The Comforters.*" *Spectator,* February 22, 1957, 256–257.

"Something Fresh: Review of *The Comforters* by Muriel Spark." *The Essays, Articles and Reviews of Evelyn Waugh.* Edited by Donat Gallagher. London: Methuen, 1983. pp. 518–519.

Waugh, Patricia. "Muriel Spark and the Metaphysics of Modernity: Art, Secularization, and Psychosis." *Muriel Spark: Twenty-First-Century Perspectives.*

Edited by David Herman. Baltimore: Johns Hopkins University Press, 2010. pp. 63–93.

"Thinking in Literature: Modernism and Contemporary Neuroscience." *The Legacies of Modernism: Historicizing Postward and Contemporary Fiction.* Edited by David James. Cambridge: Cambridge University Press, 2011. pp. 75–95.

"The Naturalistic Turn, the Syndrome, and the Rise of the Neo-Phenomenological Novel." *Diseases and Disorders in Contemporary Fiction: The Syndrome Syndrome.* Edited by James Peacock and Tim Lustig. New York: Routledge, 2013. pp. 17–34.

Wiener, Norbert. *Cybernetics, or, Control and Communication in the Animal and the Machine.* Cambridge: Technology Press, 1948.

Cybernetics of the Nervous System. New York: Elsevier, 1965.

The Human Use of Human Beings: Cybernetics and Society. New York: Avon, 1967.

Wing, Willis K., Charles Cooke, James Thurber, Harold Ross. "Talk in Dreams." *New Yorker*, October 7, 1933, 17–18.

Wittgenstein, Ludwig. *Philosophical Investigations.* Oxford: Basil Blackwell, 1958.

Wollaeger, Mark. *Modernism, Media, and Propaganda: British Narrative from 1900 to 1945.* Princeton: Princeton University Press, 2008.

Woods, Angela. *The Sublime Object of Psychiatry: Schizophrenia in Clinical and Cultural Theory.* Oxford: Oxford University Press, 2011.

Woodworth, Robert. *Contemporary Schools of Psychology.* New York: Ronald Press, 1931.

Yerkes, Robert M. "Report of the Psychological Committee of the National Research Council," *Psychological Review* 26.2 (1919), 83–149.

Young, Kay and Jeffrey Saver. "The Neurology of Narrative," *SubStance* 30.1 (2001), 72–84.

Zahavi, Dan. "Self and Other: The Limits of Narrative Understanding." *Narrative Understanding and Persons.* Edited by Daniel Hutto. New York: Cambridge University Press, 2007. pp. 179–202.

Zilliacus, Clas. *Beckett and Broadcasting: A Study of the Works of Samuel Beckett for and in Radio and Television.* Åbo: Abo Akademi, 1976.

Žižek, Slavoj. *Tarrying With the Negative: Kant, Hegel, and the Critique of Ideology.* Durham: Duke University Press, 1993.

The Plague of Fantasies. New York: Verso, 1997.

Enjoy Your Symptom! New York: Verso, 2001.

The Parallax View. Cambridge: MIT Press, 2009.

Index